THE WEB OF TEXT AND THE WEB OF GOD

The Web of Text
and
the Web of God

AN ESSAY

ON THE THIRD INFORMATION

TRANSFORMATION

Alan C. Purves

THE GUILFORD PRESS
New York   London

This book is for my sons, William C. Purves
and Theodore R. Purves, who have been my
collaborators and friends since the very
beginning. They had faith in me and this book.
Thanks.

© 1998 by the estate of Alan C. Purves
Published by The Guilford Press
A Division of Guilford Publications, Inc.
72 Spring Street, New York, NY 10012
http://www.guilford.com

Printed in the United States of America

This book is printed on acid-free paper.

Last digit is print number: 9 8 7 6 5 4 3 2 1

Library of Congress Cataloging-in-Publication Data is available
from the Publisher.

ISBN 1-57230-249-6

Preface

T his book is about the ways in which the new writing and information technologies have affected our cultural, intellectual, and religious beliefs and structures. It begins with the premise that there have been three major transformations in the way we store and retrieve information: first, the development of written language; second, the invention of the printing press; and third, the development of electronic or paperless forms of communication, including radio, film, and television, as well as the computer, the Internet, and the World Wide Web. What I want to do is to explore how these shifts in our writing, reading, and viewing have affected certain aspects of society, culture, and religion, and how social, cultural, and religious institutions have assimilated them and made them their own.

One of the key elements of the recent changes in communications technology has been the speed with which the changes have occurred. The transition from Gutenberg to the mass market book took some three hundred years. In contrast, during the past few decades we have seen the computer go from being a tool used by a small minority to one available to nearly everyone. We have moved in the past century from radio to broadcast TV to cable, from letters to telephone calls to electronic mail, from film to video to interactive multimedia story environments—all with a speed that is as astonishing as it is disorienting.

While I do not believe that technology completely determines who we are, neither do I believe that it exists in a vacuum; the technologies we create inevitably come to be seen as ends in themselves—forms of idolatry. However, rather than inveigh against the new media technologies, as some have done, I should like to understand and trace their possibilities and promises in order to see how they can be used by people of goodwill and deep faith.

The new media, I argue, have given rise to a new form, *hypertext,* and to a new type of community, the *network.* Both are characterized in part by their lack of a center, of a controlling authority, and they therefore raise questions about the source and nature of unity in the next millennium, the age we have come to call the "postmodern." Some see these questions and the new media themselves as disruptive and anarchic, as heralding the death of culture as we know it. But, although disruption and anarchy may be difficult to live through, I believe that they can have their positive effects as well—they can be, perhaps, cleansing. Thus, the network is not just a new type of community, but a new conception of community.

Although I want to look at the ways in which these various technological, social, and cultural concerns play against one another, my ultimate concern is with theophany in the electronic world. Religion and text have interpenetrated each other for millennia around the world, and our ways of reading are very much tied up with our ways of worshipping. I have therefore begun to wonder about how the new media will change the way we worship, and have come to believe that the network may be the heart of a second Reformation, or major reformulation of the nature of religious institutions in our lives. It may provide the metaphor or myth through which we come to God or to an understanding of God in our time.

In order to explore the variety and complexity of these tectonic shifts, I have tried to bring together in this book a number of facets of the new world of hypertext. I find that I cannot quite treat them in the logical order of a research report or even the rhetoric of an Aristotelian argument. I must meet this world on its own terms. Hypertext must meet hypertext. I invite you to do the same.

This book was initially composed as a hypertext, using the program Storyspace™. The program allows the writer to work on discrete segments of a book, or topics, and arrange those topics as a set of boxes, or "spaces." Within a space such as the current one, which I originally dubbed "author," I can include a number of other spaces, which then are seen as subtopics. The topics can be connected by "links," either in one or both directions. The links are named so that one can follow a single named link (such as "community") and visit all the spaces that the author has connected with that name. Alternatively, a writer may create a number of different links bidirectionally from a single space so that a reader may readily return to that space, much as one returns to a home base. *The program allows, for example, the reader to follow the text in "author mode," and the reader may create new links and/or new spaces—or add text to the spaces already there.* The resultant "reading" is less like an orderly progression through a book than it is a following of the lines and radii of a spider web; at any intersection, one is free to move along any one of a variety of paths to another section or topic—or, if in the author mode—free to launch out in new directions altogether.

The interweaving of the technologies of language and information storage and transmission with culture and religion is indeed complex. It seemed to me that this complexity is best captured by a hypertext model. Thus it was that I composed this book originally as a hypertext, as noted, and thus it is that the computer disk version of this book might be arranged. Other books that I have written have been straightforward affairs; I made some notes, perhaps, but I generally began at the beginning and ended at the end; I know that this is not the way of some writers, but it was mine for the thirty years up to the writing of this book.

This time it was different. I read a lot of new material, I had a hypertext program, and each time I had a piece to write I placed it in a hypertext space. I then arranged these spaces into larger spaces, which seemed to have a topical or thematic coherence. I also began to draw linking lines between them. Eventually I arrived at about twenty-five topics ranging from "author" to "universalism." I would revisit these each time I read something new or decided to add a piece. I decided to arrange my book into these twenty-five topics and also to suggest some major links among them. The result was a volume that might be compared to macramé: there would be dense knotted bits connected by a variety of threads into a pattern of the reader's choosing.

For many readers, however, such an arrangement is difficult and forbidding. I could not find a publisher who would consider the book in this form. I have, therefore, collapsed my twenty-five topics into seven chapters: an autobiographical introduction; a chapter on the nature of text and hypertext; one on new perspectives on literacy; one on text and image; one on text, hypertext, and literacy in a larger cultural framework; one on implications for a new sense of the church; and a conclusion. I believe that I could have begun the book with any one of them, but the order I have selected suggests a centrifugal movement of ideas. The result, I hope, is less of a macramé and more of a weaving, where warp and woof create a coherent and pleasing pattern.

To turn the macramé into a weaving is not an easy task. One of the first things one learns when working with hypertext programs is that the content that one writes is put into text spaces, together with graphics and possibly sound and digitized film as well. These spaces appear as boxes on the screen that are able to hold whole paragraphs or even longer sections of text. The boxes can be arranged in a number of different patterns on the screen. One can make pretty arrangements and displays of them.

But what makes a hypertext a hypertext is not simply the boxes but the ways by which an author or a reader can connect those boxes. There can be as many links as one wants from any one box, and the links can be hooked up to any number of other boxes. In the program I use, each link has a name, so that the thread can be followed from space to space and idea to idea. In this way, the writer can give the reader a clue as to how the writer has organized the work. In some programs the reader is able to follow only the writer's links, but in others the reader can create new links. When I first started working with hypertext, I wanted to make lots of links so that people could see the complexity of my web and so that they could go in lots of different directions. As I have come to work with the program further, I see that the most interesting links are those that can be pursued in a number of different ways so as to make up a number of complementary readings of my writing.

This means that I don't want too many different sorts of links. I may have a lot of links, but I don't want to give them too many names. Rather, I want the links that I see to represent the main threads of one of the arguments I wish to make across the spaces and the themes of the chapters.

To me, five links serve as the major connecting threads of this book and help in the weaving. You may think of them as themes by which I have conceived the sinew of the book of which the chapters are the skeleton—or they may be themes that emerged as I worked on its various parts. I do not know which, but there they are. Other themes might appear to any one of you, but I cannot anticipate what they might be. My linking themes are *anarchy, authority, community, idolatry,* and *network.* The reasons for these five are complex, but they are each tied to the idea of hypertext.

Anarchy is characteristic of hypertext; being nonhierarchical and multidirectional, hypertext at least has the *appearance* of having no order. So too does much that surrounds us in the world.

Authority is the control of content and structure held by an author, but, in being anarchic, hypertext appears to cede authority to the reader. There is a lack of authority, at least central authority, in the new kinds of text, and that lack also appears in other parts of our world.

Community has come to be a fashionable term. It suggests a commonality, a sharing among its members. A community has a lack of definable authority, but is in its collectivity the authority to those who willingly join it. As it is with the community that shares a hypertext, so, too, is it with many aspects of the current configuration of our lives, both temporal and spiritual.

Idolatry is the second term with a negative connotation, the first being anarchy. But, whereas anarchy has a positive note in my use of it, idolatry does not. I borrow the idea from two contemporary thinkers, Jacques Ellul and Owen Barfield; behind them looms Matthew Arnold. All three are concerned with the idolatry of the thing, of "machinery," of technology. It is an important and problematic issue with regard to hypertext, because the computer and hypertext deal with icons and images, as do the visual media of television and film. The icon is a way by which one may approach the world behind the image; it is a tool. It is only when we worship the icon rather than use it that we become idolatrous.

Network refers to the interrelationship of the parts of a hypertext. It is a network, too, that comes to relate the individual members of a community to one another. The members of a community retain their individuality but at the same time assert their connectedness. A network also connects communities into a larger web, the web of my title.

The five concepts can be viewed as alternate organizations of the book or as ideas that play against one another as the various topics emerge, merge, and become elaborated. They are the heart of my index.

If you were to visualize the book in hyperspace or as a hypertext, you would see something resembling a spider web (see Figure A). The essays are the meeting places in an ever widening set of concentric polygons around not a core, but a set, of ideas. The links are the major radii, but they also form the lateral tissue.

The book, then, is a network of ideas. To me the links are what make the network a network. I shall return to these five linking themes and expand on them in Chapter 7. In order to see how they

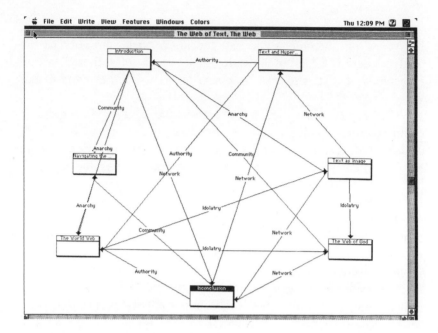

FIGURE A. A hypertext view of the broad outlines of this book.

play through the web of technological and cultural change, however, I shall spend some time discussing them in the intervening chapters, as well.

Although this book is not crammed with notes and references, as I noted earlier, I have read a great deal about this subject, though I do not pretend to be the first to explore these issues. Anyone who writes on this subject must acknowledge a number of people who have probed various aspects of the information transformation that has been happening around us, and I, too, have my mentors. I have made some references in the text to authors whose ideas I find particularly relevant but who might not be obvious. Additionally, however, there are a number of other writers whose work I have found seminal. I discuss them at the beginning of the Notes section at the end of this volume.

I hope you will find the voyage enjoyable and stimulating.

Acknowledgments

*D*etermining the precise starting point for any book may be a murky enterprise. I can think of several for this one. One early starting point was a discussion I had with Gail Hawisher of the University of Illinois about a relatively new concept for both of us, hypertext. I remember saying to her that it struck me as being like the kind of report I used to write in the fifth grade, where I copied from the encyclopedia, pasted pictures torn from magazines, and put the whole together in a binder. She laughed and said she thought it was more; I decide to plunge in and investigate further.

Another starting point, perhaps even murkier, lies in my concern with the history of literacy that began when I wrote a book called *The Scribal Society*, published in 1990. I had some idea about it then, but decided I did not know enough, so I read sufficiently to develop a course. I am still adding to my knowledge. Among the most influential readings on my own thinking were the works of Jack Goody who wrote about literacy and the mind of society. Goody is an anthropologist and one who sees the connection between various kinds of technology and social and religious practices. At that time, I became increasingly intrigued by his phrase "religions of the book." Goody is the sort of anthropologist who is disliked by many Americans who see him as being overly global. He is also, perhaps, not "critical" enough.*

---

*In the history of literacy, it is fashionable to be "critical" and to observe how literacy is a tool used by the ruling classes to stay in power. I am frank to admit that I find such a statement so obviously true as to be banal. I am interested more in exploring the workings of literacy and literate peoples than in excoriating it as a tool of monarchy, oligarchy, colonialism, orthodoxy, or capitalism (although it has been all of those things and will probably so continue). I am also more interested in exploring how our understanding can enlarge our appreciation of our present place in society and the cosmos. I am, frankly, an optimist.

Another starting point lies in my discovery of Storyspace™, the program of Eastgate systems that enabled me to write in hypertext. Through a series of conversations with its developers, notably Michael Joyce and Mark Bernstein, I was encouraged in my explorations. Others who encouraged me from the start were Karen Swan and Sarah Jordan-Miller of the State University of New York at Albany, and Robert Fowler of Baldwin–Wallace College. But the main encouragement came from my own family: particularly my sons, Will, who had helped me explore issues related to literate cultures, and Ted, an intriguing artist of print in his own right, and from my wife, Anne, who kept pushing me further.

Anne pushed me to explore the religious connection in these ideas through a fellowship in the Coolidge Colloquium, sponsored by the Association for Religion and Intellectual Life. A fellowship from ARIL in 1994 helped me to complete the first hypertext draft of the book and also gained for me new friends and colleagues and a remarkable set of insights. It was during that summer of 1994 and the experience of living, talking, and working with a score of diverse people at the Coolidge Colloquium that I discovered Jacques Ellul, Wilfred Smith, and Christopher Alexander. I also rediscovered Paul Ricoeur and many other writers whose influence permeates this volume.

Anne, together with our friends the Rev. Charles Karsten and the Rev. William Hinrichs, also pushed the theological bent of my thinking and encouraged me to spend two weeks at St. Deiniol's Library in Hawarden, Wales. This period led me once again to Owen Barfield, whom I had admired as a graduate student and whose later work has shaped the way in which I have finally produced the manuscript and the thinking in this book.

I think that my greatest and deepest debt must be to Chris Jennison, my editor at Guilford. Twenty-five years ago, he was my editor for a book called *How Porcupines Make Love*, a book on reading and teaching literature, in which we explored the possibilities of making a text that presented our ideas graphically as well as intellectually. I laid out each two-page spread on the typewriter, and a designer worked carefully with my suggestions. It was an experiment in book writing and production in which Chris had faith. The experience of producing that book has profoundly influenced my way of thinking about text and hypertext as well as about media. Chris has been my editor on other books over the years, but it was his trust and faith in this one that has helped me over many rough spots.

A NOTE ON SOURCES AND REFERENCES

I have tried to shape this volume as a set of interlocking essays. There is a great deal of reading, contemplation, prayer, and study that lies behind nearly every sentence. There are notes for each chapter as well as a chapter of general references. I have probably slighted, oddly enough, some of those writers whose work has permeated my thinking the most. One is Samuel Taylor Coleridge, whose poetry was the subject of my doctoral thesis years ago, and whose prose rests in my mind and stirs it up continually. Others include Northrop Frye, Marshall McLuhan, Josephine Miles, Marjorie Nicolson, Will Eisner, Scott McCloud, Albertine Gaur, Elisabeth Eisenstein, Louise Rosenblatt, Howard Rheingold, and Thomas Cranmer. I am sure I have forgotten others, who are in this book nevertheless.

Contents

CHAPTER SEVEN

CHAPTER ONE

An Autobiographical Introduction

In writing a book about the relationship of the new technologies used for writing and handling information to culture and religion, I found that I had to look outward at the world around me. At the same time, I realize that it is I who is looking at this world, and in order for me to say something to you about that world I think you have to know something about me. My history has a bearing on how I understand the world, and when you read my words you also have to read me—and perhaps read yourself as my coauthor.

Although I don't remember the details, I learned to read at an early age. I also learned to form letters with whatever instrument came along—sometimes a crayon, sometimes a pencil, sometimes a stick scratching in the dirt. Learning to read didn't stop my being read to by my parents or by Isabella, the person who took care of my brother and me. A good Presbyterian, Isabella every night would read to us a chapter from Hurlbut's *Story of the Bible*. On many evenings, my mother read or recited poetry to my brother and me and also read us the occasional fairy tale. Even after we children learned to read, our family would spend one or two evenings a week reading aloud.

After learning to read for myself, I read whatever came along, the funny papers, the cartons that our toothpaste came in, gum wrappers. I would read under the covers at night and early in the morning. When I could get away with it, I would read at meals. Even in the john, I would read whatever text was handy and then, after I had read it, look to see if I could find all the letters of the alphabet in the text. When we drove into the city, my brother and I could not read books because it would "ruin your eyes," so we played the alphabet game with the signs along the highway. Ours was a world of letters and print.

In school, I learned to form both print and cursive letters. At home on weekends, I also watched the lettering done by my father, an architect, and admired its clean sculptured quality, as crisp as were the clay busts that my mother made in her part of the studio. In the third grade, I was given a fountain pen for my birthday—I think it was an Esterbrook. In fifth grade, however, we had to undergo the Palmer method and to purchase a Palmer method pen. That was my downfall. I simply could not form those parallel lines or ellipses. And the pen leaked. To everyone's dismay, I failed penmanship, never to recover fully.

Almost from the beginning of our consciousness, my brother and I were exposed to "the funny pages." My father brought the papers home every evening, and we soon found "The Toonerville Trolley" and various other strips including "Gasoline Alley," "Dick Tracy," "Terry and the Pirates," and "Smokey Stover." On Sundays we had two Philadelphia papers as well as the funny-less *New York Times* (where we quickly found the editorial cartoons in "The News of the Week in Review").

Each daily paper had at least one-and-a-half pages devoted to comic strips. On Sundays, of course, the strips were in color, and there were additional feature strips like "Prince Valiant." All of these formed a major kind of recreational reading. We looked forward to them daily or weekly, remembering the segments of the serialized versions over time so that we could link our daily/weekly readings, just as we linked the frames in each strip.

We also bought some comic books, but our money was more usually spent on "Big Little Books," which had an illustration on one page and text facing it, to form a hybrid of book and comic book. It was not until the outbreak of the Second World War that the Big Little Book faded and the comic book came to hold sway. Then, when I was a teenager, one of the papers also printed a small "comic book" called "The Spirit" by Will Eisner; this notable achievement was a complete short story in the Sunday newspaper.

Reading comics got me to look at other illustrated sequential books. One was a collection of Persian Miniatures of Nizam. Another was *God's Man*, a novel in woodcuts by Lynd Ward. This adult book telling of an artist who sold his soul to the devil in exchange for talent was hardly for children, but to me it was like a Big Little Book without the words; there was one picture per righthand page. For many of the adults around me, the comics were considered an idle amusement except for certain strips that acquired a cult readership—such as

George Herriman's "Krazy Kat," Milt Gross's "Nize Baby," and, later, Walt Kelly's "Pogo" and Garry Trudeau's "Doonesbury."

I should also mention the movies and radio, both of which were important parts of my cultural life as a youth. The radio was perhaps the more important of the two media, for first it formed a part of our weekend afternoons, as we watched my parents pursue their hobbies to the sound of the Metropolitan Opera and the New York Philharmonic. In the mornings we got off to school to the sounds of WOR. And we rushed home to enjoy adventure shows like *Tom Mix*, and *Jack Armstrong*. The evenings, of course, featured a mixture of homework and adventure serials as well as the weekly comedy and drama shows, particularly *I Love a Mystery*, *Henry Aldrich*, *The Shadow*, and *Fred Allen*. Whenever I was sick, the radio was placed by my bedside, and I could listen to the breakfast shows in the morning and the soap operas all afternoon. Summers were devoted to baseball broadcasts; I can still hear the voices of Red Barber and particularly Byrum Saam, the sportscaster in Philadelphia who could make even a wire rebroadcast come alive on a rainy afternoon.

Since we lived in the suburbs and were taken to live theater a good deal, the movies were central but not a common occurrence in our lives, particularly during the war years, but we did see our share. Going to the movies once every two weeks or so was as much an adventure as going to the library. We could bring books back from the library, but we could only bring back memories from the movies—and I did so to such an extent that my trips home were spent reliving each scene, and I would often have nightmares after particularly scary films. Certain events stand out, such as the thrill of the Disney features, the tension of a Gary Cooper western, *The Wizard of Oz*, and the newsreels portraying the war. In fact, my war was one of newspapers, radio commentators, the rotogravure, Movietone News, and the Trans-Lux theaters.

For me and many in my generation, the world of books, comics, radio, and movies formed an alternative to that in which we lived and studied. From them we got our news and entertainment and our sense of the world and its different cultures. I remember listening early Sunday mornings to the folksinger and storyteller Josef Marais as he told us about African and South African cultures. I remember the voices of commentators like Raymond Gram Swing and Gabriel Heatter telling us how to think about the war. I certainly remember the images and the sound effects of radio, which brought terror, drama, and humor into our world.

Television came to replace radio in the 1950s, but by then I was in college and so was not as fully formed by it as those who are younger than I. I recognize in my children and grandchildren how it enables us to see images of people and brings us alternative worlds.

Despite my love of these other media, during my school years and on into and through the university, I was an avaricious reader, an omnivore of print. Equally at ease with textbooks and comic books, newspapers and novels, I also played the word games and did crossword puzzles. In college, I decided to make words and language my profession but was unsure whether to choose teaching or publishing. Through a series of flukes, I decided on teaching—I suppose because I was more familiar with it. Because I couldn't get a job without training, I went to graduate school.

To cover my bad penmanship, in high school I used the typewriter and managed to submit papers with no more than three strikeovers per page; they were probably barely more legible than the handwritten efforts might have been. I also took mechanical drawing and learned how to form the lettering that I had admired in my father's work (even though I had trouble with the inking). I learned to use corrasable bond paper in college, but never learned touch typing. It wasn't until I was in the army that I learned to type fast (25 words a minute with five errors)—in order to avoid having to clean bedpans in a military hospital. My typing skills improved, and I became fairly adept with the mimeo and the ditto, never getting too much blue or black on me after completing a job (having my desk opposite the sergeant major's, I also learned to read texts upside down). In graduate school I bought an office machine for my studies, one with "dead keys" so I could type accent marks. In the late 1960s I switched to an electric, and in the 1980s to a Macintosh computer. Each time I shifted, I became interested in what happened to me as a writer, how I changed, and how my perceptions of the world around me changed. Each change increased my productivity and my prolixity. Whether each enhanced the quality of my prose is another matter.

I remained fascinated by my father, who could form beautiful characters and who had written detailed and often poetic weekly letters from the front in France during the First World War. After he had retired from a twenty-year career during which he dictated his correspondence, editorials, and speeches, he appeared to have lost the ability to draft a vivid and telling sentence or paragraph on paper. I was also fascinated by the power of the drama on radio as compared to television, by the ways in which some poets and writers appeared to use the very shape of the page to weave their magic, while others remained oblivious to it. Although television certainly changed my consciousness of the world through its coverage of such events as the Army–McCarthy hearings, the Kefauver Committee hearings (with the compelling image of Frank Costello's hands), the assassination of John Kennedy, the Vietnam War and the political upheavals of the late 1960s and early 1970s, and the Watergate hearings and subsequent resignation of Richard Nixon, I was also fascinated by the power of the mimeograph machine in the late 1960s as it stirred campuses to rebellion. For good or ill, the Xerox copy worked its magic during the hostage crisis in Teheran. Later I saw how the fax kept the Chinese in the United States in communication with their comrades in Beijing— until the massacre in Tiananmen Square, at least.

I became intrigued by the ways in which people looked at the written or printed word and how it affected their daily activities and particularly their forms of faith and worship. One reason, of course, is that I am a believer, a practicing Episcopalian, and one interested in various forms of ministry. A more compelling reason, however, is that my studies have shown me over and over again how deeply rooted in religion making, reading, and thinking about books and written documents have been and remain, and how the religious use of texts and writing has pervaded the consciousness of even secular societies such as that of the United States. I have observed priests with their breviaries, Muslims with the Koran, Buddhists with scrolls, Jehovah's Witnesses with tracts; each of them and many others use the written or printed word as a central part of worship—as they have done for the past three thousand years. I still have that children's Bible—along with several others, including one on disk and downloads of various versions taken from the Web—and I regard it as a sacred text. As I have become more concerned with matters of ministry and faith, I, too, have read scripture and commentary, text and tract, of various sorts. I have noted how much our very ways of reading are tied up with our ways of worshipping. I have therefore begun to wonder about what will happen to worship as the traditional form (and perhaps function) of the book changes, and that is the donnée of this book. Religion and text have interpenetrated each other for millennia around the world, so their interrelationships are important to understand.

I became a teacher of literature, writing, and later education, worked with international groups to study the ways in which people teach the young to read literature and to write, and explored the ways in which literature is read and essays are written in various cultures around the world. In addition to being a reader and writer, I have become a student of reading and writing. And my fascination with the interplay of reading, writing, culture, and religious practice grows and keeps on growing.

As the foregoing autobiography in miniature attests, I have been a lifelong member of what I have called a scribal society, one whose very environment and livelihood is vested in print. I have lived from a time when the main sources of entertainment and enlightenment were the book and other forms of the printed word, through the growth of radio, film, and television, to where nowadays cable television and the computer form the main new sources of instruction and entertainment. I have lived from a time when people primarily wrote letters through a time when they used the telephone and into a time when they routinely communicate by e-mail.

In this book, I want to explore these shifts in our writing, reading, and viewing, and explore their interrelationships with some aspects of society, culture, and religion. I also want to explore how social, cultural, and religious institutions have assimilated the new technologies and made them their own.[1] No technological determinist, I do, however, think that technology does not exist in a vacuum and the new invention comes to support cultural and societal urges and yearnings. As Owen Barfield has suggested, the technologies that we have created have inevitably affected our consciousness in and of the world.

At the same time I worry, as have several others, about the way in which technology, the means, comes to be seen as an end in itself. Again, as Barfield and others suggest, technologies can give rise to idolatry. That is why I want to look at the new technologies and see how they can be used by people of goodwill and deep faith. I am like a fish trying to adapt to the water now that it is changing from fresh to salt—my environment has shifted. My students and my grandchildren are growing up in a different world. Rather than inveigh against the new technology and what it is doing to the world I know, I should like to understand it and to trace its possibilities and promises.

THE PLATE TECTONICS OF THE TECHNOLOGY
OF INFORMATION

In exploring this new world, I begin with the premise that there have been three major technological transformations in human history, that is, fundamental changes related to transportation and the storage and retrieval of information: first, the development of written language and the invention of the wheel and the raft, as well as the domestication of animals; second, the development of the printing press and mass print and of the steam engine; and third (which is not just beginning but rather has been in progress for over a century), the development of electric, electronic, or paperless information storage and retrieval and of the rocket and jet propulsion. This latest transformation is the main focus of this volume, but the first two form a necessary background.

Before that first shift, the human world was one of the village and one of oral communication. It was a world where speaker and listener were joined through mutual activity. This physical joining (you cannot talk to a person unless the two of you are within range of each other) has been called a world of "vatic [or oracular] communion," where physical proximity and personal relationships and connections are as important as the message. The language of communion is one of shared conventions of sound, gesture, and movement. Oral communication is suited to a village life. It is a world steeped in ceremony. Ceremony, whether embodied in story, drama, dance, or some other medium, is a way by which a community manifests its myths and lore, its laws and taboos. As Jacques Ellul asserts, ceremony is the center of learning in an oral society.

The First Transformation

The world of text is a world of linearity and order; it sets a written document, a text, between two people, the writer and the reader. They no longer need be connected to each other; in fact, the reader and writer are most often unknown to each other except by name—and that most often is only the reader's knowledge of the writer's name. There is no communion, and perhaps no communication. Texts work well in a world of towns or city-states where there is a center and a periphery. Texts give us laws and history. They give order to the world and a sense of control to those who use them. The focal point and center of learning for the world of text is the library, that archive where texts are stored so that people of several generations can have access to them.

In *The Logic of Writing and the Organization of Society* (1986), Jack Goody argues that the existence of written language has over the years enabled commerce, government, and history to develop, tribes to become states, barter to become payment, and tribal cults to blossom into regional and even world religions. Written language appears to have begun as an aid to commerce; quickly it was adapted to governments and then to religions. It was also used for art and literature much later. Writing enabled people to set prices and make bills of lading; it allowed them to enlist armies by listing names and to make treaties and laws; it allowed them to record the precise words of epics and songs; and it similarly allowed them to set down the words of the deity. The "religions of the Book" were able to transcend the local by the fact that scripture had a permanence beyond each telling of the story. The texts contained law as well as history, doctrine as well as prophecy.

The invention of writing was the first shift, but for almost two millennia writing and oral language coexisted in the West. Most of what was written was the province of a privileged group, the scribes, who had the key to the secrets of written language and who controlled the affairs of town, commerce, the religious enterprise, and even empires. What they wrote was further promulgated orally. The rabbi, imam, scribe, or priest was a person who pronounced, extolled, and expatiated upon the text to the unlettered audience. These religious leaders used other means to worship and understand what they were worshipping besides the text, including various ceremonies or icons as aids. Writing was hard to do, the materials were expensive, and copying was laborious.

The Second Transformation

Beginning around the mid-fifteenth century, Johann Gutenberg changed all that. By combining movable type with the press, he was able to make multiple and identical copies of a text, which in turn could be distributed far and wide. For the first time, texts could conveniently reach the hands of anyone capable of reading them, and within a few generations the number of readers grew far beyond the scribal minority to encompass increasingly large segments of the general populace. As readership grew, more and more libraries were founded and flourished, in turn becoming centers of learning for new universities and colleges (as did other repositories of writing). The development of the steam engine in the seventeenth century aided the spread of texts and literacy because paper could be made cheaply and thousands of copies of a book or paper could be readily generated. Further stimulated by railroads and other manifestations of steam technology, cities were able to grow, surrounded by suburbs. These urban centers became hubs in the development of nation-states and in the spread of imperial governments and religions. Such an eventual progression was to a great extent enabled by the ubiquity of text in books, magazines, newspapers, signs, packaging, legal documents, and even graffiti, all of which enabled people throughout the nation and the world over to have the same records of daily political, social, and spiritual interest.

Elizabeth Eisenstein takes up this idea in her monumental work, *The Printing Press as an Agent of Change*. She (among others) attests that, because of the mass reproduction and exact duplication of print, a whole variety of texts including money, licenses, books, and newspapers helped such modern constructs as the nation-state, scientific inquiry, and capitalism to flourish. Trade could go around the world. Scientists could make maps, charts, and taxonomies. Marriages and deaths could be certified in licenses. Christianity could be taken out of the church and into the home. By virtue of translation and duplication, the Bible could pervade Europe and travel into the New World. The Bible societies of the eighteenth and nineteenth centuries promoted Christianity through the translation and propagation of the Gospel text, believed to be as effective as the active intervention of missionaries. Not only Christianity but also the concepts of western European culture, government, and education spread throughout the world and with them the idea of universalism, the thought that there was one underlying set of principles for all humanity, as for all of nature, science, and thought.

The way in which the text bridges the gap between reader and writer is complicated and has been much studied, but one of the major principles is one of a sharing of visual conventions (the marks on paper mean roughly the same thing to both writer and reader). The fact that they are set down on paper means they have to be read in the order set down for the reader to "follow" the writer. Because writing is in visible space, it is ordered according to the three dimensions of space. This book has length and width and depth. Its pages are numbered so that you can begin on page 1 and end on page 219. You know that you are supposed to follow this order and that on each page you are to read from upper left to lower right unless told differently. You also know that these pages represent the thoughts of someone named Alan C. Purves (whomever you decide he is). If you want to find out about him, you must come in through his words, and then you will have him, literally, in deed.

Or will you simply find yourself? That question is the one raised by the third shift.

The Third Transformation

The world of print came into full flower about one hundred years ago; at the same time there came a number of inventions, all spawned by the harnessing of energy, that challenged its supremacy. Primary among these was the development of electricity and related phenomena. Thanks largely to Thomas Edison and Alexander Graham Bell, the telephone, film, and radio enabled people to bridge distances without print and without travel. With the invention of the airplane and the development of the automobile, people were not tied to a particular set of links, but could cross countryside and even oceans in any one of a number of directions. Electric light allowed for the recording of sound and image and their storage as easily as print had stored words and writing. As radio gave way to television and later as silicon chips enabled the computer to digitize information quickly, the whole world of communications could become instantaneous and not tied to written language.

Just as the advent of writing created the text or the book, so, too, the development of the new media—particularly the digitized multimedia of the CD-ROM, the Internet, and the World Wide Web—has created a new form, one with which we are just beginning to come to terms, and one which—each time we seek to grasp it—eludes us, much as a jellyfish might elude a spear-fisher. The center of learning appears to have vanished into cyberspace.

Hypertext as the New Metaphor of Communication

The world of the new media is best described as the world of hypertext, a world where a different form of relationship between people is possible. The writer and the reader may be near to each other or far apart. But the relationship is not set by the hard confines of a book or a letter. Instead, it is determined by the reader's interacting with seemingly amorphous text space. On the screen a text may appear and vanish. It may be associated with images, sound, or quick-time animations. The unit is the framed icon containing information in a digital form. It may be radically changed by a single keystroke. It may be saved or made to fit into another text that the reader has stored on a disk.

There are the letters that appear to combine into words, true, and they come in chunks like paragraphs and chapters, or documents, but there are also the spaces between them. These spaces are problematic in that they cannot be seen, as text spaces can. I type this at the bottom of my screen, I think there are several tens of "pages" of text down the scroll, but can I be sure? Where are they? They are numbers on a disk that can lose their characteristics should there be an error. I can send those numbers out through the telephone lines or the fiber optic cables to people all over the world who are plugged in. We don't have to go through my printing in a city and subsequently distributing copies along its transport routes. The world of electronic text is a world without a center—no one city is the hub of its information, just as there is no one center of transport in the new metropolis. But the cyberspace world is not a village either. It is a set of nodes separated by multidimensional spaces, a network of centers for commerce or communion. Rather than the city center or the village, we have the electronic highway and its shopping centers and strip malls of commerce, designated by cyberspace addresses.

Just as the highway is as important as the malls, so the empty spaces take on as important a role in the reading of electronic writing as do the words and sentences they separate. Such has also been true of speech (where pause and silence can be pregnant with meaning that may be fully realized only through the listener's close involvement). Such has also been true of writing, although in its earliest stages the boundaries between words were nonexistent (in languages like Hebrew, the boundaries between consonants were also not apparent). Slowly, letter, word, sentence, and then paragraph boundaries came to be used as ways of pointing to the spaces between marks and words. It is through the spaces that you as reader find order. I should note that this insight was one appreciated by artists centuries ago; it can be seen in the way they have used negative space to give sense to the painted objects, rests to give sense to the notes and chords of a musical composition, line endings and typographical space to give sense to the words in a poem, gutters to give sense to comic books and picture books, and, more recently, cut aways and fadeouts to give sense to film.

In hypertext, the spaces are less obvious than they appear to be in printed books. The text spaces can be linked in numerous ways (through a large number of dimensions), so that which link, which blank space, which connective tissue obtains is up to the reader—who thereby becomes a navigator or explorer through hyperspace and not simply a follower of a predesignated path.

There is no road map. You must make your own way, and doing so is part of the fun (see Figure 1.1).

In the world of hypertext words and pictures come together and may even overlap or be superimposed to form an overlay or palimpsest. But more, the word becomes not text but image. Writing has always been a visual medium, but in the Western world of alphabetic writing the written word has been tied to the oral. Hypertext builds not on the connection between writing and speech but that between writing and pictures. Its visual nature is not bound by three dimensions and the conventions of print, but can be changed and manipulated. As we shall see, the ideas of what texts are, what order they have, how they exist, and wherein lies their authority are all challenged.

The new electronic media have obviously brought with them changes in the ways that information is stored and retrieved. These are seen in the ideas surrounding hypertext and communication in hyperspace through the "information superhighway." With hypertext

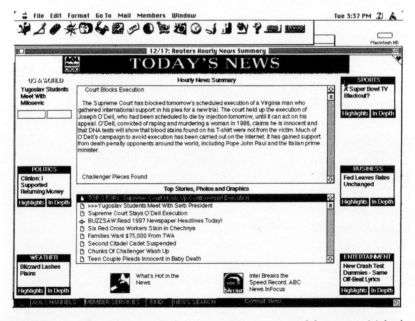

FIGURE 1.1. The American Online news page is a typical hypertext. Multiple pathways into and out of the page link it and the user to various parts of cyberspace. The page combines point-and-click technology with scrolling capabilities. ©1997 by America Online, Inc. All rights reserved. Reprinted by permission.

and hypermedia, it is possible for each reader to bring together a variety of segments related to an idea or a theme as she "browses" through them, making possible a great variety of combinations and juxtapositions of information. Some hypertexts combine both text and visual images; hypermedia can add other dimensions, such as videotapes or animations. It is possible therefore on a single disk or CD to have the text of *Macbeth*, views of the Globe Theatre or of Scotland, commentaries by various authors, segments of filmed performances of scenes, and audio commentary. These are arranged so that a reader may create any number of combinations and permutations in order to "read" the play in a larger context of his own choice.

On the electronic superhighway, it is possible to have access to hypermedia presentations; the *Macbeth* aficionado would find it possible to look through the catalogs of libraries throughout the world, check the archives of a newspaper or a journal (perhaps for a fee), see translations of the play in other languages, check a newspaper or magazine review of a new stage production, or become involved in a bulletin board conversation with others around the world who are curious about the play. The whole global library on *Macbeth* is available to a person who has a personal computer and a telephone, and the person could combine an interest in Shakespeare with one on bird watching, Argentinean politics, or any one of a number of interests. The writer, too, may use the superhighway, designing a book or poster and then transmitting that design to a printer in another part of the globe where, by electronic impulse, a four-color illustrated text may be produced. Thanks to the World Wide Web, the electronic impulses need not be printed, but can remain part of a vast panoply of images accessible in any order anywhere in the world (and out of it as well—on a space station, for instance).

Although it would appear that through such means as the Web and the Internet people can regain the direct communication and communion that may have been lost with the advent of writing and printing, electronic mail and bulletin boards offer a different sort of communion than that served by speech.

Unlike the transition from Gutenberg to the mass market book, which took some three hundred years, the computer has passed from a tool used by a minority to one available to nearly everyone in a few decades, and the Edisonian transformation is barely a century old. As a result, the change to electronic text and hypertext appears to us less as a slow shifting of the tectonics of communication, but more as a volcanic explosion. Unlike previous changes in the world of communications and writing that we can look back on with detachment, ours appears to us an eruption of change not unlike what astronomers see in a supernova. Our world today is fully as disorienting as was the early Renaissance to inhabitants of that turbulent era.

HYPERTEXT AS AN EMBLEM OF CHANGE

This book explores the impact of these new ways of storing and receiving information on cultural, intellectual, and religious beliefs and structures. My major focus will be on the United States and on Christianity (the first is where I happen to live, the second is the faith in which I am most secure), but I shall touch on matters elsewhere in the world and concerning other faiths. I shall occasionally mention geopolitical effects as well, but they fall outside my expertise. One theme of this book is that of decentralization, as represented through the ideas of hypertext and hyperspace. If space is multidimensional and seemingly infinite, it is hard to locate its single center; the center is where each of us is, but that is our center, not *the* center.

Our age is an age of decentralization in the world of text, in the physical world of cities and populations, in the world of the media, in the world of politics, where a dissident tribe can hold the United Nations (or dissident U.S. senators the national legislature) at bay, in the world of culture and the arts, where each subgroup claims its cultural niche, and in the world of the church, where supranational and ecumenical movements are challenged by local worship groups.

These changes raise the question as to the source and nature of unity in the next millennium, that age that we have come to call the postmodern. Our past unity has been so bound in the text, the church, the empire, the monoculture, that we have trouble envisioning any new unifying force or emblem.

Cultural Change

The new information technologies have come at a time of great political, social, and cultural change. Since the Second World War, numerous trends have been abetted by some of the new ways of storing and promulgating information. These years have seen around the world a resurgence of multiculturalism, or diversity in the ways we conceive of humanity and its cultures.

In the recesses of history and in the "underdeveloped" world, cultures were coterminous with villages, self-contained, isolated from other cultures. Much of our history is that of the rise and fall of nations and empires; villages were brought together into some larger construct that was termed a culture or a heritage, united by books and other documents. At the time of the building of the great library in Alexandria, Ptolemy thought he could gather together all of learning, "all that was known in the world." Of course, what was collected was all that was in Greek. He had to have the Torah translated.

Written language preserved the culture of the past and enabled people to have a cumulative record of thought, poetry, fiction, and drama. It also allowed them to coalesce around a number of texts that became totems of the culture.

When printing came, it was easy for this accumulated culture to survive and be added to. Printers began to assemble whole collections of what was important. This is the culture set forth in Europe particularly by the French Encyclopedists of the mid-eighteenth century. They advocated both deism and scientific rationalism, positing that their ideas were the sum total of thought in the world. And while they extolled science and philosophy, they also talked of universality, the application of a single cultural construct to explain all human phenomena. If something was initially foreign, it might become domesticated and assimilated into this melting pot of western European culture, which eventually allowed in contributions from Russia and eastern Europe, then the Americas, and then some of the other colonial literature and arts. The rest was treated as exotic, or foreign.

With the advent of the new media as well as with the discovery of other cultures that had their own writings and civilizations, there emerged the idea of multiculturalism. First the major empires collapsed, although their languages survived as one means of binding together people separated by vast distances. The newly independent countries of Africa, Asia, and the Pacific sought to develop their own cultural identities, either by recovering a preconquest past or by creating a new national culture. These have come to vie with the imperial and commercial cultures of Europe in their attempt to unify a population. The multicultural world is one in which some of the larger constructs appear out of place; except for such ubiquitous commercial enterprises as Nike, Benetton, and Coca-Cola, there may be no pot large enough to melt all the world's cultures. Universal concepts of growth, learning, behavior, morals, and science are all challenged by diversity. In most societies discordant cultures may not melt and coalesce but rather lie in some uneasy combination until circumstances propel them back into a traditional mode of hostility to one another. Such cultural diversity has now redirected such areas of thought as psychology, linguistics, and theology.

Social Change

One of the early changes in society appears to be that which accompanied the shift from a pastoral agrarian society with its sets of disconnected villages to that which brought the villages together under the commercial center, or the town. What towns brought with them was much greater division of labor and much enhanced possibilities for accumulating and trading goods and services.

Whether these changes helped to stimulate the further development of writing, certainly written codes of symbolism parting meaning helped to foster trade and commerce. Towns grew to become cities, even larger clusters of particular types of laborers and markets. Thriving on the written word, which enabled city dwellers to have accounts, laws, and history, not to mention a codified religion and literature, the city and the city state in turn encouraged an industry of professional writers, or scribes.

Writing served the cause of the development of larger and more centralized political and social units. The written text could travel with the king's or the emperor's messengers, and treaties and laws became a staple of the political scene. Geopolitical writing also helped to establish the domination of written codes; written languages such as Greek, Mandarin, Sanskrit, Latin, Arabic, French, and English have in their turn served the cause of expansion.

The printing press aided this expansion, for multiple and identical copies of a text meant that the rules and laws were the same wherever they went and on how many copies there were. With the printing press, writing and texts became available to more and more people, and it was possible to have a whole society literate. It was also easy for the empire to spread farther and farther. With the printing press, the empire could become global. Of course, the telegraph, better roads, and the harnessing of steam power were also instrumental to political expansion.

Marshall McLuhan wrote that, with the advent of the new media, particularly television, there loomed on the horizon the "global village" in which everyone could see and hear a potentate or a commentator simultaneously. This was true of television even when there were only a few channels available in any one area. Thanks to the development of satellite communications and fiber optics, however, multiple far-reaching channels have become available, and now, with the global electronic highway, information can be disseminated electronically through numerous modalities. Although the media bring people together instantaneously, because of the proliferation of media and of networks within any one medium, the village appears at this point to be multiple rather than single. Today's societies and cultures are suffused with media sources, and centers of learning no longer monopolize power; they are replaced by nodes on a network. Our world seems less like a village and more like a bazaar, a monstrously large shopping mall, or a Tower of Babel.

Religious Change

During the past fifty years there has been an accelerating change in the self-definition of the churches in terms of the world outside. In *The Once and Future Church*, Loren Mead sets out a series of metaphors, one of which is of the "young" or nascent church as an enclave surrounded by a hostile environment. This appears to be similar to the church in an oral or early written culture, where the church is the congregation, a group contained by the spoken word. It cannot move very far out of that containment without some sort of breakthrough in communications and storage of its records and lore. As problematic as each may be with regard to its authority and interpretation, the Torah, the Upanishads, the Gospel, and the Koran each helped the cult to become a religion. With the advent of scripture, the church can move into Mead's expansionist or imperial metaphor in which the individual congregations are bound together through a set of textual links: a scriptural tradition, laws, rules, hierarchies, and standard liturgies. In the imperial tradition, the outside world is progressively brought into a particular religion either through conversion or conquest, the two often being obverse sides of the same coin.

The growth and mutations of these religions over the centuries have, in part, been affected by changes in the technology of print. Print enabled them to spread, either through translation, as in the case of Christianity and Buddhism, or through the teaching of the sacred texts in their original form, as in Judaism and Islam. In each case diligent groups of scholars, some of them monks, some rabbis, some imams, copied the texts, commented on them, and perpetuated their own learning and the learning of the cultures that affected them. The Greek philosophic tradition, for example, was passed on through the efforts of Jewish, Christian, and Muslim scholars.

But if religions are affected by technology, out of religious institutions often emerge the people who master, transform, or re-create the new technology and rebuild themselves in light of it. The Israelites changed their way of thinking about the Word of God and of reading as they came to see the spread of the scribal tradition; the traditions of the storage, commentary, and teaching of the Torah emerged to forge a different approach to being a proper religious Israelite. So, too, as the printing press came about, people like Cranmer and Luther saw that this development had the makings of a whole new approach to the spreading of the Gospel. So, too, was it with the acceptance of written versions of the Koran by the imams. The Christian evangelical movement, too, rose on the back of mass printing, enabled by the steam-driven press. In our time, the new spirit of pentecostalism has coincided with the advent of the mass media and has even capitalized on the use of certain media, namely radio and television. The media both spawned new ways of seeing the text and the Word of the deity and heightened the efficacy of evangelism, that is, maintaining and extending the religious impulse across space and time. These parallel developments are more than mere coincidence.

It seems that today divisions between external and internal concerns are not so clearly defined as in the earlier two metaphors or traditions describing the church's development; the church nowadays is ill-defined in the sense that its walls are porous and its sense of mission is occluded. A part of its transformation consists in the growth of the home church movement, in the rise of "spirituality" (often referred to as "new age" spirituality), and in the development of a postevangelical ethos. Another part is visible in the division of denominations, sects, and parishes along geographic, social, and gender-defined lines that have become confused with doctrinal divisions. The church, which deals with the world's social and moral issues from a perspective that places great faith in "eternal verities," finds itself caught in the maelstrom of these very events. Even more than in the past, it has become the image in the mirror of society rather than the force that holds the mirror up to society. It can no longer appear universal or even necessarily the center of the spiritual empire. These phenomena have run parallel with the accelerating growth of independent charismatic or pentecostal churches, of televangelism, of numerous "twelve-step" programs, of communitarianism or Liberation Theology, and of home churches, all of which challenge the traditional mainstream denominations. I believe that these changes and the religious ambiguities they present parallel comparably radical changes in communications, culture, and society.

Change as Portent or Opportunity

To many who have recently written about the advent of the new information technologies, most changes appear to be hopelessly disruptive and anarchic in their implications. Critics have bemoaned the passing of the book, the end of writing, the death of culture as we know it, and the imminent coming of anarchy. While today's version of anarchy may be hard to live through, I believe that it can have its positive effects as well.

To most observers, hypertext represents an anarchic disruption of the book tradition, and the CD-ROM with its random access and lack of solidity appears to be a disruption of the encyclopedia and ultimately the library. As happened with the earlier changes that brought first, writing and then the printed book, this one is accompanied by a set of coincidental (or are they consequent?) changes in, or alternatives to, the way in which we view knowledge, political and social structures, cultures, and our very own religious institutions and beliefs. It is those coincidental or consequent changes that are the subject of this book.

The new social idea of community appears as an anarchic alternative to the traditional nation-state and its history of conquest and empire building.

Multiculturalism appears as an anarchic alternative to universalism and the idea of a single human culture.

Postmodernism appears as an anarchic alternative to modernism.

New spiritual communities appear to constitute an anarchic alternative to traditional churches.

But, as I hope to show, perhaps these new anarchic conditions are not so much disruptive as, in the end, cleansing. Anarchy in these terms might not isolate and divide us so much as help us to establish new kinds of connections, many of which cannot be foreseen or even imagined at this early stage of development.

Anarchies challenge old ideas of unity and authority. And in the network of cyberspace, I think, lies a new conception of unity, just as in the idea of hypertext lies a new conception of text and textual authority. Technologically, one's network of contacts and pursuits may be promoted by the modem, the hypertext web, the telephone, television, the airplane, the off-road vehicle, or the fax. Intellectually and politically, the network takes a number of forms, enhanced by these technological devices. Religiously, the network may be at the heart of a second Reformation, or a reformulation of the nature of religious institutions in our lives. Today's cyber-based network may ultimately prove to be the metaphor or the myth through which we come ever closer to God and a personal comprehension of God in our time.

At the same time, I realize full well that these new means of storing and retrieving information, of communicating, of construing society and culture, of worshipping a transcendent and immanent deity also raise unprecedented questions about the anarchy inherent in the development of cyberspace.

They raise the question of loss, of what we give up as we move into the new world of cyberspace. Some losses are harder to bear than others. Some losses are only apparent. Offices have lost the clack of typewriters. Roads have lost the healthy smell of manure. Cultures have lost the sense of a single dominant order. Religions have lost the possibility of dogma.

The world has lost the authority of the oral word.

The text becomes an image, an icon, fragile and easily manipulated; its once vaunted authority, too, is fast on the wane.

In becoming an image, the word appears to be lost, as does the voice of the speaker, and the authority of the writer.

In a world first of texts and then of images, the personal contact of human to human appears threatened by a depersonalized world dominated by technology. Truth, too, becomes harder to assert or find.

In a world of subcultures, the idea of a common heritage appears threatened.

In a world of communities and networks, the idea of a broad public or a polity appears threatened or outmoded.

But hypertext can reconnect people through the network. The virtual and the real worlds collide—and then perhaps merge. People can find communities and links in the web or the network. It is not easy; it is also less determinate and therefore more of a struggle; but it also opens up new possibilities for human communication and growth through involvement with others.

As a Christian, I find the spiritual and theological implications of the age of hypertext to be the most perplexing and yet the most pressing concerns of all. When I first explored the question in June 1994 at the Coolidge Colloquium, I found that Jewish colleagues shared many of my concerns. I also found in our common and disparate roots some of the answers that I sought. In this book I want to look at the technological, social, and cultural concerns as they play out against one another, but finally my concern is with theophany in the electronic world. How can we think of God in a world where many of the secure boundaries are gone, a world where there is not the ordered system of the sixth day but the reappearance of the chaos of the first?

CHAPTER TWO

The Nature of Hypertext
and Its Challenge

*T*o put it simply, hypertext has challenged our usual ways of conceiving of and using writing. As is often the case with challenges, the fact of a visible hypertext—something that looks and works differently from the sort of print we are used to—causes us to reconsider what we had been doing and how we had been thinking in the past. The very term *hypertext* sounds strange, spacey, trendy, and sort of "new age," but, for many, the phenomenon represented by the word has become familiar in our lives. Any person who uses a computer with Macintosh or Windows mouse-driven environments is using hypertext. The screen presents an area of spaces and texts to enter. How we read, write, and maneuver in that environment is the subject of this chapter. The challenge of hypertext also forces us to rethink how we have customarily read, written, and maneuvered in a world of pen and paper and the world of movable type, the world in which we had operated subconsciously. Some people use a computer as if they were using a fancy typewriter and believe that hypertext is simply an extension of the familiar. It is not. But it is connected to the familiar and makes the familiar new. Theodor H. Nelson has defined hypertext as "nonsequential writing—text that branches and allows choices to the reader, best read at an interactive screen. As popularly conceived, this is a series of text chunks connected by links that offer the reader different pathways." Jay Bolter, one of the creators of Storyspace, defines hypertext as consisting of "topics and their connections, where again the topics may be paragraphs, sentences, individual words, or indeed digitized graphics [see Figure 2.1]. . . . A hypertext network can expand indefinitely as a printed text cannot."[1]

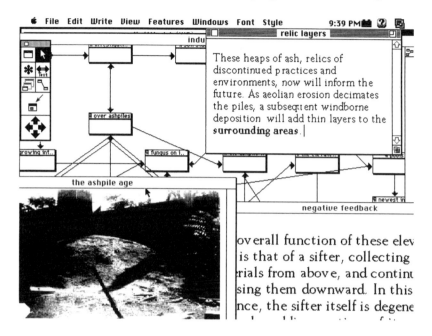

FIGURE 2.1. A view of a virtual essay (using Storyspace™), which combines graphics, links, and text in an interwoven hypertext. © 1997 by Eastgate Systems, Inc. Reprinted by permission.

I suspect that the advent of the printing press caused many people to rethink the manuscripts and scrolls they knew so well. Some probably thought of the printing press as simply a mechanical scrivener—especially given the fact that the first books were printed to look like manuscripts. Although the technology changed, consciousness of it did not change so quickly. It takes time to assimilate a new invention or discovery, and there are periods of ignoring the event and many instances of resisting it. In this chapter, I shall discuss hypertext's challenge to the way we think about the nature of the author, how hypertext forces us to consider how writing looks, and how it causes us to reconsider the conventions of texts and writing.

Before we can explore the impact of hypertext on the nature of what we write and read, I should say something about *text*.[2] Texts surround us in the Western world. When I get up in the morning, I go into the bathroom and pick up a toothbrush and toothpaste, both of which have texts on them. I find texts on all my packages of food, in the newspaper that I read with breakfast, in the book of prayers and scriptures with which my wife and I begin our day. They are part of the environment as I go to the office. They are what I busy myself with during working hours, what I create, analyze, edit, expound to my students, find on the television screen, and amuse or console myself with at the end of the day.

Put simply, texts are physical objects on which appears written or printed language. A text may be long or short, large or small. Road signs are texts; captions on television screens are texts; so are newspapers, poems, books, birth certificates, and tombstone inscriptions. Texts are both the products of and the tools of the variety of scribes who make up the workforce in the information age. They are products in that various people write, edit, print, and distribute them. They are tools in that people use them in the course of pursuing their occupations, particularly in such fields as law, advertising, management, government, education, and the church.

When texts were ubiquitous and unchallenged, people studied the content of some of them—the sacred works, literature, historical and legal documents—but, except for bibliographers, designers, and antiquarians, they didn't study the texts as artifacts of interest intrinsically (i.e., separate from their content); they mostly just churned the texts out. Most were only peripherally conscious of the beauty or ugliness of the physical text. But, as texts and the printed word appeared to be challenged by such new media as television and computers, and as people announced the death of such things as the novel, the book, or literacy, texts have become the object of study by psychologists, anthropologists, philosophers, and computer programmers. Fish don't study water until the drought begins.

Scholars have developed theories about texts and the nature of text (separating the examples and the genus). Most theories of text hold that a text is an artifact created by an artisan whom we call the writer. The writer may produce it with a chisel, a brush, a pen, a typewriter. She may put it on a stone, a piece of bark, paper, cloth, even in the sky. Then it just sits, alone, like a rock, deteriorating at the pace of whatever medium it happens to be on. When it is picked up and perused by someone we call the reader, that person, following a natural human inclination, tries to make sense of it in some way. Readers as a special breed of human and the nature of what we call literacy will be focal points of the next chapter—even though in this chapter I shall make it hard to separate writer from reader, for I face that difficulty in my very definitions of writing and reading.

RELIGIOUS TEXTS AS A SPECIAL CASE
AND AS A MODEL

In order to consider texts in general, I think it important to single out one kind of text that has had a longer continuous life than any other. Sacred texts, many of which were first composed three or four thousand years ago and first written down two to three thousand years ago, have remained pretty much as they were first inscribed. There have been some changes as a result of printing and binding, and the electronic versions of many are now quite complex, but the content and structure of many has lasted. As I noted earlier, the ways in which we think about text and literacy are intimately bound up with religion, particularly with the international religions—Judaism, Hinduism, Islam, Buddhism, and Christianity. We know of these religions and their history, as we know of all history, through the written and printed word. These religions were founded upon writing; it was written language that took them from being minor cults to regional and then global religions. The Tanakh, Rig Veda, Koran, Dhammapada, and the Gospels, or New Testament, each became the focal point of a group of believers, and to those believers and their proselytes these texts became sacred objects, perdurable and vital through all manner of vicissitudes.

These religions were spread in part by the work of writers and printers, and at the same time they were the major reason for literacy's spreading beyond a merchant or governing class. For this reason, they have affected what it means to be literate. They did so because religion was at the center of literate society in their respective cultures. Although the very first people to read and write were probably merchants, the skills and secrets of writing soon passed to priests and government officials. Since in many ancient societies the government was defined by religion (although few were the theocracy that ancient Israel was), the priestly and the governmental tended to merge. Scribes, those who could read and write and who had control of print and libraries, often had a religious status. So it was in the Middle East, and so it became at the end of the Roman Empire, when the monks, including the Celtic monks, were the ones who preserved writing, books, and therefore culture. (Islamic scribes and scholars performed similar preservational work.) So it was in the world of the Brahman and the Buddhist. The priests, monks, and scribes preserved texts so that they could be passed from village to village and town to town as well as from generation to generation. They enabled the religions to spread and prosper; they also guarded their literary skills and passed them on, as well as the texts. They established many of the practices of writing and reading we hold today. Their role held them apart from and above ordinary people.

The sacred text, or set of texts, was at the heart of these religion and their missions. The texts lay at the heart of the process of evangelizing and indoctrinating outsiders and the young into the mysteries of the religion. In order to learn of the religion, one had to read, be read to, or learn to read; in order to be considered truly religious, one of the hierarchy of the religion, one had to be a scribe. The text was at the heart of the mission of the religion; it was also at the heart of its liturgy.

It is because of the persistence of these religions and their practitioners that much of what we consider "classical learning," both sacred and secular, is preserved to this day. In most cultures of the world, the religious literates were the custodians of print, the creators of the canons, the leaders of the religious ceremonies, and the founders of the centers of learning, the libraries with their attendant schools.

When three of these five world religions began, writing was a relatively new phenomenon. Only Christianity and Islam came into being in a world where literacy and its attendant learning were well established. Although Christ and Mohammed viewed the written text and the scribal caste with distrust, their causes soon became deeply enfolded in the tradition of text and literacy. For Judaism, Hinduism, and Buddhism, the writing of the sacred text came at a time when writing was relatively young. This scribal minorities maintained the sacred texts and perpetuated themselves for generations in part because they were exclusionary and in part because they retained a part of the sacred lore not in text form but as oral tradition. The oral Torah, for example, was not written down until about 200 C.E. (200 A.D.), and much Christian liturgical practice was passed on by oral instruction and memory. To be a literate priest or scribe was to be a person of honor, a privileged one. Literacy, however, spread beyond the priesthood, and there were prophets who could write, as well as literate people who were outside of the scribal caste.

The exception to what I have been describing occurred in those two great repositories of text and literacy, Greece and Rome. Both societies had religions, and to some extent religious texts, in the form of plays and poems, but the texts do not appear to have been central to religious practice. For them what seems central was the ceremony, often captured in drama, dance, or choric song. This may explain why the Greek and Roman religions were not particularly strong and did not spread. What spread was a secular intellectual impulse contained in the written works of the great philosophers and the historians. Together with the works of those poetic giants, Homer and Virgil, these texts lay at the core of the Hellenistic and Roman intellectual and literate heritage. But history informs us that, though such was the case, the fusion of Hellenistic ideas with first the traditions of Judaism and second the offshoot of Judaism, Christianity, helped to form one of the strongest religious and literate forces history has ever known.

Christianity spread, through Aramaic and Greek versions of the Gospels; this meant that it spread through the broadest set of classes, even the slaves, who were educated in Greek, for that was the common language of the day. Three centuries later, thanks to Jerome, the Gospels appeared in Latin and thus reached the broader audience that had learned that language as a result of the Roman conquests that made Latin the new "world-wide" language. Many have noted that, as far as intellectual power is concerned, many of the best minds of the second and third centuries C.E. tended to be those infused with the new spirit of Christianity rather than with the traditional ideas of what we now call "paganism." These minds pored over and examined the texts of the Gospel and the Hebrew Testament, created the canons, wrote the commentaries, and established the practices and principles of the Church, that living body and tradition of leadership, worship, and practice. What these people did for Christianity, similar sets of people did for Islam, Judaism, and Buddhism.

In general, the transformation from simple text to sacred or holy scripture is complex. One step involves the definition of the text to be a transcription of the actual word of God or of a divinely inspired person. Another step, that of incorporation into the worshipful life, I shall describe in detail in the next chapter. The words of the text can be taken one step further and themselves become deified. In some religions, Hinduism, Judaism, Christianity, scripture is divine ("The whole of speech is Brahman [divine]"). Some within those three religions hold the view that scripture even precedes the earth. "In the beginning was the Word, and the Word was with God and the Word was God." The word, the text, the author, and the reader become fused on an eternal plane that is not like anything of the natural world.

AUTHORS AND AUTHORITY IN TEXT AND HYPERTEXT

Over the years, scholars have pondered the question of whether writing and the texts produced through writing are communicative devices like telephones and oral language. This is an important question, for it asks whether there is any direct communication between the writer and the reader and therefore what might be the identity and the role of each. The consensus is that there is no direct communication between writer and reader. The writer who produces the text on my tube of Crest (toothpaste) is not addressing me or anyone in particular. He has simply fashioned some letters and words and put them in the memory of a machine that impresses identical images of thousands of bits of plastic. Most of the millions who pick up or examine the "Crest text" will take away no more meaning than that garnered by looking at the red letters on a white background and identifying the plastic as a tube containing the brand of toothpaste they want. They can also use it each morning—that is, identify it as toothpaste and not shaving cream. A few might read all that has been written on the plastic. What further information and use they gain from that reading will vary but will not change the message or the toothpaste. Most importantly, the "Crest text" stands alone: it is an image (though marketers would dearly like it to be an idol). And the person who wrote it is not like a person to whom you are talking or with whom you are exchanging e-mail but rather has moved to a greater distance from us. That person has become not a writer, but an author.

Theorists can readily contrast text, which generally reflects this extreme distance from an almost forgotten author, to an oral performance. Text is something visible and tangible. It exists in space. A text is first of all a seen object, an image; then it comes into focus to be read. Oral performances, speeches, conversations, songs, and chants are invisible and can only be heard. They exist in time. Before the recording device, they were retained only in the memory of the speaker or listener, imperfect as that might be. But since the beginning of texts, there seems to have been an interplay between the written text and the oral performance, calling into play our evolving concepts of both scripture and literacy.

The French philosopher Paul Ricoeur defines a text as discourse fixed in writing. By being fixed it becomes particularized and separated from the author. The same might be said of the recording of a speech in that it is no longer directly attached to the speaker. Other philoso-phers have explored the implications of this view of text as an object "out there" to be seen and thus to be tangled by the perceiving eye and mind. The French philosopher Jacques Ellul sees this separation as necessarily a degradation of spoken language, for text takes spoken language out of the realm of communication, time, and truth and puts it in the realm of space, reality, and potential misrepresentation. It has distanced the text we read from the original speaker by rendering him as a mere author. Others see this separation as making any one text a mere portion of a much larger verbal landscape, and thus to be seen in relationship to its environment of other words and leaves of paper.

But this idea of separation is a fairly recent perception of writing and of various texts. Ellul cites the Bible as one source of his discon-tent, but there are occasions even there when the oral and the written can be seemingly taken for each other. One of the prime examples is in the opening of Psalm 45:

ODE FOR A ROYAL WEDDING

To the leader: according to Lilies. Of the Korahites. A Maskil. A love song.
My heart overflows with a goodly theme;
I address my verses to the king;
my tongue is like the pen of a ready scribe.

The psalmist fuses the oral and the written in the act of compo-sition such that the two are coequal in their potential for heartfelt praise. The written word served as an aid to the speaker or singer and did so for many centuries before the printing press made printed texts readily available, thereby rendering the oral reader or intoner of the text unnecessary to the community. Ellul's dissatisfaction, I believe, is with the ubiquity of print, not its existence. This act of fusing speaking with writing is one to which I shall return in discussing reading in the next chapter.

Who (What) Is an Author?

As you read this book, you are probably aware of me, Alan Purves, the author/writer of this book. I am certainly the person who entered nearly all of it on a word processor, edited it, and made a lot of decisions about it. By profession I am a writer; in your eyes I am an author, which is both a descriptive term that I have suggested and simultaneously a more honorific term. To me, an author has the charisma of an artist. I remember visiting my uncle, a successful muralist, when I was taking a painting course in high school. "I'm an artist, too," I proudly announced. "No, you're not," he replied. "No one can ever call themselves an artist. That's for others to call you." "Author" has a similar significance for me—and there's a reason for it.

The concept of the author, originator, or creator at first was separate from the writer. Writers were the people who inscribed texts from other sources or transcribed others' words. They were the scribes, the scriptors, the amanuenses, the copyists. The author, by contrast, had a voice, not a pen. We know the names of some early authors—Hammurabi, David, Homer, a Pharaoh or two, Amos. We know the names of only a very few early scribes.

It was not until writing had become fairly common that it became important for someone to be named as the writer. In the Bible, Moses is the first named scribe, taking down the commandments of Yahweh—God Himself. He is considered both scribe or "scriptor" and composer or "author" of the Pentateuch. Later named writers included Ezekiel, St. Paul, and John of Patmos.

In Genesis, Elohim "authors" the world by speaking. Adam, the groundling, was also an author in the sense of being a namer, and his naming was an act of creation. God is considered the author of the "Book of Nature" in that God created the world and all that is in it. He authored the world, creating it for the most part with His voice: "Let there be Light."

As a made being of the earth, Adam came after the first creation and was given the task of naming the animals. When the animals have names, the physical and the mental worlds come together; although the corporeal animals may have been physically present, they did not fully exist until they could be identified through language. We can say that Adam was both a reader and an author in that he had to examine the animal species and determine what they were. Several midrash treat this activity and suggest that he had to "read" the animals and determine either by looking at them or by talking with them what the appropriate name might be. We can say that this is one of the first occasions in which reading and writing come together. From the earliest of times, therefore, the reader has been an author.

This position of reading the world and reading the word is at the heart of the liberation pedagogy of Paulo Freire, which is tied to liberation theology. Freire argues that when the adult illiterate learns to read the world, to understand its nature, and to use language to describe and comprehend or surround the objects, then that person is able to see written language in a new way: not as a threat but as something that he can control. The reader becomes an author.

Both Adam and Paulo Freire's peasant are active authors who are constantly re-creating the authorial act. When they look at the world and use language to describe it, they exercise authority over the part of the world they have named. They have only to be aware of their prowess.

Harvey Cox and others argue that this cocreation is what helps keep the Judeo-Christian God separate from the deities of the ancient Greeks, of whom man was simply the passive observer. The author–reader carries on the work of the divine and is not a passive instrument in the deistic world.

Active authorship is what Coleridge described in his great statement on the imagination: "The primary Imagination I hold to be the living power and prime Agent of all human Perception, and as a repetition in the finite mind of the eternal act of creation in the infinite I AM." The act of perception, of "reading the world," is not a passive act of seeing, but an active and creative mental act. When this act is transformed into language by an author, the secondary Imagination, which "dissolves, diffuses, dissipates, in order to recreate," comes into play. "It struggles to idealize and to unify. It is essentially vital, even as all objects (as objects) are essentially fixed and dead."[3]

In Coleridge's view, then, the world of God is a world of objects, which are for us dead and inert until, like Adam, we perceive and name them, and thereby assert our authority over them by putting them in language and thus giving them what Shakespeare called "an human habitation and a name."

Language is the way in which we inhabit the world and, by inhabiting it, take on a degree of authority.

The History of Authors

Today, an author is usually associated with the written word; before there was writing, people told stories and delivered oral messages of various sorts. These vanished into thin air or remained in the memories of the listeners. With writing came a text that could be seen, touched, read aloud from, and returned to and found exactly the same, time after time. But it was not until the late Middle Ages that the person who actually made this thing that we can see and touch came to be important in the way the person was whose ideas were uttered and copied.

Up until the Renaissance, the author lay behind or under the text, not in it. This was in some respects parallel to the situation of the oral storyteller or the prophet, who was only the spokesperson for the muse or the deity, but even so was an important figure. The words were the muse's, the voice was the storyteller's. The author is the source of the Logos, the word. To some, the author and the Logos are the same.

From the time of the early Renaissance until today, the author of a text is the person who first puts ideas into a visual form. The author is a writer, that is, one who can create things that people see. The author and the scribe become merged. But the author may need a transcriber. The author creates images of words and ideas. She puts marks on a blank space and surrounds those marks with space. The author is a pattern maker. This act of authoring is an act of inscribing. In today's office with the personal computer and advanced word processing programs, this perspective changes. The secretaries are in the machine. The author is not only the author but the scribe as well.

The Image of the Author

We still hold to the idea that an author is an originator and the author can be seen through the visible writing. The author who could both set forth ideas and images has authority and thus is to be revered or respected. But familiarity breeds contempt, and as the number of authors increases, so their special powers appear to diminish. What happens to authors in a world of the information explosion? Do they disappear? Do they reconstitute themselves? We know that authors differ from scribes. The originator is not the same as the copyist. The writer is not the same as the secretary or stenographer, but, with the advent of word processors, the secretary and the copyist or scribe appear to become superfluous. Yet, the author is not alone.

There is a long-standing popular impression that authors are solitary types who inhabit garrets, striving with pen or pencil to put their ideas on paper. They cannot be successful; they do not have lives like the rest of us. They are to the popular imagination, as Jack

Stillinger reminds us, solitary geniuses.[4] That image of the inspired and impoverished solitary author has stayed with us for centuries. Many students and literary critics are unhappy that authors like Stephen King or Alice Walker can be so successful. In their view, a rich author cannot be a good author. It was so even in the time of Sir Walter Scott, the first author to make good money at the trade—or so they attest.

But Stillinger also reminds us that this primarily nineteenth-century image is far from accurate. In the earliest days the author was different from the scribe. Even though later authors physically set down the draft of their text, even as early as the time of Chaucer they were assisted by scriveners, printers, editors, and a host of other aides. Today, many books are produced by a team, a production company, that takes an idea and turns it into a book or an article. Who is the originator under those circumstances.

Traditionally, the author has authority, the right to enforce obedience, the right to influence. That is to say, the author expects readers to follow the text in the way in which it was intended. "I write; let others learn to read," Joseph Conrad is reported to have said. This is a strong call for authorial authority and readerly obedience. The author expects us to accept the given nature of the work—its fictionality, its appeal, its claims to fact and truth. That is authorly influence. It gives the author authority.

The Processes of Authoring

If we use language to author our world and so have some authority over it, how does this translate into the actual task of writing? We know something about the way people composed text in early times. It appears to have been a process in which the writer would find a formula or set of formulae whereby to make the tale or the song memorable from one teller or singer to another. These stock phrases or rhythms would be set against any new material in a counterpoint so that the author could use the phrases as rests while gathering the ideas for the next round. The stock phrases would also be known to the later reciters so that they would not have to memorize the piece word for word but chunk by chunk, using the stock phrases the same way a jazz piano player uses the "vamp" to move from melody to melody or theme to variation.

Anthropologists and folklorists have shown how this use of stock

phrases enables oral storytellers and bards to go on reciting for hours.[5]
The Hebrew psalms are good examples of this sort of authoring with
such phrases as:

> Ps. 33:3 Sing to him a new song; play skillfully, and shout for joy.
>
> Ps. 40:3 He put a new song in my mouth, a hymn of praise to our
> God. Many will see and fear and put their trust in the LORD.
>
> Ps. 96:1 Sing to the LORD a new song; sing to the LORD, all the
> earth.
>
> Ps. 98:1 Sing to the LORD a new song, for he has done marvelous
> things; his right hand and his holy arm have worked salvation for
> him.
>
> Ps. 144:9 I will sing a new song to you, O God; on the ten-stringed
> lyre I will make music to you.
>
> Ps. 149:1 Praise the LORD. Sing to the LORD a new song, his praise
> in the assembly of the saints.

or:

> Ps. 18:2 The LORD is my rock, my fortress and my deliverer; my God
> is my rock, in whom I take refuge. He is my shield and the horn of
> my salvation, my stronghold.
>
> Ps. 19:14 May the words of my mouth and the meditation of my
> heart be pleasing in your sight, O LORD, my Rock and my
> Redeemer.
>
> Ps. 27:5 For in the day of trouble he will keep me safe in his
> dwelling; he will hide me in the shelter of his tabernacle and set
> me high upon a rock.
>
> Ps. 28:1 To you I call, O LORD my Rock; do not turn a deaf ear to
> me. For if you remain silent, I will be like those who have gone
> down to the pit.
>
> Ps. 31:2 Turn your ear to me, come quickly to my rescue; be my rock
> of refuge, a strong fortress to save me.
>
> Ps. 40:2 He lifted me out of the slimy pit, out of the mud and mire;
> he set my feet on a rock and gave me a firm place to stand.
>
> Ps. 42:9 I say to God my Rock, "Why have you forgotten me? Why
> must I go about mourning, oppressed by the enemy?"
>
> Ps. 61:2 From the ends of the earth I call to you, I call as my heart
> grows faint; lead me to the rock that is higher than I.
>
> Ps. 62:2 He alone is my rock and my salvation; he is my fortress, I
> will never be shaken.
>
> Ps. 71:3 Be my rock of refuge, to which I can always go; give the
> command to save me, for you are my rock and my fortress.

These stock phrases, like the stock descriptions of enemies, or of specific historical actions, or of the sea or the vineyard, were used not because the reciters or authors were lazy but rather because they formed a pattern that would be useful to the audience as well as the reciter. In the Hebrew case, the reciter also used the second part of the verse to repeat and extend the first, as is evident in a number of these examples. The repetition helped the hearer recapture what had been heard before and connect it to the new material.

The oral author, then, used a technique of theme and variation in which the shape of the whole could be derived from a template and thus create a new story. In writing, people do the same with form letters or templates such as the ones that exist for many companies and government agencies. Novelists, short story writers, playwrights, and essayists use them as well. The author is, like Adam, a reader and reuser of words, phrases, metaphors, and stories.

When people talk about the process of writing, they refer to it as a "mental" and "linguistic" process involving a set of operations that appears to be invariant. There is the stage of planning, or thinking about what one is going to write and finding the language to have authority over the subject; drafting, or setting the initial verbal reconstruction of the word; revising, a form of checking the text against the mental model one has of what one wanted to say; and lastly, editing, making the final version.

This view of the process of writing suggests that each piece of writing is new and that the writer starts from scratch with ideas and then finds the linguistic form for them. It separates the composing from the inscribing and uses a model of the publishing world that places editors between the author and the final text. Such a view works if one thinks of writing either in the medieval fashion of a reader intoning the text to be copied by a group of scriptors or scribes or as the composer putting things down in longhand on a yellow pad and then getting someone to type them up or print them, going over the typed version to make major corrections, and then releasing the whole to a set of copyeditors. It works as a model in the world where the author is separate from the secretary. It works for the author as dictator. That was real authority, and the language would show it. But even these authors were not originators, but readers who reorder and recombine. And this view of the process only skims the surface of what goes on with the one who reads and then writes. The hypertext model may catch the complexity more fully.

A Surfeit of Authors

In the world of hypertext there are a number of authors as well as scribes. There are the authors in the machine, the programmers and keyboarders, and the readers who rewrite the text each time they read it. In this world, there is a surfeit of authors—everyone is an author.

There is an originating author, but the originator may simply set forth the pieces of the game or the spaces of the hypertext and create the web, drawing from a large number of diverse files in the computer's hard drive. The successive users (readers) can re-create, change, and reorder the spaces. By creating weblets within the web, they, too, are authors of their part of the hypertext web. The hypertext is highly mutable. Given the fact that it consists of a set of spaces and links between them that different readers can combine in different ways, the hypertext is not the set production of an author; rather, it is mutable in each reading, thereby creating a new web. Just as Adam read in order to name, so the reader of a hypertext simultaneously reads and composes. The activity is a tangible version of what authors have been doing for centuries. With hypertext, the operation is patent not hidden.

That being the case, the following questions apply:

Where is authority over the text?
Where is authority in the text?
To whom or to what is there to be obedience?
Who is the originator of influence?
Where is the orderly process?

It would seem to be an anarchy.

The Authority of Authors

Do authors today have the same sort of authority they did in the past? Has the author disappeared or receded in the contemporary world of hypertext?

Actually, the author lost authority before the advent of hypertext—at least the literary author lost it. From the time of Aristotle, Western critics have focused their concern and research on the action of the author or the action of the reader. Modernist critics sought to focus on the text itself, to strip away the perceiving self so as to see the object as it really is, but their efforts have since been seen as fruitless. They kept finding themselves.

The object is hard to isolate from the artist and the viewer. Yeats asked, "Who can tell the dancer from the dance?" We might also ask, "Who can tell the reader from the text?" In the heyday of modernist criticism, the poem was an autonomous object whose meaning and value could not be authorized by the writer. The author creates a work of art that remains immutable and silent, like a statue. Then the author steps aside. The text stands alone and in this modernist view the immutable text is an object for criticism and remains, in a sense, dumb. Archibald MacLeish summed it up with the expression from "Ars Poetica":

> A poem should not mean
> But be

Later, as modern critics gave way to postmodern ones, there came to be an emphasis on the reader as the authority for meaning.

Who is in control is a perplexing question. Equally perplexing is this question: who are the authors of word-processed text? Who is the author of this book? Me, the programmers, colleagues who made comments and suggestions, the spell-check, the editors, the printer, you who reads it?

The author can do nothing to control the answers to that question, and perhaps does not want to, for the creative act of coauthoring is finally liberating. But some authors find it discomfiting and use various tricks and devices to assure the reader that they are in control. There has been a spate of books in which the author (or the assumed author) becomes a character in the book, telling the reader that he or she is really in control over the characters and their lives. This phenomenon occurs in the fiction of Umberto Eco, Michael Ende, Salman Rushdie, and others. They are following the lead of Laurence Sterne and Jorge Luis Borges, who developed the idea of the author as master trickster, the person who controlled the whole illusion of the fiction. They tried to claim authority, but in so doing they raised the question as to whether the author had any control or not.

The originating author (if such there be) has not surrendered authority but rather is sharing it with the readers.

Author! Author?

The author is displaced. The reason lies in part with the dilemma I have cited above, but it is also a feature of the ways in which the mass media have tended to treat the author. Nowadays the author may not be the central figure in conceiving a film or a television script—often, it is an actor or the director who is the true stimulus. The director is often seen as an "auteur," but it is often hard to assess how thorough-going the control wielded by a Steven Spielberg or a Jane Campion really is, film by film. One must consider the cinematographer and the editor, as well. In the cases of both Woody Allen and Spike Lee we seem to have a sense of clear authority. For Allen, additional authority may derive from his often being the star of the film. Thanks to the star system, authority in the media may largely gravitate from the author/director to the leading actor, that is, the most visible and thus identifiable figure involved in the project.

In the world of mass media, authority accrues to those most visible or audible in the final product and not necessarily to the originator, scriptwriter, director, or camera person—those who most surely determine specifically what we see and hear. The emphasis is on the *who*, not the *what*. So it is similarly with our perception of hypertext.

Hypertext Authors

In the world of hypertext, there are a number of authors:

1. the program authoring team;
2. the writer of the original text;
3. the mechanical "writing" done by the program itself (the sorters, spelling checkers, organizers, editors, search engines, and converters, for example);
4. the networked coauthors, external editors, and formatters; and
5. the readers, who redact the text as they read.

Hypertext is in some sense never finished.

This does not mean that we cannot identify authors 1 and 2. Authors 3 are invisible. Authors 4 are also elusive. Authors 5 fill the role that most of us inhabit, although we may occasionally shift into any of the other four roles.

Authority and Control of Hypertext

Who controls the reading of the hypertext? The writer clearly established the spaces in the first place and also forges the links.

But each reader can take a variety of different paths and ignore, reorder, change, delete, and supplement spaces and paths.

Who is the boss, anyhow?

Is being the boss the right question? Is it even a relevant question?

Have we all along avoided the question? Isn't the hypertext question simply a bringing into plain sight a series of questions we should have been asking all along about all sorts of texts?

If the question of control and authority changes with respect to text, what are the broader implications in society? What are the theological implications?

The writers control the text; the text controls the readers; the readers control the text and the writers; convention controls the writers and the reader through the text; writers and readers can invent and play with convention and the text. The whole is an apparent anarchy.

Invisibly, the text controls how we read. As we shall see, the comic book is a useful example of how this control operates but also demonstrates how we maneuver through the apparent and invisible controls.

Hypertext changes the form of control as well as the nature of control.

In electronic space, where simultaneous text spaces surround the reader and writer or are displayed on the screen, the motion of reading or writing is not determined by the left-to-right, top-to-bottom, front-to-back fixity of the book. One may float through the spaces in a number of different orders and skip from the inside of one space to the outside of another. This skipping occurs for both writer and reader.

The number of dimensions of movement expands.

It is unlikely that any two readings will be precisely the same. The fixity of print controlled writer and reader. No such control now exists.

There are other kinds of control: the memory of the machine, the nature of the program, the size and resolution of the screen.

But writer and reader can surf on the text just as they can surf on the Internet or cable television. This means that hypertext differs from traditional text in being not nonlinear, but multilinear—perhaps multidirectional is the better word. It also differs in that the visible text and the conceptual text are not coincident. Interactive hypertext enables readers to take the spaces and make new connections, to add spaces, or to add to the space. In this circumstance the reader becomes an author and a group of readers, coauthors. The reader/author creates a new text order.

THE LOOK OF TEXT AND HYPERTEXT

If the idea of hypertext causes us to reconsider the nature and role of the author, it also brings us to look once again at what we have been looking at almost unconsciously all these years. Seeing text on the screen causes us to think about what it means to look at and see the text on a page or on sheets of paper. For me, one of the key aspects of a text is that it must be seen to be read, unless it's in Braille; then it must be felt. In traditional texts, the visible text is read in two-dimensional space that has an invariant sequence according to custom. In one of the oldest incarnations of language, Chinese, the written language and its surface features derive from a variety of visual and iconographic sources that bear little connection to the spoken language. It was designed to be read equally well by people who spoke languages that were distinctly different, and it developed a calligraphic style that focuses on the surface, the brush stroke, as well as on the grammar and syntax. The relationship to the oral equivalents is virtually nonexistent. The Chinese writing system reminds us who use alphabetic systems based on phonetic relationships between squiggles on the page and both the sounds and the sense that we make, that our written language need not have been that way and that the visual design of the text is a great part of our understanding its message. Too often we tend to think of writing as if it were devoid of pictures, when in fact it is itself a picture (see Figure 2.2), a point I shall return to shortly. (I note that I use a metaphor of time that implies that you will read the text in order, although I realize that you can skip to page 157 [or whatever] in a second. This act of moving in space rather than being bound to a sequence is one of the key aspects of hypertext, where I could have given you a link at this point so that you could move instantly to that discussion.)

One attribute of written language and text is that their two-dimensional nature may limit conceptual space as well as text space. By limiting conceptual space, I mean that, because we begin reading

FIGURE 2.2. Here the content of the text and the physical condition of its appearance are interwoven. After the text was printed, it was left out in the rain until the ink began to run. Though "Rain Work" is clearly a text, it is also a picture.

at the top, we may well be conditioned to think hierarchically out of habit. This habit based on our sense of the page helps set the patterns of lists and classification systems. We may alternate between a top down and a bottom up approach, but this is a minor variation. Because we also read left to right we have tables like calendars and grids that enable us to look at things in cells and we see things as cross-related. The horizontal–vertical relationship, however, is but one of many. We can simulate cubes, but we cannot easily indicate shifting relationships in that context. These limitations brought about by the fact of the text on the page may have rhetorical consequences in what we consider as important in the disposition of ideas on the page or pages. Besides alluding to bodily imagery, the ways in which we attach "headings" and "footnotes" to texts also may suggest a visual metaphor of hierarchy that sees the bottom as lower in importance than the top. As a result we perceive the top of the page as containing the important components of the text; we also see the beginning and the end of the message as having greater import than the middle. These are the parts enclosed by the large blank spaces. This favoring of the beginning and end again, is a visually based preference, and it is one that in part determines how we arrange our ideas into an order that is widely understood.

When the text becomes electronic, what happens? We see a part of the writing on a screen, but it is not like looking at the pages of a book or sheets of foolscap. Actually we see a set of contrasting spaces or pixels created by a complex combination of digital commands so as to give one the illusion of seeing letters, words, fonts, paragraphs. These images can be saved or discarded with a single keystroke. They may be moved and manipulated in any one of a number of ways. With my word processing program, I can see them as a scroll, as they might be pages in a book, or as a running outline in which I can hide from my own view large amounts of text still resident in the machine. I can change fonts at will. One feature of the electronic text is that, although we see it on the screen—or at least parts of it (we assume it is all there)—it is viewed as text but in truth generated as a collection of pluses and minuses—"on" and "off" signals—in which we place blind faith. The text is simultaneously visible and invisible.

If I put the text into a desktop publishing program, I can take the separate parts of what I have written and move them around on a mock-up page. I can surround the text with illustrations, or surround a picture with the text. I can put the text into a number of columns or rows. But I cannot do much more than that. What emerges has to be looked at as if it were a virtual set of pages in a book or magazine. I can open a number of different documents at once and move back and forth among them, although with some difficulty.

This difficulty changes if I put the same text into a hypertext program, I can take each paragraph or chunk of text that I want to keep and have it appear as a separate segment encased in a box or "space." These then appear as an array of spaces on a screen, and I can go into any one of the spaces with the click of a mouse. I can also drag the spaces around on the screen, nest inside each other, or link with any one of a number of devices to other spaces. I can create different pathways between the spaces so that a reader can follow any one from a particular space and go to as many as a dozen other spaces. And my readers and I can become lost.

The relationships among parts are multidirectional and instant, not simply up or down or across and sequential. And the parts themselves change from segments of words and phrases to collections of words, images, moving pictures, sound, or the like, all stored in a binary fashion, all able to be called up as a succession of images on the screen, perhaps never to be printed—for such would hold them in a static form (whereas they are moving, always in a complex network of relationships with one another)—a web of internal connections that can be linked to ever expanding webs in cyberspace. Always and never there at the same time.

The limits of hypertext are also the limits of the screen, but one can have multiple windows and screens and thus appear to move through a third dimension and perhaps even into other dimensions.

The largest unit of a hypertext is a web, which could theoretically be arranged as a single visible hypertext were the screen large enough, but is usually portrayed as a series of windows within windows, each window containing a network of what is contained below or within it. One must usually move through the web sequentially in order to encounter the various weblets, but one may also go back to the larger web. The web exists in a self-contained hypertext but is at its most potent and far-reaching on the World Wide Web, the electronic master web accessible through various on-line services. This web is constantly expanding.

In a web, the links are multiple and not necessarily hierarchical or cross-tabbed. The movement from place to place may be in many directions. One is taken out of two-dimensional space, at least metaphorically.

The Virtual Simulacrum

We believe that what we see on the screen is the text, but it is only a simulacrum of the text, just as a copy of the book is only a simulacrum of the text. In the literate world before print, a book was what one copied down from an oral recitation or what one had copied from a manuscript. It was a record of an oral performance and was often used to summon up a subsequent performance. With print, there came multiple copies of a text that were identical and thus not tied to performance but to manuscript or "true copy." In the past century, scholars, led, perhaps by biblical scholars, have sought to identify true texts, their work taking the form of critical editions, variorums, and other types of textual scholarship (this was perhaps a wild-goose chase, for there was no more a source manuscript of the Bible than there was an original draft of Homer's *The Iliad*). All of these searches were for the source or immanent text, which is the one from which all others are either simulacra or debased copies. In many cases, the search has proved fruitless, for if an author revised a manuscript to create a printed version and then corrected the printed version several times for subsequent editions, there is no clear rule for determining which version is the immanent text. Recent editors of writers like Samuel Taylor Coleridge or Dante Gabriel Rossetti have found it useful to have each of the versions available on disk or at a site on the World Wide Web rather than decide that one version was the true one. What they have amassed is a compilation of textual images that can be manipulated in multiple ways.

If the immanent text is hard to pin down in the case of printed books, it is even harder to pin down in the electronic world, because the electronic text and the hypertext has less semblance of permanence than the written or printed "hard copy" ever seemed to have. One can copy disks, of course, but hypertext changes with each reading, and if it is added to or manipulated by readers, a modified disk can prove an unwieldy object through which to retrieve an "original version." Similarly, no two readers move through the web in the same way, and even a single reader is hard put to retrace his journey.

Understanding Hypertext through Its Forerunners

There are many discussions of the forerunners of hypertexts. Some would argue that the commonplace book or compendium of aphorisms or maxims has some of those qualities. These are discontinuous text fragments that ask us to make the connections that we see fit. When Montaigne and Bacon strung the items of their comoendiums together in the form of essays, they invited us to look at the connections they saw as well as at individual ideas. We are given spaces and asked to link them. Laurence Sterne is often mentioned as having produced an early hypertext.

Holy Hypertexts

It appears from the work of a whole variety of scholars of religion and of scripture that the texts of various religions prove to be good examples of forerunners of hypertext. These texts tend to be plural. "Bible" comes from a plural for books; other words have a similar thrust—Koran, Upanishads. They are seen as forerunners to a great extent because of the ways in which they were written and the ways in which they are used.

The point is that these seminal texts are not read in the monolinear fashion that we read novels and stories. The texts themselves are compendia, collections for dipping into—or, in the parlance of electronic media, surfing.

Take the Talmud. It is a set of text spaces, written at different times, meant to be read against one another. It is established and laid out on the page in just such a way that it must be seen as hypertext. Certainly it is not to be read in the customary sequence of novels or essays, but in a variety of configurations—each depending on the reader and the occasion. In that way the reader turns the Talmud into a scriptural event. It becomes a web of text spaces. For the Talmud, this weblike nature is apparent at a glance. The Bible, the Koran, and other scriptures are similar even though they may appear as more conventional. So, too are adjuncts like the Catholic Breviary or the Episcopalian *Book of Common Prayer*, which despite its title is hardly a common book. It is a compendium that one has to move through in a variety of ways skipping from place to place in what seems a haphazard fashion.

Like other religious texts, the Bible is a compilation that is intended to be seen less as a linear or hierarchical text than as a collection of pieces assembled in an order that is meant to be violated. The Christian testaments are designed so that the New Testament refers to the old and is often set up in a three-column format with the middle column containing the references from the present text space to others before or after. The actual verses and images refer outward to other verses and images, so that the Gospels present a set of glosses and reworking of the earlier books, songs, and prophecies. The four Gospels of the Christian New Testament are a special case of scripture and of hypertext. These are, we know, four accounts of the life, death, and resurrection of Jesus. They appear to be independently written, although there is some evidence of borrowing as well.

It is possible to see the four Gospels as hypertext rather than as text. That is, they are four text spaces that can be cross referenced and that lead to one another and also lead to various parts of the Old Testament. For years there have been attempts to make a synoptic or single Gospel, but given the nature of the four differing views of the events in the four writers (five if you add James, and six if you add the other Gnostic fragments), any attempt to create a single text would be inappropriate.

The final book of the New Testament, Revelation, is rife with references back and forth through all the earlier verses of the two testaments, arranged numerically so that parts of it refer to other parts but are immediately linked—in the mind of the knowledgeable reader to three or four other sections of the Bible. The whole is a dazzling illuminated kaleidoscope of verbal motion and self-reference. It is truly a hypertext, although one that is seen as static on the page despite the fact that it seeks to leap from the page back to other pages and verses and thus into the mind of the reader who is open to making link after link. The human mind creates a continuity on the discontinuous. That is the link. We need to create coherence. It's in the genes. That is why we have been called grammar-making animals (although probably all animals use pattern recognition to deal with their perceptions).[6]

Comics as a Way of Understanding Hypertext

In the textual world, I think, the best example of the combination of image and text occurs in comic books, creating a complex of cross-reference and motion. Many of us who grew up in the world of print find an analogy in the newspaper and particularly in the comic pages of the newspaper or the comic book. Certainly this is true for me, as I observed in Chapter 1, for the comics were central to my education in the world of text. These are clearly the print texts where the visual is most clearly and obviously a key component, as they are based on a combination of printed word and image and are laid out in a manner that requires a particular sort of visual layout and processing. Marshall McLuhan has observed that newspapers' juxtaposition of article and advertisement represents a curious junction and disjunction of bad and good news. I find a similar point of reference in comics. Comics help me and many others understand what it means to have the spaces and links of hypertext and to comprehend the nature of printed texts and how they work.

Comics were a staple of the recreational diet of most of those who grew up in the thirties and forties. We could read about sports in comics, follow the war in comics, learn about the forces of good and evil in comics, and even read most of the classics in a comic book version. The military even used them to explain the principles of war machinery and field sanitation. Print comics were supplemented on Saturday by the movies and particularly the serial and the news and cartoon that went with the feature, but the staple diet was the comic. It is still with us in the child's picture book, just as it has been with people since the caves of Lascaux, the tombs of the Pharaohs, the Bayeux Tapestry, or books of the hours. In India, comic book versions of the *Ramayana* and the *Mahabarata* are popular versions of the texts—or were so until the videos appeared. They are popular because they do not pretend to be other than visual, and they combine the graphic system of written language with another graphic system, that of a thoroughly visual medium. They are, perhaps, the Western version of Chinese calligraphic writing, as certain as scroll paintings. The comic is built on an interplay of picture and text. The two may enhance each other, support each other, explicate each other, serve as metaphors for each other, or undercut each other—to name but a few of the potential relationships. It is an entirely visual medium in that the eye must be used to make sense of the relationship between picture and text. And the text must be seen in order to know who is speaking—if indeed it is speech that is in the bubbles.

The comic strip and the comic book are both print precursors of hypertext—or perhaps are themselves an early form of hypertext. The major theoretical work on comics has been done by Will Eisner in *Comics and Sequential Art*, Scott McCloud in *Understanding Comics: The Invisible Art*, and Robert Harvey in *The Art of the Comic Book: An Aesthetic History*.[7] I think that exploring these sources will help us to understand not only hypertext but also the world of texts and writing more fully.

How Comics Work

Comics work by taking text out of the lockstep convention. They do so by adding space to text and most clearly by treating the text as but a part of the iconic complex.

Traditional texts are framed in dimensions. They go across and down. Of course, the pages add thickness, but how does that figure in, when we see only one double-page spread at a time? Generally the thickness of the book is not a factor in its imaging of reality. The reader and the writer are forced into a cross-linear pattern. And the pattern is generally rigid—left to right, top to bottom, and so on to the next page of the codex, recto, verso, recto, verso until we get to the thick cover and are let out.

If we think of traditional written texts, we realize that they exist in two-dimensional space—three-dimensional, allowing for the multiple pages through which one may flip. By the tradition of the Eurocentric world of text, this means that the reader is meant to go from the top left to the bottom right. That is how you are reading this text now.

Comics provide a chance to break and to understand this configuration. The gutters between the panels and the positioning of the panels on the page form a hypertext configuration. That is, the reader (guided in part by the artist) may connect the panels in various ways. The connections may be temporal or visual. The resultant pattern on the page may be horizontal-vertical or it may be circular, or (using arrows) a criss-cross or boustrophedon (the form of text that reverses itself at each line like the movement of an ox pulling a plow). In the newspaper, the separate strips form a tapestry of two or three dozen separate patterns that one may read in any order. Some readers tell me that they scan and search for specific strips, others tell me that the read them in a vertical boustrophedon, down one column and up the next, and thus four times on a double-page spread.

In another way, comics resemble hypertext. In the newer comics, particularly those created by Stan Lee and in some of the serial strips like "Doonesbury" or "Prince Valiant," the basic narrative conventions have been changed so that there is no story with a beginning, middle, and end. The reader can come into the book with any issue or the strip on any day. The characters come in and out and the relationship between volumes or weeks is one of associational links in a web, not a sequenced short story or novella—the preferred form of the earlier comics.

Comics use pictures and words to form a series of text spaces (to use Jay Bolter's term) that are themselves icons, a feature to which I shall devote most of Chapter 4. Here I am concerned with the disposition and arrangement of the panels or frames rather than with what is in them. It is the gutters that form my focus here.

Gutters

The frames of a comic contain the images and words, and the space between the frames, usually marked with clear lines although sometimes not, is called the gutter. The gutter is where the reader interpolates a connection between frames. The gutters are to the frames as the spaces between words and sentences are to the black marks. These spaces form the connective tissue, the link, the grammar by which we make sense of the welter of separate bits. The grammar is, of course, not in the space, but we put it there.

According to McCloud, the most common types of connections implied by gutters (see Figure 2.3) are:

- moment-to-moment
- action-to-action

FIGURE 2.3. The major types of gutters, as described by Scott McCloud. From Scott McCloud, *Understanding Comics: The Invisible Art* (Northampton, MA: Kitchen Sink Press, 1993), pp. 51–52. © 1993 by Scott McCloud. Reprinted by permission.

- subject-to-subject
- scene-to-scene
- aspect-to-aspect
- non-sequitur

The reader, of course, can make other connections or break them.

The gutter serves some of the functions of the rest in music or more particularly the silence between movements. It also serves the function of the space between words in a sentence, or between sentences in a paragraph, or between paragraphs in text—or between the text chunks or spaces in a hypertext.

The connections and links are made by the reader, who then works together with the artist to be a re-creator of the comic, the book, the hypertext.

Sequence

The connections that are made by the mind in looking at a gutter are such that the reader creates a sequence from the arrangement of spaces on the page. This sequence can be from top left to bottom right, as is the normal sequence in the West. But it need not be. There can be arrows that lead the reader through a serpentine or counterintuitive path. The sequence helps us to relate the space of the picture to the idea of time, which is contained in the pictures and often between them.

Comics and Hypertext

In their great variety, comics help us to understand the ways in which hypertext and writing on the screen work. They do so by showing us the intimate relationship of text and picture and therefore of the pictorial nature of text. They lead us to an appreciation of the icon and the image (as we shall see in Chapter 4). They particularly lead us to appreciate the white space, the gutter, and its part in our making sense of the relationships among objects; and they point to the ways by which the writer and the reader work together to make meaning. But comics go further than that. They lead us back to an appreciation of the image as a positive and integral part of our use of written language; they reconnect us with the world of the picture and the icon. Through comics we can see the roots of our highly visual world of text and hypertext in proto writing (the cave drawing, the pictograph on a stele, the Native American sand painting, the patteran, the calligraphy of the handwriting on the wall).

The new form of communication on and off screen is iconic. Since it is iconic, it causes us to rethink the iconic nature of texts as well as hypertext.

CONVENTIONS

The third issue that hypertext raises about text is that of conventions. By presenting us with a new form of writing, storing, retrieving, and reading, hypertext helps to make us aware that we may well have been prisoners of, or slaves to, a set of textual conventions that were so ubiquitous that we barely recognized our condition. In fact, we came to think of ourselves as free and those who could not read or write as being the real prisoners. Yet, one of the defining attributes of human language, whether it be oral language, bodily language and gesture, or written language, is that it is ruled by conventions. When people talk to each other, they use conventions of sound to indicate the meaning of their utterances. "Tsk, Tsk," the old comic book phrase, represents a conventional sound that people in the English-speaking world share when they wish to express concern, caring, or chiding. It is an aspirated clucking of the tongue that conveys to the hearer something of the nature of the feelings of the utterer.

Nods of the head also have meaning that is conventional, as do shrugs of the shoulders and other gestures. Speech, the use of consonants and vowels, is highly conventional so that a particular combination of sounds has a nearly uniform meaning within a community or even within a language-using group. As children learn language, they are learning conventions. The process is one of coming to a shared understanding of a particular set of sounds. For the young child, the parent is extremely helpful in that the parent will often perceive a "pre-meaning" stage in an utterance like "dat" (as my grandson often uttered) and turn it into an adult convention by responding, "That's Daddy."

As the child learns to write and read, the child learns that there are visual conventions as well. Some of these are in the shapes of signs. Often a child's first reading experience will be a reading of signs or logos. The patterning of marks and spaces in text is governed by conventions, some of them centuries old, some set by writers and editors, some by printers, others by the limits of the medium.

Conventions are the rules of a code, and codes are a necessary part of dealing with information, as Jeremy Campbell pointed out in *Grammatical Man*.[8] As with the gutters in comics, so with white space on paper and with subtexts on a web page, we use these to make and to understand a pattern.

DNA is a code. Language is a code. Traffic patterns on a freeway system are a code. A library uses a code. Codes are conventional sets of rules for dealing with information, and it is their conventionality (i.e., the fact that they are agreed upon) that makes the codes work. If we did not have codes with their conventions, we would be unable to deal with the information that comes to our senses. We could not use language or any of the language tools. We could not think (as we conceive of thinking). If we did not have codes with their conventions, we would not have any collective social memory—all would be individual.

Who Sets Conventions?

Most of the codes that we use are not programmed by some external or biological source like DNA; rather, most are made by people's conscious decisions. In their various dealings with one another people establish codes of behavior or communication that operate by convention. A convention is a coming together of opinion, that is, operation by consensus. Conventions can thus be those of a relatively small group (the "fraternity" of the tractor pull) or a relatively large one (for example, the speakers of English). At times the conventions seem dictated by a technology, such as the conventions related to starting and driving an automobile, but these conventions are nested in the larger system that we call "the rules of the road." Print is a good example of a technology that over the years has developed a number of conventions imposed by particular groups of users.

Print Conventions

As a neophyte moves into the world of print, she becomes progressively aware of an increasing variety of print and text conventions. These include the order of letters in the alphabet, the conventions of text shapes to signal different genres, the conventions of page order and direction of turning, and later the conventions governing when it is appropriate to write or read certain kinds of text.

We know by convention that we may send cards expressing our

love to people we do not know very well or even wish to know intimately—but only once a year, on Valentine's Day!

We know by convention that roadside signs in the shape of a red octagon are meant to give us a strong warning—STOP!

We know by convention that poetry is "prose with wide margins" and that it is all right in certain places but not in others.

We know by convention how to recognize which parts of a form we are supposed to fill out and which are to be filled out by the administrators receiving the form.

We know by convention the difference between envelopes with windows and those without. And we know by convention that the placement and configuration of the stamp or mark in the upper righthand corner above the window may indicate whether the windowed envelope contains something worthwhile or mere "junk mail."

We know by convention that a scholarly article has small print and begins and ends in a particular way using headings and titles differently from the way they are used in, say, directions for assembling a toy.

We know by convention which portions of the newspaper are imparting information, which giving opinion, and which seeking to sell us something.

What we call rhetoric is primarily a set of conventions about how to go about organizing our thoughts in written form so as to tell stories, present information, and persuade other people to do what we want. The principles of rhetoric have less to do with any universal patterns imprinted in the brain through DNA than they have to do with a set of accumulated (i.e., established) conventions that a particular society values. Beginning at the beginning and ending at the end are matters of convention, as is the common practice of presenting ideas in terms of comparison and contrast or cause and effect.

Many of these conventions are quite old. Certainly the conventions for presenting the Bible and other religious texts have a long history. Chapter and verse divisions come from the time of original inscription; the capitalization practices emerge from scribal practices of various times, such as the capitalization of all letters of the tetragrammaton YHWH and the later Christian practice of capitalizing the first letter of certain names such as "Holy Spirit." The use of red letters for marking certain portions of the text derives from medieval practices related to notes for the oral reader, and the double-column format harks back to times well before Gutenberg's first printed Bible. These conventions are almost as rigid as those surrounding other sacred texts, such as the Koran which can only be printed in certain scripts, and in fact could not be printed until four hundred years after the invention of the printing press. All of these conventions and others may have emerged as a result of practical or religious considerations. They are now deeply ingrained in the minds of writers, printers, and readers. To alter a convention is to tamper with history and "truth."

There are thousands of conventions in and about print that we have learned and that we use to enable us to navigate in the sea of paper and text that surrounds us. We are unaware of many of them simply because they have become part of our habitual behavior in a world of print. Many of these conventions have accumulated over the years, and many appear to have lost their purpose, but there they are. A large number of the conventions are social conventions; others arise from the perceived function of the printed or written page. Anthropologists have explored the ways in which different social communities have established conventions concerning who reads, what sorts of letters are written and what is in them, and how people are to talk about what they read. Shirley Brice Heath found that in many cases the conventions that children had learned at home were not what they were expected to follow when they went to school, and so they were labeled as ignorant or remedial. Another group of psychologists, led by Sylvia Scribner and Michael Cole, found that the Vai people in Liberia learned to read in three different languages, Vai, Arabic, and English, but that they learned not only different scripts and languages but also different conventions of reading and writing.[9]

Conventions are necessary if people are to use written language to communicate with one another. They are just as necessary as the conventions of talking and driving and many of the activities we perform as citizens of the state or members of the community. Generally we have only a small degree of tolerance for the unconventional. I cannot break too many of the conventions of grammar and spelling in this book if I want you to read it. I am perhaps stretching those limits when I appear to range among the topics in a haphazard manner rather than presenting the material in a so-called logical argument. Some of you may go along with me that far; but I need to watch my spelling and my syntax, and I should not include too many pages that are out of order, if I want people to think me at all sensible.

Criminals of Convention

Small children may break conventions. We grant them that license because we know they are ignorant and we think they are struggling to learn the rules. But, once they get beyond a certain age, their rule breaking is no longer seen as merely "cute," but thereupon potentially becomes a problem to society. School staff and much of the public see slow learners as "dumb," "retarded," "dyslexic," "remedial," "different," "deprived," "special," or "challenged," depending upon the specific observer or the temper of the times. The nature of the child's deviance may be as simple as spelling errors or as complex as interpreting the text literally when society wants it read metaphorically.

If the deviant child adopts a chronically bad attitude toward language, she or he may be labeled illiterate. But there are some who can be seen as escaping this sort of penalty. Over the years, some people have developed an interest in the writings of "certified" psychopaths and schizophrenics, with some serious commentators studying their writings as clues to mental disorder. When a paranoid schizophrenic starts writing letters to God, for instance, the writings may be highly relevant to understanding the subject's mentality. There may be disjunctions of syntax or even telltale misspellings that can enable professionals to understand the personality disorder better.

Poets

Occasionally deviant learners are elevated to an entirely different rubric in regard to their writing: they are called poets. In the eighteenth century Christopher Smart moved in and out of the "madhouse" called Bedlam and supported himself as a hack writer in his saner moments. One or two of his works have been preserved as poetry, particularly his *Jubilate Agno*, which contains these lines:

> For I will consider my Cat Jeoffry.
> For he is the servant of the Living God duly and daily serving him.
> For at the first glance of the glory of God in the East he worships in
> his way.
> For is this done by wreathing his body seven times round with
> elegant quickness.
> For then he leaps up to catch the musk, which is the blessing of
> God upon his prayer.
> For he rolls upon prank to work it in.
> For having done duty and received blessing he begins to consider
> himself.
> For this he performs in ten degrees.
> For first he looks upon his fore-paws to see if they are clean.
> For secondly he kicks up behind to clear away there.

For thirdly he works upon it stretch with the fore-paws extended.
For fourthly he sharpens his paws by wood.
For fifthly he washes himself.
For Sixthly he rolls upon wash.
For Seventhly he fleas himself, that he may not be interrupted
   upon the beat.
For Eighthly he rubs himself against a post.
For Ninthly he looks up for his instructions.
For Tenthly he goes in quest of food . . .
Is this madness or poetry?

Many other poets have gotten away with defying convention
without being committed to mental institutions. One of the more
famous in the United States in this century has been E. E. Cummings;
in the preceding century, Walt Whitman and Emily Dickinson come
to mind. Whitman broke with the ruling tradition of poetry to write
confessional verse using long unrhymed lines that were reminiscent of
the Old Testament. Dickinson wrote in hymn stanzas with her own
form of punctuation. E. E. Cummings went further by blending odd
typographies and settings of words. For instance, here is "Poem 33"
from *No Thanks:*

emptied.hills.listen
,not,alive,trees,dream(
ev:ry:wheres:ex:tend:ing:hush

)
 andDark
IshbusY
ing-roundly-dis

tinct;chuck
lings,laced
ar:e,by(

fleet&panelike&frailties
!throughwhich!brittlest!whitewhom!
f
 l o a t ?)
          r
      hythms[10]

Such deviations from convention attracted attention not only to the words of the poem but to the very conventions of language themselves and helped Cummings develop an aesthetic in which convention is part of the obvious aesthetic matrix.

For poets, as for artists of all sorts, conventions have always been important; it is against the background of conventions that they seek to work their magic. For artists there is a constant interplay of accepting and working against existing conventions that is a form of revolt that at the same helps establish new conventions. At the end of the eighteenth century, William Wordswoth and Samuel Taylor Coleridge boldly announced that they were defying the conventions of poetry by writing in "the real language of men." But they tended to use the prevailing stanza shapes and meters accepted by the generation before them. In doing so, and in moving to scenes of rural life and nature, they helped establish the new conventions of romantic poetry. Similar revolt helped the metaphysical poets craft their poems of conceit, the modernist poets establish free verse, and helped the imagist poets of the middle part of the century and the poets and artists of the Fluxus movement—to name but a few.

Poets from minority cultures in many societies have often had to write according to the prevailing conventions of the time in order to be published. For the African American poets of the late nineteenth century, there were two ways to be published; one was to write dialect poetry, the other was to write in one of the conventional forms about conventional subjects. Only slowly did the African American poets develop their own idiom and sets of conventions. And the younger poets of those groups tested the conventions set by their seniors. The same has since been true for poets of other groups, so that now schools of poetry and the arts exist for many cultures and subcultures around the world and even the conventions they establish are used, challenged, and broken by their followers. It's a major feature of the creative spirit.

Electronic Conventions

The new technologies of writing have brought with them new conventions. When papyrus scrolls were first used, they forced writers to divide their texts according to the manageable length of the scroll. The early users of the printing press followed the conventions of manuscript until they began to develop their own. Many of these had to do with the limitations of typesetting and printing, such as the numbering of pages, the use of signatures and chapters, and the placement of particular segments of information like the title, printer, date, and acknowledgments. The newspaper format brought with it one set of conventions if it was a large sheet and another if a tabloid.

To writers, the computer started out as a fancy typewriter, and many of the word processing programs were initially designed to emulate electric typewriters as closely as possible. But all that has changed.

In the first place, there has emerged a whole set of conventions about how to use the computer. In 1993 I first taught a course in which all students had to use the program Storyspace™ as a notebook and as a means of presenting their papers. Several of the students had not used a computer before or had used it only to play games. Three in particular did some of the work, but the disk they returned to me at the end of the course was totally unchanged from three months earlier. I found out that, after writing on it, the three students had simply turned off their machine. They never checked the disk. Nothing was saved. It is not that they are to be ridiculed; they followed a convention in which "Off" was the same as "Save." Unfortunately, it was the wrong convention.

Other students had trouble learning the formatting commands and the various techniques for getting in and out of the program. Thinking the machine was nothing more than a typewriter, they thought they could use it as such, and when it did not respond correctly (as they put it), they decided that the computer was at fault. The machine would put their sentences inside other sentences, would begin writing at the beginning again, or would make unpleasant noises if they tried to follow some of the conventions of typing. I have also noticed that many secretaries accustomed to the electric typewriter use the formatting conventions of the typewriter when they are using the computer; in particular, they use the tab key for indentations and columns. The conventions are seemingly ingrained in their nervous systems. As a result, they often encounter difficulties in changing the format when merging documents.

Most computer users know that each program has its conventions that set it apart from others; the conventions may be determined by the operating system or by the individual program. Learning the conventions involves a combination of practice and reference—it's no different from any other code.

Internet Conventions

In addition to the regular computer codes, there are codes and conventions involved in signing on and using the various features of the Internet. Many of these are determined by the host. Once on, however, the user of a bulletin board or a list-serve faces a new set of conventions.

There are clearly programs on the network that have their own sets of conventions. MUDs (multi-user Dungeons) and MOOs (MUDs that are object-oriented), the places where people can enter an alternative (virtual) world, have complex sets of conventions that the neophyte must learn.

A number of commentators have observed that the style of the messages left on the bulletin boards on the Internet differs from that of either speech or writing. For me, this results from the speed with which I type and the fact that I am on "real time" for which I am paying, and so I simply drop a note to the other person without going back to correct even the obvious errors. In part, it also results from the fact that, even though I may never have met the person in real time, I have a sense that we can chat about a topic and so be less formal than with others.

Beyond this stylistic convention, others have emerged. There are rules of conduct about "flaming," the use of abusive language on a bulletin board or a chat. Those who abuse the rule may be barred from a board or chastised by others on the system.

Character conventions have also emerged:

:–) is the "smiley face" of pleasure;
:–(is the frowning face.

These face symbols—and hundreds of variations on them—have become a separate code from the text code or the numeric code of the message.

As people learn these conventions they become full-fledged members of the world of hyperspace. They have learned to read and write in the system.

The Conventions of Hypertext

Beyond the conventions of the program or the Internet, there are beginning to emerge sets of conventions surrounding the technology of hypertext. Again, these are set by the designers and the first users of the programs. The programs have a grammar and syntax, but these are not the key conventions of hypertext.

Those conventions have to do with what is nested in what, what is linked to what, and how the whole web is configured. There are emerging conventions on such matters as: how many windows on a screen may be scrolled; how links are to be indicated; where to place text and subtext; and where to put pictures or quick-time video.

The conventions that are emerging are coming from a melding of the conventions used by advertisers, illustrators, comic book artists, writers, and programmers. They borrow from the conventions of television and film as well as from a variety of forms of business communication. At this point, the conventions are beginning to establish themselves and are going through a necessary period of flux and revision. From this version will emerge a set of conventions that will build upon the conventions of print and film but at the same time transform them into the new merged medium. Just as it took several centuries for printing to develop conventions that were appropriate to the technology, so, too, will electronic conventions find their own particular niche.

We are, then, settling into the world of hypertext as authors and users. Like pioneers we are somewhat wary and unsure, and we seek the familiar in the book and the written text, even though these may not be the best guides for us. In doing so we are confronting who we were as authors in the world of text and print, and we are seeing that, although things are changing, indeed some points of continuity persist. We are in a new world and beginning to get our bearings as we learn to be part of the new community of scribes—authors, coauthors, transcribers, denizens running along the filaments of the complex web of hypertext. But how have we changed?

CHAPTER THREE

What Is the Literate World Now That We Are Leaving It?

Y ou and I live in a world that has been dominated by print; because we do so, we are joined together in a literate society. That means we read and write as a matter of course, we store and retrieve information in print or text form, and we see the storage and retrieval of print as a necessary part of our very being. People who cannot read and write are treated as members of a nearly criminal class. We read (and some of us write) from the moment we wake up in the morning to the moment we go to sleep at night; some of us even read in our dreams. We have written words all around us: on our clothes, in our medicine cabinets, at the kitchen table, in the car, in almost any public space. Literacy defines us as human beings; it is a part of our being "civilized," "cultured," and members of a "community."

Some people claim that literacy is on the decline and that the world is what is fashionably known as postliterate. I don't think we have left that world yet, nor are we about to for the foreseeable future. But we are changing and expanding our views of literacy. One reason for this change is that print on paper is no longer the sole means of storing information, and it is information that defines our society, not the medium through which we garner it. The means has been seen as the defining element, but we are coming to see that it is the content, not the container, that is most important. Just as we no longer need coins and bills to buy and sell goods, so we no longer need paper or even words in order to record and retrieve information.

Having already observed that in this new world of hypertext the nature of the author has changed and the reader becomes a coauthor, in this chapter I shall explore other aspects and ramifications of the changes that have been wrought upon the act of reading and being literate, looking first at the nature of literacy, the relation of the reader to text and image, and finally the centers of our literate societies—our temples, as it were. I shall examine these even as they undergo rapid change and translation into new forms wrought by the electronic media.

Before I begin this examination, however, I want to spend some time on a particular kind of reading: scriptural reading, or reading in religious contexts. I make this seeming digression because I believe that we have forgotten how central religious reading is to our notions of reading in general. It is in religious contexts that reading has been practiced by a large part of the population over the years. Church reading was the first introduction to reading for countless generations, and for many it is so still. We can learn much about the secular views of literacy by first examining the religious ones.

THE NATURE OF SCRIPTURAL READING

I count myself a member of the Episcopal Church in the United States, which is probably one of the most text-ridden churches in the world. In front of every seat in every Episcopal church are a prayer book and a hymnal. When I walk into a service, I am handed a leaflet of some two or three folded sheets, which not only contain the news of the week in church but also provide an index, table of contents, or "cheat sheet" to the service that is about to begin.

One day, visiting a chapel in Wales, I noticed that our leader in Evening Prayer, a rather short and simple service, had in front of him not only the prayer book but also a couple of sheets that indicated the appropriate readings for the day, two Bibles (each a different translation), and a second book of prayer with both a Welsh and an English version. Five books and pamphlets for a half-hour service, the order of which most of the attendees knew by heart, as they knew many of the prayers, but each of the texts was used and manipulated in proper sequence. Some of the items were read aloud by one person, some by the whole group, and some antiphonally with the two sides of the chapel alternately reading sections of a psalm. We skipped around in the books, reading none of them for more than a page. The texts were often marked with regular and bold-faced type to indicate who was to read what, and there were italics that served as stage directions, telling us to sit, stand, or kneel, read, talk, or keep silent. All of these texts together formed the worship, and the worship was smooth, without interruption, and it was a time in which most of us felt close to God. This was a corporate reading of a complex of texts.

To me it is a model of the nature of hypertext in use, and it serves to show how the new forms of text illustrate something of how the religious world interpenetrates the world of technology and the world of text. To do so, we need to reevaluate the concept of a holy text, or, to use the common word, "scripture."

Scripture

When we hear the word *scripture,* many of us think of the Bible or some other holy text. We tend to think of scripture as having a certain importance as an artifact regardless of what it says or which religion it comes from. A scripture is sacred; after all, we often hear the phrase "Holy scripture." But the phrase came about because scripture first meant simply that which is written. "Holy scripture" came into being to distinguish sacred from profane writing. As often happens in the history of language, the sense of the adjective in the phrase got transferred to the noun. Scripture is now thought of as a specialized form of text. How is it special?

To some theologians, scripture has come to mean that text which takes on a sacred definition apart from the circumstances of its writing. Although some scriptures may have been the work of an inspired writer or even assert to be the word of God, others might have more mundane origins and yet still become a part of scripture. The letters of St. Paul, for example, were written by a man who had a holy mission—to spread the Gospel before it was written—but they are often very practical and down to earth, even at times testy or sardonic. Nonetheless, they have become a part of scripture and take on a different existence from that of their origin. Scripture is seen as having been endowed with an existence as if it were a living, breathing thing, and so it becomes transformed and transforming. Those books that are referred to as scripture take on a special way of being and acting in our world.

We tend to think of scripture as the physical book, the sacred text. Scriptures are printed and bound in a special way; they are sometimes restricted in their format; and they are often treated as holy images. In many countries people put their hands on Bibles or other scriptures in order to take oaths. Students I have interviewed over the years are shocked at the thought that they might throw out or destroy a Bible. According to Islamic doctrine, the Qurran has to be printed with special fonts and cannot be translated. The same text might take on a different scriptural nature depending on the sect or culture of the readers. If a religion were to die out, its texts would no longer be scriptures. The Gilgamesh epic may have been a scripture at one point. Now it is read as an interesting myth or legend.

Recently, however, scholars have come to argue that it is not the books themselves but their sphere of existence that is scripture, and that is the meaning I shall pursue in discussing this topic. Scripture becomes a term like literacy, involving both the text and the set of relations to it that specify who treats the object in what particular way.

Scripture as an Activity

In a recent volume one of the major comparative theologians, Wilfred Cantwell Smith, argues that "scripture is a human activity."[1] His point is that humans engage in converting a text so that it takes on scriptural characteristics.

Since it is the case that a people make a text a scripture, "scripture" implies a relationship between a text and a people. In this way we can say that scriptural activity is a special form of literacy, the human habit. Scripture is the religious version of literate habits.

That is to say, the people decide to confer authority to a particular text to make it scripture. Their way of doing this is to use the text in a ceremonial fashion. It is not simply the object of study. It does not sit in a library. It becomes a part of a liturgy or ceremony of some sort. Often this means that a particular form of recitation or reading is part of the scripture. In Jewish, Christian, and Islamic ceremonies, certain portions of the text are chanted or intoned. Often the beginning and the end of an oral reading of the text are marked by the uttering of some formal comment or prayer. In some Christian churches, the sign of the cross is made over the lips of the person designated to read the Gospel. This person must be a priest or a deacon of the church, someone specially trained to read in the ceremony. In other churches the Gospel is carried over the head in a procession. Carrying the Gospel, like carrying the cross, is a symbolic way of carrying the presence of Christ.

The sacred text is read differently from secular ones in another way. It is seldom read consecutively. Usually the selections of the text read are short. Seldom are long stretches of the text read straight through in a ceremony. In any one ceremony, different segments of the total text are read, and not necessarily in chronological order or even the order of the pages of the book. The way of reading a sacred text is close to the way of reading hypertext. It is approached in a fresh fashion each day and recombined to form the scripture of the day or the occasion.

One could argue that it is through becoming scripture that a text can make communities; but it is not the text that does it, it is the readers.

Text and Scripture

What is the nature of the sacred text in relation to its character as scripture? In asking this question, I mean that the text of scripture may be thought of as being like any other text that was described in the preceding chapter, or we may conclude that it bears another relationship to author and reader, one that is defined by its circumstances, just as its readers and editors are defined by those same circumstances.

If it is like any other text, it has a writer whom we know by entry through the words, an intended audience as well as a set of real, live readers, and the fictional relationship between writer and audience. We can pick it up and coauthor it, as we do any other text. We see that it has a number of interpretations, depending upon our nature as readers and our community. That the text has a history that is both oral and written and that it is often read communally in a liturgical setting—both features change the text's particular qualities, since we normally think of text as an inert document or object. But the change is not that great, and it becomes more like a play script than a novel or book of philosophy. It is possible, therefore, to think that written scripture is an ordinary text and subject to some of the same rules of reading and criticism. The recent Jesus Seminar is a case in point, where a group of scholars are determining on the basis of "internal evidence" which sayings of Jesus are most probably historically accurate and which are dubious in being attributed to Him. The scholars are treating the text as a text. So too are the people who worry about its having inclusive language or not.

But we can also argue that the printed or written part of scripture is not the same as text. Smith argues that scripture is not the same as text and that the equation is false. "The idea of a text, as an object to be understood," says Smith, "is modern and impersonal and subordinating, characterizing present-day culture's objectivizing orientation to the world."[2]

In scripture, the printed text is but part of the total religious experience. We use the text as an entry point to understand the meaning of the history, or the divine. We do this through ceremony, the ceremony of reading in a religious or theological fashion. We do it within a religious community as participants in and of that community. The text is reauthored by the community to make it scripture.

Oral and Written Scripture in the World of Hypertext

Scripture, therefore, can be seen as having both oral and written aspects. In many religions, the oral tradition precedes the written one. But that sequence may raise the question whether the concept of scripture can antedate the concept of written language. I think it can, if we see the text from the perspective of hypertext, that is, as a combination of word and icon. As I have noted earlier, the center of oral religion and oral culture is the ceremony. Ceremonies may contain dances, songs, recitations, stories, and other activities. They are oral and visual and they are designed so that they will be memorable and thus capable of being transmitted from person to person, generation to generation. Ceremonies are the libraries of a culture that has no written text.

In ceremony, the oral is primary. The oral word is related to the idea of the Logos, the Word that John's Gospel opens with and that is seen as the creative naming of the universe and thus the formation of a cosmos out of chaos. When writing is introduced, it is often as a way of recording the creative Logos, and thus in the most basic sense the oral component lies at the very basis of scripture in that the ceremony persists unchanged over time; yet, the written text is subsequently brought in as another and major reference point of the ceremony. The interweaving of the oral and the written contains the paradox that, although the oral part is temporal and is transmitted through airwaves and thus is evanescent, the oral word of scripture is also eternal. The oral aspect of scripture is seen as primary and a part of the Logos; although it appears to have the stability and permanence that a tangible text affords, the written part of scripture takes on a secondary importance—as a script, a mnemonic, a source of doctrine, a means or tool of conversion and instruction. Only later does the text of the written part become as important as the oral ceremony.

The tablets of the Ten Commandments are important as a symbol and an icon. They were, in the first instance, actually written by YHWH, being His own secretary. Around them there is ceremony, talk, and sacrifice. Although the Torah existed in the service and was carried in the Ark of the Covenant, the oral tradition remained at the center of the worship of the Israelites for a long time before the written text itself became a serious object of study and contemplation. In fact, the oral Torah coexisted with the written Torah from the time of Ezra well beyond the life of Christ, when it was finally written down as the Mishnah. Before that time, rabbis were expected to carry vast parts of the law in their heads and be able to retrieve and recite the relevant bits at the merest hint of need. How they were able to do this remains something of a mystery, but it is probable that they had elaborate mnemonic schemes, perhaps verbal rhythms and repetitions like those described in Chapter 2, perhaps iconic ones like those used by medieval monks and scholars.

In most religions, then, there is an interplay between oral and written traditions. In religions where the written text exists, the oral scripture works around that text liturgically and also through exegesis and recitation, which impart the deep structures of the scripture into the minds and hearts of the hearers.

To many there has been a perceived danger in the written scripture: it supplants the oral scripture, that which is written in the heart. Aware of this danger, St. Paul raises the question about the letter and the spirit (as do various other commentators in Hinduism, Islam, and Judaism). As we have seen, the physical religious text is often assumed to have properties as an object. There are many tales of people being healed by touching the physical book or finding the answers to questions by sticking pins in it. In some instances, then, the sacred text becomes not a text, not a vehicle for scriptural use and an entry to the divine, but an object, or idol that is itself divine. This problem is one to which we shall return later in this chapter and in the next. At this point, I shall only remark that the oral part of scripture then has a special character that needs protection. This danger to the oral scripture persists, although I think it takes a different form in the idolatry of the text and the literal.

To some commentators and theologians, electronic text appears to be even more removed from the human heart than written text. It becomes even more detached from us. The written scripture is information, not knowledge, the electronic text is a large body of information, but we must translate it into our knowledge. It must be brought into our hearts. How is that done? It seems so distant from us on the screen; even more distant than in the book.

If we assume the primacy of the oral word, that which exists in time and in communion, then we acknowledge that the written word, by visualizing the oral and making it eternally present, changes it. The written word is continually repeated and always identical. This is not possible of the oral word.

This transformation to the electronic word, however, is not a degeneration of the written word but a transformation or a combination of the written and the oral. The evanescence and ephemerality of the oral word and the permanence of the written word are both possible in the electronic word and at the same time both challenged. The word is both everywhere and nowhere at once.

In hypertext the truth of the word and the reality of the text come together, shimmer, and perhaps disappear. They also become combined through the icon and mixed with the frozen voice in hypermedia.

Hypertext and Scripture

Some have argued that scripture is hypertext. By this is meant that there is a unique set of relationships among writer-text-reader.

This is an attractive suggestion in that we can say that the Torah/Mishnah is clearly a hypertext, and so too appear to be the writings of Buddha with their successive editions and glosses, the I Ching, and possibly the Christian Gospels.

This would follow from Smith's notion of scripture as an activity. The text only takes on a scriptural nature in the reading of it and the handling of it. As an object, it is inert—simply a book until it is picked up as *The Book*.

How does this relate to the definition of hypertext? If the hypertext is continually (written)(read)(rewritten) in the particular cultural community, it can be seen as taking on a scriptural cast provided the participants see it as engaging them in questions of meaning and spirituality. The hypertext members could be a spiritual community. A secular community participates in a hypertext in a parallel fashion but without the spiritual impetus to make the hypertext scripture.

The different readings are formed by the community. As we read within a community and coauthor the hypertext by making our own pathways through the web of words, we may transform the text into our scripture. How broad can a scriptural group be? Probably relatively small in the detail but perhaps broad in the generality. Authority devolves not to the reader alone but to the community of readers participating in the scriptural act.

At the same time that there is the temptation to see scripture as hypertext there are some legitimate questions about whether the view of hypertext that we have advanced lends itself to the notion of scripture as coeval with the Divine.

In one sense it makes sense to think of the Divine as not writing what we usually think of as a treaty or contract, but as being the author of a set of text spaces (revelations or prophecies) in a discontinuous mode (or in a rhetorical form that is not what we normally associate with text) and left to the reader to construct the web.

At the same time there is the question as to whether the liturgical use of oral and written scripture can coexist with hypertext. It seems an interesting possibility. Of course it can and does, and it could clearly be the case that the new electronic networks have the potential to create virtual spiritual communities. They would do so through a combination of the written, the oral, and the iconic.

THE COMPLEXITY OF LITERACY

I have come to learn that literacy has meant and still means many things to many people. For some it is the capacity to sign one's name. For others it is the ability to read a particular text, like the Bible. A group of women in Bombay may define it as the ability to know whether the vendors in the market are telling the truth when they give the price for a kilo of lentils. A group of employers in upstate New York may define it as being prompt and faithful in coming to work, being clean and polite, and managing the till honestly. A number of people equate it with correct spelling. Others equate it with being able to read and write particular kinds of technical texts (such as the manuals for repairing automobiles, or articles in sociology, or the tax code). Students in most schools around the world equate it with handwriting, spelling, grammar, and the ability to answer specific questions about the text when the teacher asks them.

The one thing these definitions have in common is that they assume that there is a group or communal aspect to being literate. This is a secularizing and generalizing of the scriptural aspect of text. Reading and writing are not merely being good at figuring out print or writing a sentence; they involve a number of social activities, as well. We think of reading and writing as being solitary, but they prove not to be. I shall take this point up later in the discussion of religion, but I would say that, like scripture, text is less an object than it is a human activity. Any text is a thing, yes, but a thing around which people behave in certain ways. These ways are defined by the community in which the people and objects find themselves. They also define the community. Groups of writers who share certain assumptions about what they write and how they write form what are called rhetorical communities. Groups of readers who share certain assumptions about what and how they read form interpretive communities. Joining the writers and the readers together, then, we can consider the fact that people are not simply literate or illiterate but that they become members of particular literate communities. Like many other technologies, text or print has become encrusted with entire social and private rituals.

Critics and philosophers who call themselves "postmodernists," meaning that they are critical of the ideas and practices of the world that we refer to as "modern" (for a fuller discussion, see Chapter 5), have raised questions about the nature of literacy and its effects. There are those, particularly the Brazilian Paulo Freire and the Frenchman Michel Foucault, who see it as giving people the chance of assuming or asserting power.[3] But I think it is a question of how one interprets the notions of freedom and power with respect to literacy. Literacy clearly enables some people to become free of certain kinds of constraints and free of the power of particular hierarchies (if you can read, you can vote and perhaps you are no longer trapped by what people tell you is happening). At the same time, literacy binds people to its own set of conventions and constraints, as I suggested in the preceding chapter. And certainly becoming literate in the context of being an engineer is not the same as becoming literate in the context of becoming a priest, an accountant, or a chef. The context (or should we say "circumtext"?—that set of conventions that is in and around the text) imposes constraints on the reader and on the writer. Each sophisticated reader becomes free and bound at the same time. One kind of bondage is substituted for another, one kind of freedom for another. (Power is involved—that is, not power in simple but rather in complex terms. I would further say that it is less power than it is authority—that which is conferred rather than asserted.)

Literacy as a Habitual Activity

Many sociologists would agree to the preceding statement, and some of them use the word *habit*, saying that a social habit overtakes us when we enter into a literate world. This habit defines each of us as we go through a set of practices that accompany picking up that thing called a text. To sociologists like Robert Connorton and Pierre Bourdieu, all of the different views and definitions of literacy that I gave above would apply equally—and many more.[4] Literacy is not a state or an ability but rather an habitual activity that is social as well as private and involves both oral and literal components, much like scripture. An activity, according to many psychologists, is a complex of separate acts, so that literacy involves selecting what to read, finding a site in which to read it, reading it, and then sharing the reading in some way (if not sharing it, then somehow memorializing it). As an activity, then, literacy may best be defined as the general term encompassing the specific religious activity which we called "scripture." For the greater part of its history, literacy as a practice has derived its nature from being an extension of the activity of scripture.

As with any human phenomenon, the activities that surround reading and writing take place within a complex social framework. As a tool, written language both has been incorporated into and has changed the fabric of that social framework in many subtle ways. Once having been developed and put into use, it could not readily be abandoned. Those who became literate found written language all too useful in their daily commerce, in their capacity to record history, stories, lists, pronouncements, ephemera and eterna, or to codify other kinds of religious and secular lore. They found it impossible to renounce literacy once they had it. I cannot think of anyone who has relinquished reading and writing voluntarily. On the contrary, there are countless tales of people who exerted every ounce of their being to read or to write. People in prison or stranded in an isolated spot have composed books on scraps of paper or whatever surface they could find with whatever tool would make a mark; several holocaust survivors tell of those who recited what books they had memorized.

Although the first literates may have shared their capacity with others, people soon came to see that being literate conferred both power and privilege. From the very earliest times, across civilizations as diverse as the Chinese, the Hindu, the Mesopotamian, and the Greek, scribal communities emerged, and literacy came to be associated with castes and classes, to be guarded through various systems of gatekeepers. In most of these societies and well into eighteenth-century Europe and America, this caste was also the caste of religious leaders. Most of the universities in Europe and in the Islamic world were established for the training of clergy, and scriptural practices led into secular ones. These communities set the rules and standards for levels of membership, and they continue to do so, although the scribal communities in a technological age have become highly complex, more secular, and more diverse. We don't call them scribes today; we call them accountants or advertising specialists or professors or lawyers, but they are not different in function from the ancient scribes. They too are jealous of their scribal status and erect various barriers to make it difficult for others to join them. Even schools that claim to be open to all erect barriers of academic literacy to make success difficult for those who are unwilling to accommodate to the system.

The kinds of practices scribes developed included: whether they would write or read a text from left to right or bottom to top; whether they would sit or stand when reading or writing; which texts they would save and which they would throw away; how to shape their letters and words, how to talk about what had been written; how and where to store documents; and, not least, which young people would be trained to read and write. We live in a world where some form of literacy is taken for granted for everyone in most industrialized societies, at least, but there indeed remain groups who have specialized types of literacy and who, in fact, control the flow of information to the broader populace. So it is that we all expect to read and write, and we have come to consider illiteracy a kind of mental aberration or illness.

As I have described myself in the Preface, we who have grown up in a world where the tool of written language and various texts were readily available and some form of literacy is taken for granted have found our world shaped by the assumption and habit of literacy and have been concerned now that our world seems challenged. Just as people who cannot drive nonetheless find themselves thrust into an environment where roads and automobiles are the custom rather than the exception, where not to own a car or to be able to drive are seen as aberrations—so, too, those who grow up in a literate environment cannot ignore it. Indeed, it permeates their very lives to such an extent that they may not be fully aware of it. In such an environment, literacy becomes such a social habit that an individual may paradoxically be seen as unable to use the tool of writing but yet able to participate in the activities of the literate social world. The literate environment exerts its influence on everyone from the newborn child to the aged, from the remote rural dweller to the urbanite.

One of the more radical thinkers, Paulo Freire, argues that, not having acquired the habit, "illiterates" cannot simply be taught the rudiments of reading, but rather they must be exposed both to the tool and to the power that it confers. The printed word is the source of temporal power.[5] It represents a command over the phenomenal and political worlds. The neoliterate must become aware of the political as well as the technical aspects of literacy. This pedagogical approach coincides with the approach to theology espoused by the "liberation" theologians.

What happens to being literate when the nature of the text is transformed into hypertext, when the world of books and the library become the screen, the Internet, and the Web? I think that as these materials change and as the nature of the text is transformed into hypertext, so, too, the nature of the literate community changes. To explore this change, we need to go back into history and see something of the past as well as the present in order to observe the future. A literate community develops habits of reading, habits of thinking about what is read, and habits of thinking about what it is important to read. It is these habits that appear to be disrupted.

THE NATURE OF READERS

What is it we do when we read a text? What are you doing as you read this book?

The simple and immediate answer is that you are a person who has picked up this book and is looking at it. You see the various marks on the page—letters, groups of letters we call words, groups of words we call sentences and paragraphs, groups of sentences and paragraphs we call chapters and sections. You see them and you work at making connections across the blank spaces between them. That is reading.

After you make those connections, you make others between what you know and remember and what you see. People who write about reading use the term *response* to describe these connections between the text and the reader's mind and memories. But, as I suggested in the preceding chapter, the word *response* is too passive, too behavioristic. I prefer now to use the term *coauthoring* or *reauthoring* for that is what the reader does.

The Reader from the Writer's Point of View

Who are you, the reader? Do I know you?

Like the Author, the Reader (as an idealized construct) is a fiction; there are millions of readers who tend to look at texts in particular ways, depending upon their particular perspectives and needs. Of that large group, a smaller number are those of you reading this book.

Some of you swallow what I write, hook, line, and sinker.

Some of you are skeptical. Some may even doze off from time to time. WAKE UP!

Some feel confused, amused, bemused, abused by this text and by the very idea of hypertext.

You readers of my text necessarily take a stand in relation to it. Your position may range from absolute ingestion to critical distance and dislike.

You bring yourselves to this book. Your selves are many and varied, strange to me and to one another. You have some common points, however. You are human. You are living at a period surrounding a millennium. You know some things about reading and writing. You have some command of what is called "standard written English," the medium in which this book is written. You have some knowledge of things like computers, literature, comics, pop music, cable television, and world events. You probably have some knowledge of and interest in culture and religion.

All of these things make my writing of this book and your reading of it a little bit easier. They help you coauthor the book with me.

After you have finished reading this book, you and I and the other readers will all share some common knowledge of what I wrote. How much is a matter of debate. It is an important debate particularly for those who are concerned with special texts such as the sacred ones that bind together the members of a religion or a denomination within a religion.

Reading Text as a Special Sort of Reading

Some people have argued that, when you read this book, you are not doing quite the same thing that you do when you read a billboard, a toothpaste label, or a shopping list. They believe that there is a special kind of writing called a text. Others, myself included, think that the billboard, label, and list are texts too. My definition is broad, but I certainly agree that there are special kinds of reading that we reserve for what we think are special kinds of texts, although it is possible to extend that specialized form of reading to a broader range. People who are trained as lawyers read legal briefs and opinions differently from ordinary people. So, too, with the clergy, with accountants, literary critics, and engineers. This fact would suggest that certain designated texts serve to define and be defined in a special way by certain communities.

Those who hold the more limited definition of a text would claim that, to be called "text," a piece of writing must have the capacity to be interpreted and, therefore, any text attracts interpretations. This limited definition, I think, comes from the habits of reading sacred texts, but it extends itself to certain secular texts as well, particularly literature. A text in this limited sense is a piece of writing upon which commentaries can be written. Texts are therefore read, and in being read become rewritten by whosoever reads them. The toothpaste label probably does not invite a large number of interpretations; its meaning remains pretty much the same no matter who reads it. And most people take the same implications from it. They know the label tells them that what's inside the tube is a particular brand of toothpaste, and they don't think much more about it. A poem is different; so is an editorial in the newspaper. These are *real texts*. Therefore, "text" takes on a privileged status within the broad world of writing by virtue of being that which can have one or a number of interpretations attached to it. It is something that has that particular characteristic that we call meaning. And interpreting and looking for meaning are some of the main ends of the activity of coauthoring.

When we think about interpretations, we think about them in relationship to the thing we call a text. The text is the common element of a large number of interpretations (or perhaps one of the common elements). But how we think of a text can vary; we can see it in relation to the author, to language, to other texts, to the world, and to the reader. That is, the text can be seen as an expression of an individual whose name we may know; someone wrote a letter or a book, and we can wonder what she meant. But we could simply see it as a selection of written language, in which case we would just examine the vocabulary and the grammar and see what meaning emerges from them. That is what people do when they try to decipher a strange or mysterious text like the Rosetta stone. Another way of looking at any one text is to see it in relation to all the other texts that have been written, as if it were a part of a large jigsaw puzzle of texts. Scholars of the Bible do this when they try to determine the relationship of one Gospel to another, or to determine where one group of prophets fits into the larger scheme of prophecy literature. Still another way of viewing the text is as a point of reference to an external world; for example, we assume that a set of numbers in a telephone directory is a signal for anyone to punch those numbers on a phone and speak to the person listed. We make the same assumption about history and many textbooks, that is, that the events they describe are what actually happened. Finally, we may think of text as being intended to affect an audience, that is, what happens to us as readers is what is important. Any text can be interpreted with reference to any one or more options in this set of relationships. None of them is any better or more correct than any other, but scholarly wars are fought over which should prevail; and which one does prevail at a given time can affect a great number of other aspects of our mental and spiritual lives.

The Relationship of Interpretations to the Text

Critics and philosophers have worried and disputed long about the relationship of interpretations to the text. There are thousands of interpretive articles and treatises on *Hamlet* and even more on the Book of Job. Many of them attack previous works in order to build their case. When I was a graduate student working on my dissertation, we had to establish first that no one had ever written on our specific topic and second that we had read all the other commentators and either could refute them or use them to support or extend our argument. I remember a philosophy graduate student's telling me I was lucky, to be working on Coleridge; he was thinking about working on Immanuel Kant—but that meant three years of reading just to establish his topic.

One question that interpretations raise is that of validity. Is one reader's interpretation of either *Hamlet* or Job closer to the true meaning of the work than others' interpretations? Or is each one as probable as any of the others? These raise the questions of whether there is a true meaning and how we would know if we found it. The answer to those questions depend in part on how we view the text. The argument is whether the appropriate metaphor is that of an onion or that of barnacles.

If we see the text as an onion, we see the interpretations as peeling away the protective layers of skin until we arrive at the kernel or essence of the "true meaning" of the text. This position is expressed by the philosopher Hans-Georg Gadamer, who argues that the text has a deep meaning that can be uncovered by the hermeneutic method.[6]

If we prefer the barnacle metaphor, we are in the camp of the French philosopher of deconstruction, Jacques Derrida.[7] This school of thought posits that the text is a surface upon which interpretations attach themselves. The result is soon a complex of texts superimposed upon texts. We cannot say that any of them is closer to the center, for the hull of the text is impenetrable.

Or we may take the position that a text is a space in a hypertextual world. In that case, Gadamer and Derrida are held in balance. Within the text-reader space there is the hermeneutic approach that seeks to unfold or create or coauthor a deep meaning; simultaneously the meaning of that coauthorship is necessarily piled onto or related to other hermeneutic attempts in a larger web of meanings that constantly unfold and expand and become interrelated and attenuated.

The world of hypertext suggests that, as we read we peel the onion, but a part of the outer peel is encrusted with apparent barnacles that prove to be onions themselves; and to the next reader who visits the text space and sees what we have done (provided we left our mark), we too are a barnacle and perhaps an onion; and so on, ad infinitum.

Finding the Reader in the Text

Hypertext, therefore, sharpens the question of the relationship of a reader with the text by raising and treating as a paradox that the reader is both passive and active: the reader both makes meaning of the text and takes meaning from it.

For a long period in thinking about literature and writing generally, the focus was on the writer. Aristotle had spent some time in his

Poetics thinking about the audience, but his work was interpreted as being focused on what authors do to create plays that affect audiences in the ways that they do. Such Romantics as Coleridge and Shelley focused on the writer and the nature of the poem, but they also began to think about readers.

The Victorian and early modernist critic Matthew Arnold tended to focus on the reading public in his concern with the ways in which literature might bring a culture of readers together. He was a forerunning advocate for seeing a text as an external object, a datum, something out there beyond writer and reader, something that had its own meaning and identity. But it was not until the twentieth century, particularly with the budding interest in psychology, that critics focused on the reader. The main figure in this sea change was I. A. Richards. In *Practical Criticism*, published in 1929, Richards reported on his studies of a number of Cambridge undergraduates and their readings of unfamiliar poems, where he found that many of them had difficulty making sense of the poems and many made unexpected judgments of them. The key reason, he found, was that they brought a lot of preconceived ideas to what they read. What was in their heads before they read the poems largely determined what they said about and thought about them. As John Updike once said in an interview, "You can trust the reader's head to have something in it." Richards often didn't like what he saw in readers' heads.

The American critic Louise Rosenblatt carried the ideas of I. A. Richards further and argued that what was in readers' heads was a necessary condition of reading. In *The Reader, the Text, the Poem*, Rosenblatt argued that, when the reader meets a text, there is a transaction or an interchange between the written marks and the ideas and feelings of the reader. The reader looks at the text in the light of her own set of lenses and thus makes meaning or sense to her. The Canadian critic Northrop Frye argued much the same point in *Anatomy of Criticism* when he said that the text was like a dumb statue and that critics put different lenses on texts (such as historical, metaphoric, linguistic, stylistic, or mythic). Each lens refracts the text in a different way, and all the ways are appropriate and add a complexity to the text.

Out of these positions grew a whole field of criticism called reader–response criticism. It has held sway in Europe and North America for a whole generation. The focus is on how readers (either "ideal" readers or real readers) construe or make sense of literature.

Reader–response theory makes the reader into someone who is important, someone who is in control of the reading.

Many of these critics moved into their own heads to fashion their criticism. Their followers have done the same so that theories of criticism are fashioned from the question "how do I read?" We can say that this is typical of so much of what we think of as postmodernism. As the surety and security of world outside the perceiving self becomes less and less, where else can the self turn but to the self? This seems to be the starting point for reader–response criticism. Hypertext takes us further, into the world of the coauthoring reader.

When we read a poem, we make connections to our understandings and feelings of each of the words and of the ensemble of words, images, shapes, voices, and themes and allusions. We do not read the poem passively, but we write a new version and bring out our particular poem. If we insist on the validity of our particular poem, it is because that is all we can know, we who are trapped inside ourselves.

For many people this solipsistic world, the world of the narcissistic reader, is perfectly fine. We are happy in it. The poem means what I think it means, and you are entitled to your opinion too. This is a friendly counter to the idea that the text has a definite meaning outside of ourselves or that the text means what the author intended.

The individual reader has authority.

There is no other authority than the mind of the reader. But the reader is not free. Readers are prisoners of their culture.

Hypertext holds that all of these critics and theorists are right; much of what is on the page controls both the sense we make of what we read and how we make sense. But there is a remainder that we do. We fill in the blank spaces and read between the lines; in doing so, we are authors.

Reading between the Lines

Reading between the lines is a phrase that is often used to describe the act of interpretation. But there is nothing between the lines except space, blank space. How do we read blank space? what do we read?

Readers, like nature, abhor a vacuum. So, readers look at the space and make connections between the lines. Readers use the white space of text to make sense of the connections and gaps between the words, phrases, and sentences that are printed (see Figures 3.1a and 3.1b). So, too, readers use the white space of hypertext. So, too, readers use the

a.

CONSENTING TO LOSE SIGHT

FIGURES 3.1a and 3.1b. These two poems use their relationship to their position on the page and the space around them to make a point. Part of their effectiveness is in what they imply by their position; this adds to the actual text and changes our understanding of their meaning.

gutters of comics. This is a part of reading, the making of connections between groups of black marks on white space. We read the white space as much as we read the black marks. So, too, we read the rests in music.

It is this act of reading across space that makes us grammatical people, that is, people who seek to find a pattern in ourselves, our language, and our world. But, though there may be some common elements in the process by which we read, we read differently. (For a fuller discussion of this phenomenon, see Chapter 4.)

Sacred Texts and the History of Interpretation

The place of the text in that complex activity called scripture has shaped the ways people read secular texts. As I wrote earlier, the center of learning in the nonliterate world is the ceremony, often a religious ceremony. Through it people learned about the gods, the tribal history, the moral and ethical injunctions, and much else that was necessary to be a full-fledged member of the ceremony. We see this phenomenon today in a variety of ceremonies such as initiation rites into a fraternity or church. When texts are introduced, ceremonies don't disappear; rather, the ceremonies enfold and involve texts and books. Ceremonies remain.

In the world of the text, ceremonies may appear to have moved somewhat to the periphery, as the center for learning and transmission of the culture and the religious tradition seemingly shifts to the book itself, and from the book to the library, which contains the sacred (or

b.

LEAP

profane) text and the commentaries on that text. Ceremonies around the use of libraries and books persisted and grew into such elaborated ritualized institutions as the monastery and the university. The way people read and the uses to which they put the texts they read became and remain a focal point of the habit we call literacy. So, to ceremony was added the library, and ceremony shaped the way libraries are conceived and used in the practice of scripture and literacy. The tension between the oral and the written persists.

> The Bible, and the reading of the Bible as an instrument of instruction, may be said to have begun on sunrise of that day when Ezra unrolled the parchment scroll of the Law. It was a new thought that the Divine Will could be communicated by a dead literature as well as by a living voice. In the impassioned welcome with which this thought was received lay the germs of all the good and evil which was afterwards to be developed out of it; on the one side, the possibility of appeal in each successive age to the primitive undying document that should rectify the fluctuations of false tradition and fleeting opinion; on the other hand, the temptation to pay to the letters of the sacred book a worship as idolatrous and as profoundly opposed to its spirit as once had been the veneration paid to the sacred trees or the sacred stones of the consecrated groves and hills.[8]

This passage, written over a century ago, tells us much of what the change from the oral ceremony to the book-centered world must have been like. It also suggests one of the problems that emerged very shortly after the introduction of the sacred book, namely, that it came to be worshipped as an object rather than as the vessel of the divine word. Such worship did happen, and it persists, but idolatry takes a number of different forms, as we shall see.

We know something of how the sacred texts were read ceremonially. The rabbis developed a dual system of reading the Torah. One, the Halakah, was a legal interpretation of the Torah and produced extensive commentary on how the laws were to be read and interpreted. The other reading of the same text, the Haggadah, was a more homiletic or pastoral one. In addition, there developed a series of comments and explanations of what the meaning might be.

Without a doubt the most radical interpretation of these texts was that of Jesus and his followers. Instead of taking the Torah and the prophets as had the Jewish scribes and Pharisees, they offered through the Gospel, the proclamation or Kerygma, a new interpretation of major segments of the traditional text. This reading was not legalistic or homiletic, but metaphoric, or at least so the early Christian writers claimed.

Influenced by the Greeks, many of the early Christians, such as Clement of Alexandria and Origen, argued that the laws of Moses contained a fourfold significance: the natural, the mystical, the moral, and the prophetic. In the late Middle Ages, Dante held that there were four ways of reading: the literal, the allegorical, the moral, and the anagogic. Some form of multiple reading formed part of the tradition of worship and particularly of preaching. The oral presentation was a reauthoring of the text in one of these ways, or in several.

This view of reading—that the text was to be read in the fourfold manner—suggests that the four are to be held in suspension and our readings are to shimmer among the four as if the text were a palimpsest. The text was seen as the springboard for contemplation, preaching, and devotion. It was the way into the Word, and it formed an entry point similar to the icon, the statue, and the very design of the cathedral, church, or mosque. The important focus was the memory and ceremony of the devoted, for the text, being rare, was an aid to the mind and not the mind's sole focal point. This view was common to Islam, as well. In religious thinking, the text is simultaneously a sacred object and the center of religious ceremony. And this ceremony provides a way for the worshipping community to reauthor the text in a mixture of interpretation and performance.

But many readers today have predilections toward one particular kind of reading; they seem to have lost the capacity to suspend and balance multiple ways of reading. I think that the reason for this loss arises from the fact that printing changed the way texts were produced and made them identical to one another across thousands of copies, and thereafter the idea of the authority of the text as an object came to dominate the thinking of many. It worked its way into the popular imagination, as it was led by the thinking of such influential teachers as Peter Ramus and John Calvin.[9] They seemed to distrust the mind, the memory, and to some extent the scriptural ceremony, and they placed their trust in the external text, which they saw as the map to lead the reader and the soul to God. From this view came the idea of sola scriptura. Sola scriptura remains popular and is threatened by the counter view that I suggest throughout this book should obtain, a view that gives authority and autonomy to the reader and that coincides with the concept of hypertext. To me, the reader is an intelligence that brings something of his or her past experience to the text and so modifies it rather than being a simple responder to the unchanging words on the page. Such a participatory view is in accord to with the contemporary ideas that the knower is the one who makes sense of the world. This is akin to Coleridge's view of the imagination and of coauthoring.

Sola Scriptura, Literal Reading, and the Source of Authority in Reading

The idea of sola scriptura holds that the scripture is the sole authority of doctrine and faith. It has carried with it the corollary that reading the scripture in order to ascertain matters of faith and doctrine can be done unaided. To hold such a belief is also to hold a view of the text that it is not a metaphor or an icon, but an exact picture, that it is to God and God's plan as the periodic table is to chemical elements. It is to view the tool as an end and not as a means of stimulating the imagination and devotion of the reader. This was a way of reading encouraged by many of the Protestants. It is claimed as the hallmark belief of some of those sects that are called "fundamentalist" but should rather be called literalist in that many people who call themselves fundamentalists do not subscribe to the concept of sola scriptura.

The literal reading of the religious text—or any text—is not a new idea, but to hold that only the literal reading is legitimate is relatively new. With the coming of print and the Reformation came the idea of the authority of the text and the belief that it was not the reading but the text that was important. This meant that the literal

reading came to predominate in the world of the Reformation, particularly in such writers as John Calvin. But their meaning of literal
is not quite what was later thought of as being literal. The English
reformer William Tyndale wrote:

> Thou shalt understand, therefore, that the scripture hath but one
> sense, which is the literal sense. And that literal sense is the root and
> ground of all, and the anchor that never faileth, whereunto if you
> cleave, thou canst never err or go out of the way. And if thou leave the
> literal sense, thou canst not but go out of the way. Neverthelater, the
> Scripture useth proverbs, similitudes, riddles, or allegories as all other
> speeches do; but that which the proverb, similitude, riddle, or allegory
> signifieth, is ever the literal sense, which thou must seek out diligently.
> . . . We say, 'Let the sea swell and rise high as she will, yet hath God
> appointed how far he shall go:' meaning that the tyrants shall not do
> what they would but only that which God hath appointed them to do.
> . . . All fables, prophecies, and riddles are allegories; as Aesop's fables,
> and Merlin's prophecies; and the interpretation of them are the literal
> sense. . . .
>
> So when I say, 'Christ is a lamb;' I mean not a lamb that beareth wool,
> but a meek and patient lamb, which is beaten for other men's faults. . . .
>
> Beyond all this, when we have found out the literal sense by the
> process of the text, or by a like text in another place, then go we, and
> as the Scripture borroweth similitudes of worldly things, even so we
> again borrow similitudes or allegories of the scripture, and apply them
> to our purposes; which allegories are no sense of the scripture, but free
> things besides the scripture and altogether in the liberty of the Spirit.[10]

Over the course of the first two centuries after printing became
established, the idea of the strictly literal reading took hold. The reason
for this was that the texts slowly began to contain information that
required a person to follow exactly what the words on the page signified.
We can see this in the history of navigational maps, which changed from
being general depictions of the outlines of a land mass to precise charts
of water depths and shoals. Similarly, scientific writing began to take on
precision, and with the work of anatomists like Vesalius a map of the
human body could be used as a guide to those who would trace various
bodily functions. The same held true of rules and charters. Cookbooks
began to take on precise measurements and sequences of directions. If
one strayed from them, the cake might not rise.

So the literal reading became the central one by which knowledge was accrued. Texts, taxonomies, maps, and other plain documents represented the world in a single vision. It was a world that required close and exact attention. No metaphorical or symbolic meanings need apply. The spiritual was out of the question.

Many poets railed against this view. William Blake wrote:

> Now I a fourfold vision see,
> And a fourfold vision is given to me;
> 'Tis fourfold in my supreme delight
> And threefold in soft Beulah's night
> And twofold Always. May God us keep
> From Single vision & Newton's sleep.[11]

Blake, who knew Dante's writings well, sees the fourfold vision as like Dante's anagogic view, but this is seldom to be reached by humans. They can attain the mythic or innocent vision of the child, where the literal, imaginative, and moral all come together. Adults make the dual reading of the literal and the metaphoric, and the vision of empiricism's and Newton's sleep is that of the single minded who take the world only literally.

Blake also wrote, in "The Everlasting Gospel":

> Both read the Bible day & night,
> But thou read'st black where I read white.[12]

Blake's reading was a reading of the spaces in the text, the links in the hypertext, the gutters of the comic book of the Bible. From what I have argued about the nature of scripture and of hypertext, I would concur with Blake that the reading of the Bible in the scriptural sense is to take an active role in the coauthoring or reauthoring of the text rather than the passive one that is suggested by the concept of sola scriptura and Nature's sleep. I would extend this view beyond the religious text to most texts (in the restricted sense of the term, of course, I am not yet up to an anagogic reading of my Macintosh manual or help notices).

Nevertheless, a large number of readers have persisted in reading the Bible as if it were a timetable for the train to heaven. It is perhaps not coincidental that a large number of those who make up the literalist camp are technicians, people whose daily lives are spent in following the book.

The idea of sola scriptura is continually defended and continually critiqued. In part it is a Catholic–Calvinist debate, but it is more. The "postmodernist" theologian Stanley Hauerwas is among those who see authority residing not in the text but the community interpreting it. These critics take their cue from reader-response theory and the idea of the interpretive community, and they argue that the reader may think she is accepting the text as authority, but in reality it is the community of readers that exerts its pressure on those who are brought in as catechumens.

Hauerwas "challenges the assumption that communities can exist without authority"[13] and suggests that the community authors or gives an authoritative reading of the text, and in that authoring is itself the authority, not the text. The illusion that the text of the Bible is the authority neglects the scriptural role of the Bible. It is convenient, if not necessary, for certain Christian communities to treat the text as having no symbolic or mythical meaning but to be a road map for the soul. That is the way the text becomes scripture in those communities.

Hauerwas further asserts: "What is at stake (in preaching) is not the question of 'the meaning of Scripture' but the usefulness of Scripture, given the good end of the Christian community. The Scriptures are exhibited in communities that are capable of pointing to holy lives through which we can rightly see the reality that has made Scriptures possible."[14] He is arguing that scripture when seen as scripture is so read; the text is not scripture, but the community of readers makes it scriptural. And the scriptural nature of the Scripture changes as the community of readers changes. We cannot argue that Torah means what it did to Hillel or to St. Paul, nor that the Gospels mean what they did to Augustine or Aquinas. If God is the Word, the Logos, then the text is the record of those who have somehow "heard" or perceived that Word. The text is divinely inspired, but it is not divine. In one sense it persists through time; the marks and spaces remain; in another sense it changes as the community reading it changes. We may, and many of us do, find divinity through, but not in, the text. We are seeing that scripture is not out there, but in us, that it is indeed the activity of worship with and through the text— which is no longer a traditional text, but the hypertext that many had long ago realized. In this sense, the idea of salvation through the scriptural activity makes sense, but that is not the same as salvation through the words on a page.

Once we adopt this view of text and hypertext, once we link text, word, and image and see ourselves as participating and creating coauthors of the scripture, we also tend to rethink who we are in terms of that important feature of religion, doctrine, an issue that I shall take up later, in Chapter 6.

Types of Readers

There are a number of different types of readers. In the time of Dante or in the time of the Talmudic scholars, there were relatively few readers, and these few tended to be taught a variety of different approaches to the literary text. As we noted earlier in this chapter, during the late Middle Ages, the Jewish mystics referred to reading through the acronym "PaRDeS." It derives from the first initials of the name of each level of meaning: *peshat*, the literal level; *remez*, allegory from which philosophic and scientific truths are derived; *derash*, the rabbinical interpretation for laws and instances of faith; and *sod*, the meaning revealed to the mystic. Dante's version, as we have seen, argues that the Bible, and particularly the Old Testament, is "polysemous," having a literal sense, an allegorical sense about the life and works of Christ, a moral sense, and an "anagogic" sense. The astute reader juggles these four possibilities or moves among them in an ever widening set of circles. But this reader was scrupulously trained in this technique of reading and authoring the text.

As the number of readers grew and as many of them became specialized in one field or another, they appear to have separated the variety of reading styles and become specialists in a certain kind of reading. Most have learned to make certain assumptions about the nature of the text and what they can do with it. These assumptions are ingrained because they help the reader get on about his business of using texts in work, study, worship, or recreation.

One group tends to see all texts as metaphoric or allegorical. Such people are always digging for the hidden meaning deep down underneath. These people are ones who see the text as being some index to a hidden reality. They are looking for implications, the ponderables. They see the text as bearing a code.

A second group sees many texts as the subject of eternal speculation and mystery. They are looking less for the ponderable than for the imponderable. The mystical readers tend, more often than not, to be persons who are accustomed or attracted to poetry, philosophy, or myth.

Another group tends to see all texts as maps whose surface corresponds to reality. These map readers are literal readers, ones who accept what is said and take it at face value. What they are used to reading and doing with their reading is adapting action to the text, as when they assemble something or follow a set of directions.

Another group can be said to treat texts as textbooks, to want to take something away from what they read. Reading is homiletic. These are people who sermonize the reading.

Most of us, of course, are mixtures of these four types. We may read some texts in any one or a combination of these four ways. How we read what we read depends upon the circumstances of the reading and the nature of the text. But in different situations or different social settings the reading may shift. I read a computer manual differently from the way I read a poem. And I talk about poems differently with my colleagues in the academic world than I do with my wife. I shift communities and ways of reading. In each community, however, I am a creature of my training. How people read depends in part on their personalities; to a greater extent it depends upon how they are trained to be members of communities.

THE FORGING OF READING COMMUNITIES IN A WORLD OF HYPERTEXT

Literacy is a social habit challenged by hypertext, and since readers are trained to be readers within their communities, how has hypertext challenged and shed light on their training? Hypertext leads us to rethink and reexamine the nature of different reading communities. It also leads us to think about how they are forged into communities, given the changes that appear to be resulting from the coming together of a variety of new forms of communication, wherein text is transformed into image and communication becomes instantaneous. The fabric of the traditional reading community appears to be sorely rent.

Common Texts

But if rent, the fabric is not tattered into a world of a million different interpretations, one for each reader. The onion remains essentially an onion; the barnacles are affixed to one rock or oyster. So it is that a group of readers may have the same reaction to a particular poem or story, even if the hypertext format allows for reauthoring and recon-figuring. This is where convention comes in, for as humans we share much, and much that we share is conventional wisdom. People might say different things about a story, but they will share a sense of who the hero is, and who the villain, whether they are to laugh or cry, and what the general gist of the story or poem or essay might be. This similarity in response is what makes a community of readers. These communities have been forged not only in shared suppositions and ways of reading, but also through the sharing of a common text or group of texts, what is known as a canon. This is the notion of the people of the Bible, or the people of the book, or the members of a particular cultural group such as those brought up in the "classical tradition."

It is a fragile bond.

The tie is not simply that of the text, but of the human culture of the reading of the text. The tie is in the reading or interpretive community.

In the world of hypertext, this community coauthors the text, so the book is the occasion for community but not the cause of commu-nity in this realm.

The Reader and Hypertext

Hypertext has helped sharpen the discussion of interpretive commu-nities.

In the world of printing and modern literature, the various editions of a novel or a poem generally had the same text printed in the same order (although there might be variations in type size, leading, font, and trim size of the book).

The differences among readers, then, are differences about what was assumed to be a common physical object.

But in the world of hypertext, readers clearly create different orderings of the text spaces from one another.

They do not have the "same" text to talk about. The occasion wherein a variety of readers (and readings) focus on one text has disappeared. Hypertext reasserts the equality of the authors and the readers as coauthoring the text. It appears to be a commonsense solution to the problem of the failure of the unassailable monumental text and to the narcissism of the individual reader.

We know that certain sets of relationships appear to exist and that these help ground the reader. We know from the fact of printing and reproduction of disks and programs that the text is the same through all its printings even though a part of it is changed when even the font is changed. We know that the text is the product of a person or group of people whom we call authors.

We know that a group of people sharing space–time will have certain common tendencies when they read a text. We also know that people can talk to one another efficaciously about a text if they share a common frame of reference. They can come to a consensus. They reach consensus most clearly when they place the text in the context of scripture and see themselves as community.

The Commonality and Community of Readers

As I have noted, there are a number of situations where the community of readers (those gathered at a point of space–time) have authority over the text. They come to a consensus. There may be a leader, but there need not be. These communities do indeed rewrite the text in terms of the larger discourse with which they are concerned. As the critic Stanley Fish noted, a group of linguists will look at a text from a linguistic perspective, psychologists from a psychological perspective, and literary critics from whatever is the critical perspective of the moment.[15] The text appears to remain the same, but does it?

Ceremony, and ceremonies of print, reinforce the idea of the interpretive community. But in the world of hypertext, where each reader has a different re-creation of the text, community seems difficult to attain. It is made more difficult if the readers share their readings in hyperspace or in the virtual world, which may or may not be synchronous.

Consensus and community are indeterminate. The readers themselves become nodes in a web. They are connected or linked in more or less strong ways. We appear to have only sensus not *consensus*, and unity not *community*.

Is there only fragment and nonsense?

Yes and no, One group's sense is another's nonsense; one person's community is another's heterodoxy.

The Hardening of Readers through Ceremony

Although many would say that the kind of reading depends upon the circumstances of the text, the reader, and the situation, many readers develop approaches to reading in those situations where the text becomes part of a communal activity. Schools, churches, and other institutions help them become set in their ways.

In the international studies of literature that I was involved in during the 1970s, we asked the students to read short stories and then select from a group of twenty questions the five that they thought most important to ask. The students at the end of secondary school were consistent in choosing the same questions across the texts that we offered them. They had established a style of reading.

We also found that the students within a country were remarkably similar to one another. They appeared to establish national styles of reading, regardless of how well they actually could read. The styles sorted themselves along two continua: a personal—impersonal continuum and a form—content continuum.

These two continua can form four quadrants of readers: personal–form, personal–content, impersonal–form, and impersonal–content. These quadrants have a rough correspondence to the PaRDeS of Jewish mysticism; at least one can see analogues for the literal and allegorical resembling impersonal–content, the moral resembling personal–content, and the mystic resembling personal–form. But such analogues are rough, at best. I would simply say that, at school, students learn how to read in particular ways, and for many of them this way of reading shapes the ways they deal with texts in later years.[16]

I would go further and assert that these ways are shaped both by school and by forces outside of school that affect reading: religious training and family and community culture are a part of that shaping force. In all of the following situations, students learn not only how to read or decode the text but also how to put that text into a literate or scriptural ceremony: reading aloud, answering questions about the text, listening to discussions of it ("sermons"), or participating in discussions themselves, or writing commentaries of one sort or another. The text inhabits a scriptural space, and the ceremony of reading is a ceremony of talk and interpretation.

Some of the ceremonies in different institutions lead to a similar view of reading and talking. This is particularly likely when the same kinds of "sanctioned" reading are perceived in two or three institutions where the text is important. People who tend toward the sciences or technical subjects and occupations are map readers. People in the social sciences and many journalists tend to be homiletic readers. The diggers often learn their craft from novels and certain kinds of religious tracts, and the mystics may have learned this form of reading from pondering and talking about aphorisms, gnomic utterances, and fortune cookies.

It seems that people are inducted not simply into a broad world of literacy but into a specific world or community within the literate society. That has been the case in the past. When we become literate, we have the potential to be free and to cross into a larger world of print, but many of us become trapped into a smaller world of being a particular kind of reader in a particular language, a particular profession, with a particular set of habits.

Whether we see ourselves as free or trapped may finally be irrelevant. The basic fact remains that, whether or not we have learned to use the system of inscribing ideas in a written language and are able to make sense of those things we call texts, we are all in a literate environment. We cannot escape it. From the moment we get up and look at our digital clock or hear someone read the news on the radio, open the toothpaste tube with writing on it, face the dials and buttons in our kitchen, get into our automobiles with their numerous dials and icons, drive down streets marked by signs, pass billboards and buildings with advertising and neon lights on them, go about our shopping or work, return home to watch television with its various captions until the moment that we fall asleep, we are in a literate world and partake of it. Written or printed words may even inhabit our dreams.

The world is a world of written words as well as a world of sounds and talk and music. It is a world made up not only of words and letters, but of particular texts that our community values and the knowledge of which marks our entry into the specific community. These form our canons, and they are important to us. They are one of the forces that bring us together into communities of readers. Not just reading texts in the same way, but also reading the same texts, both work to create our habits and ceremonies of literacy.

Canons and Shared Values

A great deal has been written about canons in the past decade or so. One whole part of the discussion has concerned the limitations of the "traditional canon" of literature as it was taught in courses in the humanities or the "Great Books." The canon appears limited to "dead white Males," according to the critics. An occasional female was admitted to the ranks of the greats, Jane Austen or Emily Dickinson, most notably. There were few authors from outside of western Europe and later America. Such a restriction of the canon is a form of censorship: one keeps in, the other keeps out; both are exclusionary. The challenge to the canon is a part of the broad challenge to modernism and universalism that I shall take up in Chapter 5.

To understand a canon, we have to understand something about how a culture or a society perpetuates itself. Jacques Ellul has argued that cultures do this through what he calls "centers of learning."[17] As he has described in some detail and I have alluded to, in an oral society the center of learning is embodied in the ceremony—the ritual dance, performance, worshipful service, or pattern of activities that are a central part of the life of that culture. Ceremonies may be related to seasons of the year, stages in the life cycle, or some other set of important points of tribal or group memory, such as the Hebrews' Passover or the Christian Nativity. With the advent of writing and written records, the center of learning became vested in the library, the place where books were kept. Just as village schools were built around ceremonies in certain tribal cultures, so latter-day schools developed around libraries, and they continue to be so developed to this day and build their ceremonies around the library. But, since their very founding, libraries have been faced with the problem of both what to keep and what principle should determine what should be kept as the core of the "center of learning." This is where canons come in.

Traditionally a canon was an external rule by which was determined which texts were considered authentic, authorized, or standard. The problem was an extremely simple one. Given a limited number of copyists, given the limitations of papyrus or mud, or whatever surface, and given the rather high cost, how does one determine what shall be kept and what thrown away?

One of the first determinations of the canon took place at the Library of Alexandria in the Hellenistic period. The idea of canon came to be applied to religious texts and then to secular ones. The following legend of the great library of Alexandria is instructive:

> "Demetrius of Phalerum, as keeper of the king's library, received large grants of public money with a view to his collecting, if possible, all the books in the world; and by purchases and transcriptions he to the best of his ability carried the king's purpose into execution. Being asked once in his presence, about how many thousand of books were already collected, he replied: 'More than two hundred thousand, O king; and I will ere long make diligent search for the remainder, so that a total of half a million may be reached. I am informed that the Jews also have

certain laws which are deserving of transcription and place in the library.' 'What is to hinder thee then,' replied the king, 'in this task? For all the necessary means are at thy service.' And Demetrius answered: 'Translation is also required. For in the Jews' land they use a peculiar script. . . . ' And when the king had learnt all the facts, he gave command that a letter should be written to the high priest of the Jews, in order that the proposal of Demetrius above mentioned might be carried into effect."[18]

The problem of keeping texts is no different from the problem of deciding what stories or charms to remember except that the texts would not necessarily go away simply because people forgot them. They had the habit of sticking around—so they had to be kept somewhere, and if they were kept there had to be some principle of storing them and of retrieving them. Thus developed the idea of the library and the canon, the set of rules for making these decisions. What to keep, of course, includes what to read and what to sanction as worth reading. The canon, therefore, leads beyond issues of storage to issues of promulgation.

In earlier times a group of priests, scribes, or librarians had determined canonical rules. There were few to question them since they were the ones who knew how to read and write and they had custody over the materials. They were accepted as long as people had little access to text. With the development of printing and mass production of texts, restrictions determined by the economics of copying, printing, or storage slowly faded into the background; others could check on decisions of particular canon setters by going to another library or by buying a book on the black market. Also as more could read and more was produced, there were increasing chances that control over the canon was less sure.

Why Canons?

Canons exist as a way of dealing with information. They serve as measures to limit information, to authenticate it, and to serve as rules for admitting new information. Canons are corporate extensions of the human faculty of knowledge. Each of us determines what is worth knowing and selects and chooses information accordingly. So, too, communities, nations, organizations, and institutions establish canonical rules.

Every society and culture has a canon—that body of artistic works that are considered central to a group's self-definition; some were formed as deliberately as that of the Alexandria library, while others were formed much more haphazardly. Petrarch and his successors formed the canon of Roman and later Greek literature by what they could salvage from monasteries and nunneries. Their success depended upon happenstance and the vagaries of the abbots and prioresses as well as the ability of the searchers to copy materials quickly before they deteriorated or were destroyed. As Wendell Harris observes, there are several operating definitions of *canon*, each of which can be seen as the product of an individual's or a group's defining a body of texts that serve a particular function. In a sense the term is as slippery as *culture*. It may be seen cynically as *what we believe should be read, viewed, seen, or listened to by those who would join us*. What makes the issue more problematic and political is that it has come to form a part of a national debate on the nature of our society and the government's role in defining that society. It has become reified in a way that far exceeds the historical reality of what we know about canons.

How Canons Are Really Made

In few cases is there an easy consensus as to what belongs in a canon, what is excluded, and what is marginal. The makers of canons include editors, reviewers, librarians, historians, and others concerned with the determination of what shall be known of a culture or a society. In our society, literary canons are determined by diverse forces; the critic Janice Radway painstakingly described canon formation among a group of Midwestern women who meet through a bookseller to determine the "classic" romances.[19] Others have described the ways by which the canons of popular culture such as film, television, and music are created through various combinations of market research and promotion. These, too, share aspects of canons, as do comic books and commercial juvenile and adolescent literature.

At times, as in Radway's example, those who set a canon are members of a particular culture; more often, they are external to it. Such is true of Renaissance scholars and archaeologists, who have to be content with what they can find and decipher. All we have of the "literary canon" of certain Mesopotamian cultures is a collection of tables of the price of corn. Let us hope that those who could read had something else to amuse themselves with and that mothers had tales to be read to their children.

Another group of external definers of canons includes folklorist-anthropologists who determine what they preserve of various dying cultures and societies throughout the world. At times, they make their own selections, but at other times their informants—who might have many motives for their selections—make them. We must remember that for many societies the very idea of recording folktales and folk songs is new, less than a century old; what is recorded is but the tip of the iceberg and probably not fully revelatory of a particular culture.

The group determining a canon in many societies is the committee appointed to help the librarian. The group determines what should remain and what should be jettisoned. Often the determination is economic. What can we afford to keep? Can we supply what there appears to be a demand for, and can we keep the low-demand items, as well?

If we examine the body of texts from the past two centuries in the United States in order to select representative texts of a cultural group, we are again at the mercy of printers and booksellers, of magazine and newspaper publishers, and of the marketplace. Even in the "dominant culture," canon formation is about as scientific as the stock market or the "Top 40" in pop records (itself a "nonce" canon, to use Harris's term). Whether the canon represents the best, the "classic," the most representative, or the most popular is arguable. We know that in England F. R. Leavis led a propaganda campaign to get Lawrence into the educational curriculum and Tennyson out of it; similar campaigns have been waged in this country. Scott, Hardy, and George Eliot have been driven out of the school curriculum by various groups. The inclusion of one writer is subject to fashion, and writers blossom and fade based on the taste of editors and teachers, not to mention students. Contemporary writers are promoted and sold by cartels of agents, publishers, reviewers, teachers, and librarians.

Sometimes the determination is by some principle of collective authority. Is there a way of determining the appropriate texts of a particular author? Is there a way of determining what is necessary for salvation? In recent years there has existed the "Jesus Seminar," a committee of scholars that meets to decide which words in the Gospels are indeed the words of Jesus. This is similar to the committees established to determine the entries in an encyclopedia, or an anthology of American literature, or on a list of what every student should know. Approaching the task from a variety of perspectives, the group makes its best guess.

Canons are capricious human selections among artifacts and are subject to change as the criteria change. Matthew Arnold's list of the "best that has been thought or said" contains such obvious gaps as the works of the eighteenth century, and it took the popularity accorded T. S. Eliot and Archibald MacLeish to bring John Donne and the metaphysical poets back into favor. Whatever approach to the canon one adopts, one is always subject to criticism on specific authors and titles, and one can never *fix* what is most important for young people to read from whatever heritage. A particular canon is probably not adequate to the culture at large nor even to the "elite" within that culture. Curriculum planners need to acknowledge and accept the limitation of what is selected; they should never be seduced into defending it as the best and most enduring monuments (as William Bennett [1988] and Allan Bloom [1987] have done) nor attacking it as being a monolith that excludes minorities, women, and homosexuals (as some of Bloom's and Bennett's detractors have done). Some texts and writers have greater staying power than others—that is about all we can say. Why they stay is partly a matter of intrinsic quality but mostly the result of fashion. Because of their staying power they have had greater influence on other artists and on the culture.

Electronic Canons: Everyone Is Her Own Librarian

Canons extend beyond text to film, audiotape, videotape, and other media. In fact, for many of my students, the canon is less a canon of literary works than it is a canon of film, comics, or music. This canon is just as strong a cohesive force and to them and to many at least as important as the canon of the humanities course that I have taught. Canons are determined in many of the popular arts by commercial criteria, again a matter of supply and demand. But as storage of materials becomes easier, the criteria for canonicity become more vexing. In the world of hypertext and the hyperspace of information, the canon becomes indeterminate—and perhaps superfluous.

It is true that canonicity in the sense of authorship and attribution is still possible. Owing to computer concordances and other aids, it is possible to make more accurate guesses as to who wrote what when.

But in the broader world of canons, a group may bring in new texts or ones that had been previously omitted. On the Internet, one may browse in any one of the world's large libraries, and then call for the text, which if it has been scanned can be brought forth and downloaded within a matter of minutes. All texts are potentially available, and not only all texts but also manuscripts and multiple editions or versions of those texts.

The reader is not limited in access to any material. The physical presence of the book does not make the canon. Any reader can create a personal canon that selects from different nodes on the web of information. Censorship also becomes more problematic, since there is potentially unlimited access to whatever texts, films, tapes, or discs are available in any one of the countless repositories in the world. The only censor that seems to be operative is the practical consideration of cost.

The issue of canons, then, becomes not an issue of access but an issue of what a community or an individual values. Canons become more clearly a matter of choice and a question of who chooses. Sometimes in the electronic world the individual or group forms the canon, but there is also the force of the large commercial providers of Internet services who decide what the canons shall be. My American Online web browser has a list of preferred places that it thinks I want. I can and generally do ignore its canon and make my own selections, some of which I share with my different interest communities.[20]

Canons, therefore, remain an important part of the formation of communities and the particular types of literacy that those communities value, but we can see that they are breaking down with the advent of the electronic library and the Internet and Web. All is available to anyone who has a modem and the time and inclination to access it. As the major libraries continue their practice of digitizing their collections, the world's libraries become an invisible and universal source.

Particular communities will still establish particular subsets of this panoply of texts and hypertexts as the operating canon of their group. There will be certain texts that are the sine qua non of being a mycologist, a geographer, or a devotee of a particular form of evangelical activity. But these texts will become joined by videotapes, CD-ROMs, and other forms of storage. They will also be available as icons on the screens of the home computer or portable television. Whether this will produce a new virtual-world "tower of Babel" remains to be seen. Certainly, the center of learning is no longer the library. As I shall argue in Chapter 5, the center of learning now exists somewhere in cyberspace or in our hard drives.

Being literate in the world of hypertexts and hypermedia, then, involves a rethinking of how the reader behaves toward the text, that is, how she thinks of herself as a coauthor within a community of like-minded beings and how that membership both restricts and enhances her capacity to make the text meaningful in her life. Even though we may sit at our terminal alone, we are sharing with others who have clicked on the text space and put it into their own mosaic of hypertext. We are also part of the mosaic of readers that forge and form a community. To an extent we are members because we have entered the same space—even though it may be at different times or from a variety of locations on the globe. We have all penetrated to a particular node on the web, and then we recede or follow different filaments to other spaces. We have become—if only fleetingly—part of a community, and what we do is shaped by that community. At this point, we are probably shaped more by the institutions and ceremonies that surround our being readers of print than our being readers and viewers of hypertext images. But that is in the process of changing.

As members of this new community, we have come to share a particular body of text space that forms our canon and helps us to have the common knowledge that binds us to others. We have read some of the same spaces, seen some of the same images, and these form our common frame of reference. How large that point of commonality is will depend. I am a subscriber to America Online and I certainly share a whole iconic and text world with my millions of fellow members. I also share to a greater extent the common bond of the subscribers to a particular list-serve or the readers of certain home pages. This canon is part of our communal binding. But so too are the information sources, books, films, images, and other parts of the canon that we share off-line. How the two come together remains an object of exploration.

CHAPTER FOUR

Text as Image

The Picture of the Web

One of the words that has accompanied the advent of computers and hypertext is *icon,* a word coming from the Greek which means likeness or image. To many among the Christian world and the art world as well, the word has come to have associated with it the tradition of a religious image, particularly that of the Eastern Orthodox Church. The religious icon is usually a painting of one of the major Christian figures, particularly Christ or Mary, and includes some of the symbols around the story of Christ, such as the lamb or the fish. Icons also represent certain of the major saints, as well as Old Testament stories (but usually with a Christian point of reference included). Icons helped form the basis for worship among a people for whom the reading of the written text seemed remote.

Icons were a central part of the design of the church, which was also seen as an image through which one could approach divinity. The visual environment of worship was itself a doorway to worship and a way toward the real presence of God. People could move among the icons and, through what they saw, reach an appreciation of and perhaps even a communion with the divinity. The role of the Christian icon is paralleled by counterpart icons in both Hinduism and Buddhism. In two of the major religions, however, icons are banned, and the icon has not had an easy time of it in the Christian world, either.

The word *icon* has surfaced in the technological world as a key term in computer language, referring to a schematic figure that appears on the screen to represent a function, program, or file. The icon and the menu of icons have come to be staples of personal computing on both the Macintosh and Windows visual display as well as on the Internet. All three are icon-driven in that it is through the pointing at and clicking on icons that people navigate through the network of commands and menus that are the hypertext of the screen.

Scott McCloud argues that one of the powerful features of the comics is that they do not use pictures but icons, that is, a distillation of the pictorial so that it is less directly representative and more universal.[1] They may also use caricature, that which focuses on a particular feature and exaggerates it. Caricature moves the icon toward the abstract, where the representational is distorted in order to emphasize some other visual point (see Figure 4.1).

A drawing selects from a photograph the most salient details.

If more and more of the specific details are removed, the details that remain come closer and closer to becoming an icon. The ultimate icon of a face is a circle with two dots and a line (see Figure 4.2).

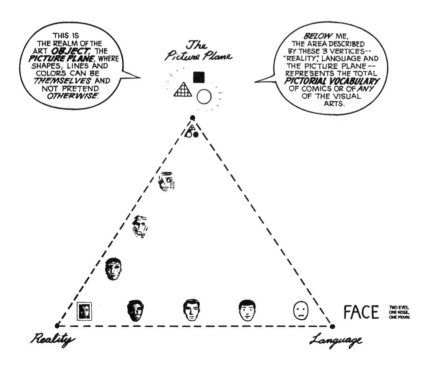

FIGURE 4.1. Pyramid of abstraction and iconic representation, according to Scott McCloud. From Scott McCloud, *Understanding Comics: The Invisible Art* (Northampton, MA: Kitchen Sink Press, 1993), p. 51. © 1993 by Scott McCloud. Reprinted by permission.

FIGURE 4.2. The icon at its most basic level.

Whether we talk of the religious icon or the computer icon, both tend to avoid photographic representations for schematic ones that eschew detail and realism in favor of generalizations that enable us to see ourselves reflected or portrayed in them.

Iconic depictions enable viewers to identify with the picture more, to see the picture as an extension of the viewer rather than as an object. By manipulating the icon, the reader–writer exerts control and has authority. The icon is the first step toward the symbol, when the abstracted picture becomes constant over time, space, and circumstance and the writer/artist can use it knowing that it will be understood in the same way time after time.

ICONS AND SYMBOLS

The icon is an image, a representation of the general. It is often confused with a symbol, the visual representation of an abstraction, of something that is generally unseen. Of course, comic strips use a variety of symbols (see Figure 4.3.). The light bulb, the motion line, stars around the head, and many other visuals serve as symbols, but the main symbol is the bubble.

Bubbles are the spaces that contain written language that expresses the speech of the character—that is, if it's a straight-line bubble.

A wavy, cloudlike bubble is, of course, a representation of thought.

A zigzag bubble connotes something electronic as the source.

Language outside a bubble is ambient noise or perhaps commentary.

Language can also be in a legend bar.

But the written language itself is also a set of visible symbols and icons.

FIGURE 4.3. Some symbols from the world of the comic book. From Scott McCloud, *Understanding Comics: The Invisible Art* (Northampton, MA: Kitchen Sink Press, 1993), p. 129. © 1993 by Scott McCloud. Reprinted by permission.

The Iconic World

Just as we inhabit a world of words and text, we inhabit worlds of images. What we see is to some extent what we know, and we are both impressed and motivated by the images of things. To say this is to say that we are a species that observes the world and comes to understand that world in terms of what we see. When we look at something, the light from that object comes through the lenses of our eyes and forms an upside-down image on the back of the eye. The brain then takes this and turns it around again so that we see it rightside up and then enables us to connect it with other images that have already been stored there. It is by these images in the brain that we sense where we are, where we are going, what time it is, and who we are dealing with. It is as a result of images that we are able to view something resembling as a box on wheels that we have never seen before and say to ourselves, "Oh, yes, a car." We have matched the visual image of a specific car with the icon of cars. These icons may become more detailed and specific so that we are able to identify Maseratis or Volkswagens as such, just as people in rural societies can identify different types of berries and plants (see Figure 4.3).

Icons are central to our whole way of thinking and acting in the world. When we fit an image to an icon, we are acting not simply as an independent eye, but we are also acting socially, for we have been taught which distinctions to consider important and which to see as trivial. We assimilate the new into the known; matching and sorting images perceived with images stored in the brain, we make our way through the world. As in writing, we coauthor the world, and both perceive and create simultaneously. The next box on wheels that rolls along the street might be physically distinguishable as a totally new object; but we are now able to place it into a category, name it, and assimilate it into the world we know. If we do that, we are performing Adam's original task of coauthoring by reading and naming.

Besides the images of the world around us that we see and turn into icons in order to make sense of our environment, there is a second world of images. For centuries, people have created a world of manufactured icons: the cave drawings, the Byzantine icons, the paintings of Rembrandt or Picasso, the comics of Al Capp, and those pictures that we see on television or our computer screens, in books or photograph albums. Some of these icons are icons representing the world around us; many more are icons of an imagined or idealized world. We see icons on the sides of buildings or the packaging around toothpaste or soap. Many young children appear to read because they can look at a package and tell what is in it or at a sign and tell the name of the company. They are reading images, not words. We continue to do the same as we shop for labels and wear T-shirts with images on them. Like the children, we arrange and inhabit our world on the basis of logos rather than *the Logos*. We put these icons into patterns, and from those patterns we make meaning.

These images have become the objects of study and of controversy. Because they are central to the electronic media, particularly television, but also computers, they have become the centerpiece of that field of study called communication. In an interview in *The UNESCO Courier*, Régis Debray observed:

> Edison once said that "whoever controls the cinema industry will control the most powerful means of influencing the people." Today he would have to say: all peoples. The image governs our dreams and dreams govern our actions. Images are indeed powerful, perhaps they have always been powerful, but because they are so easily reproducible and transmissible, they have taken on a new importance which has made them controversial.[2]

The Reputation of Images

Images have a mixed reputation in the philosophical and cultural world. Plato saw them as being on the side of the cave we can see—"shadows" of the true world of ideas. They are divorced from reality, from the True, the Good, and the One. Moses and Francis Bacon referred to them as idols; Moses saw them as unholy, Bacon saw them as misleading. The characteristic of the idol is that people see the icon and fail to see it for what it is, a way of representing the reality beyond what we see through what we *can* see and of treating it as an object in and of itself. For centuries, the icon has served people as an aspect of myth or of metaphor. To see the icon of the yang and yin is to see the whole concept of duality and unity playing itself out throughout the cosmos; to see the crucifix is to enter into and reenact the whole story of the death and resurrection of Jesus. Such is the mythic view. The metaphoric view of the icon is that, by seeing it, we are able to identify some quality of the maker or the holder of the object. The sign of the fish on a doorway is the sign that a Christian lives there. It is still a fish, but it is a fish that becomes a metaphor for a way of life and belief.

Idolatry, however, is not a mythic or metaphoric view of the image, but a metonymic view that asserts an actual correspondence between the image and the thing signified. By being copyrighted and designated a trademark, the corporate logo is tantamount to the actual company. It is not a metaphor for the company. When some people see icons as metonymical, they see the image as the object of reverence, not the world that is supposed to shine through it. The icon is no longer a lens but an object. Thus the Golden Calf built by the Israelites was the actual god Ba'al. When in the late Middle Ages a woman pressed a copy of the life of St. Clare to her diseased breast and reported that she had been cured, the physical book became an idol rather than the words of the text being an icon through which to understand the saint.[3] In the film version of The Wizard of Oz, the wizard tells the scarecrow that he does not need a brain, but he needs the idol of knowledge—a diploma—and with it the scarecrow immediately is able to spout impressive-sounding truisms. Idol or parody of an idol?—it is hard to say. Seeing the image as an idol is like reading the text literally.

Many contemporary writers, including Jacques Ellul, Gregor Goethals, and Ivan Illich, take umbrage at the fact that the electronic world is a world of images more than a world of speech or text, and therefore they hold it as suspect. These images, they argue, particularly those purveyed through the commercial media, are both misleading and unholy; they represent, in Ellul's phrase, a "humiliation of the word." They see the images of the media not as icons but as idols.[4]

But there have been others who see the images positive side. Prince Trubetskoi, the Russian philosopher who rediscovered and wrote about the icon in the horrific period of the First World War, at a time when the new medium of film was just getting under way, argued in his essay "A World View in Painting" (1915):

> If indeed this apotheosis of evil [war] is the crown of all human life and history, where is the meaning that makes life worth living? I shall not try to answer this question myself. I would rather remind the reader of answer given our forebears. They were not philosophers, they were seers, and they put their thoughts into colors, not words. Their painting directly answers our question, for in their lifetime, too, the meaning of life was a burning question. . . . The kingdom of the beast even then

tempted people with the same eternal bait: "All these things will I give thee, if thou wilt fall down and worship me." [Matt. 4:7]

The ancient religious art of Russia grew out of the struggle against this temptation. The old-Russian icon painters countered it with striking power and clarity by embodying in images and colors the vision that filled their souls—the vision of a different truth of life, a different meaning of the world.

Anticipating the discussion of icons by McCloud, Trubetskoi continues by asserting that "an icon is not a portrait but a prototype of the future man-within-the-church. Since we cannot yet see this man but only divine him in the present sinful people, an icon can only represent him symbolically." Icons are not based on realism or on life figures: "There is no room in that church for the uncircumcised heart, the fat complacent body. That is why icons must not be painted from living people."[6]

Icons have an architectural function in the church and are part of the total design. They present the world of the spirit and thereby a rejection of the worldly rather than the worldly. They are not literal, for to be literal they would become idols. They are, rather, thematic and emblematic, both of the world of sin and of the world of transcendence and salvation. The working of an icon is twofold. First, it works through its participation in a pattern of images that are interrelated and that form part of a broader tradition. This is the allusive character of the icon, which appeals to the more rational part of the soul. The second means is affective, as we go through the image to the feelings that it evokes in us.

In *The Art of Memory*, Frances Yates quotes Thomas Aquinas as saying, "Man cannot understand without images [phantasma]; the image is a similitude of a corporeal thing, but understanding is of universals which are abstracted from particulars."[7] This view would suggest that the image is a necessary way to get to the Logos. Yates argues convincingly that for centuries people held that the image was the key to memory and that images are the key to ideas and through ideas to truth and to God. Speakers and poets and bards used a series of mental pictures as the way to remember the poems or stories or speeches they wanted to tell. Buildings such as churches were designed as mnemonic aids. The statues, windows, and reliefs of the Stations of the Cross were for the "unlettered," or laity, to "read." Even the floor plan of Chartres Cathedral was seen to represent the body of Christ, with the choir His throat and the altar His mouth so that people could reenact the actual feeding at the Eucharist.

In the early Renaissance, people created large "mental" churches, or theaters of images by which they could recall all sorts of things, particularly scripture, but also philosophy, rhetoric, and science. The icon was the lens to the whole world of knowledge and thought. Such a use was particularly valuable in a time when books were scarce and belonged only to the rich or to the ecclesiastical library. The iconic theater was a mental library in its own right. It, too, of course, could become idolized, as may have been the case with a person like Giordano Bruno, who represented portions of Copernicus' cosmology as controlled lay individual deities.

The books of the hours and the "paupers' Bibles" that contained picture versions of the testaments, so popular in the early Renaissance, are collections of images by which the semiliterate nobility could reach scripture through that which they understood—pictures.[8] In the sixteenth century, when printing had made texts and print more readily available, the mental theater of images came under fire. Influenced by such thinkers as Peter Ramus and his followers, people came to see the image as less important than the text. The text could order ideas logically into columns and tables to which one could always return and refer. The order of words was important because writing could fix ideas on the page for all to study and manipulate. Memory was enhanced not by images but by lists and taxonomies.[9]

But the world of writing is necessarily and essentially a world of images. So was the world of the cave drawing. So is the world of film and hypermedia. Images have always been with us, or at least since people began making visual representations of the world around them. These images were sometimes direct copies, such as the handprints found in early cave drawings. Some were representations, drawings, or paintings of objects in a two-dimensional space; others were three-dimensional—statues, bowls, and bas-reliefs. Finally, some images have been four-dimensional: dances and other ceremonies that took the image through time.

The image is visual and is the way in which we see the text and get to the words and meaning in or behind the text. The billboard, museum, film, newspaper, comic, and photograph are all images.

We have become (have we not always been?) members of a universe of images, and at this juncture our knowledge is expressed predominantly through them rather than through the text.

The Authority in Images

The image is usually what lasts in the retina of the observer, just as the voice of the commentator or speaker is what lingers in the eardrum. One of my most vivid memories of childhood is of the last page of Lynd Ward's God's *Man*, which was a wordless novel illustrated in woodcuts. I used to go to the bookcase in the living room, get the volume out, and read to the last page, a figure of Satan with a death's head. I hated turning to it, yet I was compelled to by the image. Another experience conditioned my understanding of the First World War, in which my father had served. He had a book of photographs called The Horror of *It,* and its graphic images of mutilated soldiers impressed themselves on me and remain with me.

We are aware of the image rather than of who has made it. Most of us are unaware of the camera work, the sound synchronization and mixing, the script. We are caught up with the face or the voice, the scene. As a result we tend to focus on the images and the actors rather than as the writers and directors. We are aware of Bill Cosby or Mary Tyler Moore as actors rather than in their other roles as producer/ directors. When there was concern over the possible cancellation of the television series *Northern Exposure,* one of its most visible actors— not one of the creators, writers, or producers—became the show's instant spokesman.

As a result the image, what is most visible on the surface of the page and particularly of the screen, assumes an authority that displaces those whom we have been used to thinking of as having authority, the creators or authors. This displacement of creator by creation is a phenomenon of the mass media, where advertisers seek to seduce the public with "glittering images" of celebrities and of logos. Politicians, lawyers, doctors, and professors seek to create images of themselves in the minds of the public in such a way that that they become better known than what they do or what they produce.

There is a subtler use of the image in the non-mass media, as it becomes the guide to moving through hypermedia. The image takes on the role it had in the time before print, when people used mental images and physical ones as well in order to remember what they wanted to know.

The world of print and the written word that exists in a "transparent" text that one does not see but reads is receding to a great extent. That world, the world of Peter Ramus and the advocates of sola scriptura, is giving way to the world of Giordano Bruno that it had displaced. The world of the image is now returning and is shaping the ways in which the new literate world operates.

ELECTRONIC IMAGES

Much has been written about television, of course, and most of the commentaries focus on its visual nature. Television images can become powerful mnemonics and have the potential even to become icons or idols. Television is made up of pictures, and the recurrent pictures have the effect of staying with us and becoming a kind of visual shorthand or code. Some of these familiar television images arise from news coverage—the assassination of John Kennedy, the resignation of Richard Nixon, the fall of the Berlin Wall, Baghdad under siege, for example. Other iconic images may come from commercials or even from situations comedies or variety shows.

If one closely observes the pattern of those images—such as by watching a show with the sound turned off—the images appear in discontinuous sequences, not unlike the gutters in a comic book or the frames in a film (except that the continuity is longer, up to four or five minutes). There are few dissolves, so that the visual impression is cut against cut. When the sound is turned back up, this sense of visual discontinuity may still appear, but on-camera sounds or voiceovers facilitate transition. Thus, television "text" is closer than we might initially think to a comic book or a hypertext, where the reader must make certain connections and thus coauthor the show.

The image largely supplants the real product in television. That is to say, what we take away from the TV commercial is most often the most powerful visual image—of a particular soft drink, say, even if we are not then consumers of that particular brand.

Images of the event can sometimes transform the event in the popular mind into something greater, over time. Images of the Vietnam War—the first "TV dinner war"—linger on even today, thirty years later—as do vivid images of the Persian Gulf war, Bosnian atrocities, and the explosion of the *Challenger*. Eventually, the image may even become more important than the original event itself because it becomes the icon of a whole collection of ideas and emotions. One of the most powerful of contemporary American images is that of the girl kneeling beside the body of a student shot by National Guardsmen at Kent State University in 1970. This image sums up for many their collective feelings about the Vietnam War, the government, protest movements, and the political tensions of the time a sense of distraught horror of it all.

The television image tends to be secular in origin. Yet, it takes on something of the character of a religious icon in that, like the Kent State image, it can conjure up a whole set of parallel images, feelings, and associations. It facilitates mentally reentering an era through which people have lived. Even those who have not lived through the period may use the images to make a connection to the unknown or unexperienced other (just as I used photographs in a book to connect to my father's wartime experiences).

The Television Curriculum

Radio and television offer a way of reaching people that has leapt over most of the institutions that had provided the basic shared information and the shared ceremonies that constituted learning and acculturation in an era dominated by print. In the print era, one had to learn a special skill, reading, in order to become a full member of the culture. That requirement may no longer be sufficient. Over the past five decades, both radio and television have been able to reach out ever increasing numbers of people who had the means (an increasingly modest sum) so that these two technologies of purveying information, learning, and culture have become ubiquitous. For the past thirty to fifty years, virtually every child in the United States has been exposed to either radio or television, or usually both. In order to participate in the information society fully these days, it is not only necessary to be able to read and write but also to log onto a computer now and then. Much of the information once thought to be available only through print and the eye is now available through electronic media, tape, disk, and the ear. Today's cultural canon is not simply a canon of books and authors but also one of images and films. Orson Welles's *Citizen Kane* is probably more central to the American cultural canon of today than is Ernest Hemingway's *A Farewell to Arms*. This means simply that nowadays the library of print is not the sole repository of culture. In fact, for some cultures, and subcultures of our multicultural world, print is comparatively *irrelevant* as a medium for acculturation. So, too, by extension, is the institution that is founded on print, the school. But hypertext and hypermedia provide a new technology that may have the paradoxical effect of saving and extending print and literacy.

Hypermedia

As I write this book, one of the fastest-growing technological phenomena is hypermedia, the bringing together of such media as text, pictures, animation, and sound through the process of digitization. Although I use the word *hypertext* as an image of the new world, *hypermedia* is perhaps the better term, for it comprehends a blending of text, still image, moving image, and sound, all arranged through a series of controlling icons. In 1992 I served as general editor of an encyclopedia about the teaching of English. Despite our best efforts to persuade them otherwise, the publishers wanted to produce only a book. In 1995, I received a call from a colleague who was about to begin a similar project in another area of education.

"Don't you think," he asked, "that it would make sense for the dictionary to be on CD-ROM so that people could not only read a definition of a concept in teaching but also see a 20-second clip of someone practicing what they preach?" I agreed, and so did many of his contributors. The dictionary will now be a hypermedia package rather than solely a textbook.

In the 1970s I worked on a series of anthologies for secondary schools; in addition to the texts, we also had some related long-playing records, which was considered a daring departure at the time. I am working on another set of anthologies as I write this book, and the publishers have added a CD-ROM with additional text selections as well as a series of hypermedia CD-ROMs with material on authors, productions, and backgrounds. Some of these, primarily those on Shakespearean plays, include the full text and notes of the play, a video of the BBC production, a commentary by a noted scholar, taped readings, and background stills of London and other historical material related to the play. The viewer can move among these media in countless ways that create a more sophisticated appreciation of the play and its production than could be acquired through print alone.

Hypermedia can be seen as combining in one source the network of existing electronic and print media. Through a procedure known as digitization, the text, the score, and the performance in sound and visual image can be juxtaposed at will, the senses thereby becoming more interconnected.

Early Precursors of Hypermedia

The interconnection of the senses is not new, of course. When we consider classical Greek theater, for example, there were words, sights, and music. There was a combination of dance and drama. Such combinations have long been a part of that form of entertainment we call spectacle. Opera, for example, was seen as the major art form to bring together a number of senses so that the entertainment could affect as much of the human sensorium as possible. In the eighteenth and nineteenth centuries, theater itself worked toward this combination of media, as well, and at times the spectacles on royal barges or in palaces would go beyond what we even imagine to be in opera.

This same sort of spectacle and emphasis on pleasuring multiple senses has appeared in a variety of cultures and societies. The opera and drama of many societies has involved catering to the audience's senses. So did the vaudeville show.

One might well argue that the typical religious ceremony has more of the elements of hypermedia about it than does the typical secular performance. A single religious service of yesterday or today might well combine the reading of texts, the performance of music, dance, the smell of incense, and the ringing of bells.

Earlier and more static versions of hypermedia have included the picture book and the pop-up book as well as some of the early book-and-record combinations. Even educational films and television documentaries have sought over the years to combine reading insights with their own by giving specific reading recommendations of their program's close.

These are precursors, but they are not the same as hypermedia itself. In all of them the audience remains an audience, a spectator, rather than a coauthor or coproducer.

The Role of the Viewer/Player/Reader

Without being technical, hypermedia has the ability to put in one place—a disk or a CD-ROM, for example—a variety of modes of expression. Each of these is digitized and then inscribed on the disk. A disk might contain some segments of text, such as a whole book. There could also be some audio recording of music, a number of drawings or still pictures, and some "quick-time" film or animation.

Each of these is contained in digital form so that the user can switch relatively effortlessly from one to another.

When we open up a CD-ROM containing hypermedia, we are not simply reading. We are watching and listening, as well. But, as with hypertext, we are not doing these things passively (i.e., in the manner of a television viewer. With hypermedia, it is impossible to be a "couch potato." The relationship is much more dynamic and active. We might liken it to being in a museum or a cathedral. We can move around in it, stay in one place, ignore certain parts, or participate fully in others. We move from image to text to sound and back to image. Each icon presents a menu that takes us down a different corridor, or along a different strand of the web. We are controlled by the network of relationships that has been created, but since we are offered continual choices, we have at least the illusion that we are in control. To a great extent, of course, we are solitary viewers or participants; we have not yet fully developed or adapted the ceremonies that bring us together as a community of readers of hypermedia or even of hypertext, for we have not shared the same thing or have shared it only nominally. I suspect that soon there will emerge a new dynamic of the community of hypermedia participants, just as, subsequently, there will emerge a new canon and probably new interpretive modes.

WHAT HAPPENS TO LITERACY WHEN THE TEXT BECOMES AN IMAGE?

As we saw in Chapter 2, one of the effects of hypertext is to cause us to think of the text not as a set of recorded words but as a complex of images. That change may not be profound when taken by itself, but when we begin to think of how hypertext fits into the broader spectrum of media based primarily on images or icons, we need to consider how literacy itself has changed, both as the ability to use a technology but moreover as a social and communal activity. That is to say, writing on the screen is perhaps more like television or a film than like a book. That is why thinking about the comic book as a precursor of hypertext is as important as thinking about a printed volume as its precursor. It is in the comic book, comic strip, and cartoon that we see the way in which writing and text are themselves images and should perhaps best be viewed as images.

Writing as Image

When writing was first invented, the originating scribes developed a pictographic language in which each icon represented a particular object. This form of writing evolved into a variety of systems, such as the hieroglyphic, the ideographic, the syllabic, and the alphabetic. In the latter two cases, the icon became increasingly dissociated from the object and more closely related to oral language and thus to the word for the object rather than the object itself.

But the written language was still a visible representation, albeit a rough abstract representation of human sounds in all their complexity. In English, *you* represents a variety of sounds from "ya" to "ye" to "yaw" to "yoo." Far from being precise phonetic transcription, writing is, at best approximate representation. For many learning a language as difficult as English, this imprecision is one of greatest difficulties in going from icon to speech. The comic icons of the light bulb and the question mark don't present this problem. That may explain why so many who have difficulty reading written language take to comics like ducks to water.

Yet, writing itself should be seen as iconic. We notice it most clearly in such art forms as pattern poetry, concrete poetry, and to some extent in comics, where the shape of the lettering becomes an icon of loudness, intensity, and other aspects of meaning. But the iconic is, in fact, a part of the very definition of writing.

Instead of the circle, two dots, and a line, we could write the word "FACE" and put it on top of a stick figure, and most people would see the word as a true icon (see Figure 4.4).

So a word, particularly a printed word, is an icon in that it has a visible abstracted shape persisting through a variety of typographic manifestations. **Face** is `face` is **face.**

But various iconic representations, such as boldface, italics, and

FIGURE 4.4. The icon of an icon.

capital letters, can change the meaning of "face" in the context of other word images. So too, can the particular placement on a page or even the size of the type. The icon's various representations do, in fact, provide nuances of meaning. As in all design, the modification of one part of the pattern affects the whole.[10]

Icons are never quite what we seem to experience, but they are the ways by which we move from the particularities of experience to a more general or abstract level. They are one of the principal ways for connecting our individual experiences.

The Patterning of the Icons of Text

Writing is, first of all, marks on a field. We normally think of it as black and white, but that is simply a function of the ready availability of ink and paper.

Marks on a field form patterns. They do so by virtue of the fact that the mark occupies space and, in its relation to the space around it and other marks separated by the space, a pattern is produced. And it is in patterns that we make or decipher meaning. As in the comic, the spaces form the semantic and syntactic glue of the marks. Their conventional uses form the grammar of written language.

Take this most simple example (see Figure 4.5). In the frame are three shaded boxes. They are in a line and they are separated by white space. They appear to be aligned horizontally and to be spaced nearly so as to be equidistant. The three boxes form a pattern. That pattern has a potential meaning. The meaning is derived from the boxes and the space between them—both are integral to the meaning.

Here in Figure 4.6 we have three letters in a column. But, more

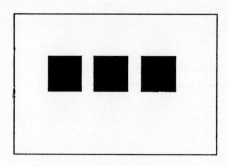

FIGURE 4.5. The basic pattern.

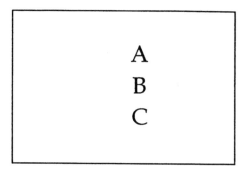

FIGURE 4.6. An alphabetic icon.

than just any three letters, these letters are evenly vertically spaced and are the first three letters of the alphabet, in order. Their typeface is a font called Ultra Shadow. It is a display font, used often for signs and advertisements. The arrangement, size, typeface, and spacing all help us to determine meaning; in other words, meaning is derived comes from the pattern. We can look at these three marks and observe that they most likely signal an ordered list.

Let us take another example (see Figure 4.7). We now have a combination of marks and spaces formed into three groups or chunks. The marks are in a sans serif typeface. They are what we refer to as letters, and each group has taken on a meaning as an image containing letters. We refer to these groups as words. The groups themselves are arranged in a column, centered. The size of the first word in relation to the next two indicates its greater importance. The fact that it is in a sans serif typeface—which indicates that the three words is highly legible even at a glance—may well constitute an instruction or warning. The first word is a member of that group which we call an adjective and could be a modifier of either the second or third word or a predicate adjective. The size and placement indicate that it is probably the latter, following an implied "You, BE . . . "

The point of these three examples is that the simple display, separation, and arrangement of a few letters and marks contains a great deal of information and, moreover, that we are conditioned to create meaningful patterns from visual information. Written language is a complex iconic system that has evolved over the centuries in such a way that the pattern of icons (read, letters) conveys complex meaning and can be used in a great variety.

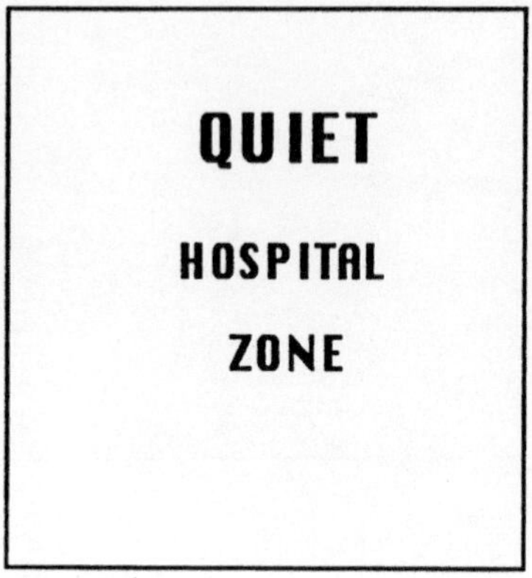

QUIET

HOSPITAL

ZONE

FIGURE 4.7. Words in an iconic form.

As segments in a text space, the icons of written language can be shifted around in their dimensions just as any other space can be shifted. They can be stretched or shrunk on the screen. Their colors can change; so can their fonts. Individual segments can be highlighted. The text becomes an object, manipulable. With hypertext, the capacity of text to be manipulated extends to readers, whose relationship to the written word appears to shift, for we appear to be in greater command. We are not slaves to the words on the screen, but, rather, we can assert our authority.

This is true in the world of hypertext. But, what are we manipulating other than our view of the text? What is on the memory of the disk may not change, only that which is in the "memory" of the reader.

Iconicity of Text

Just as the word can become an icon, whole texts can be an icon in a book, a magazine, or a hypertext (that "nonsequential writing, text that branches and allows choices to the reader, best read on an interactive screen," to invoke Theodor Nelson's definition, from Chapter 2). Pieces of text are referred to as text spaces, and they have equal weight with pictures, quick-time video, charts, or other spaces. Jay Bolter refers to these as "writing spaces" in his book of the same name.[11]

As spaces, they can be shifted around in their dimensions just as any other space can be shifted. They can be stretched or shrunk on the screen. Their colors can be changed as can their fonts. Individual segments can be highlighted. The text becomes an object, manipulable. Of course, for a writer and a printer, such was always the case. I wrote a book twenty-five years ago in which I not only wrote the text but set it up so that I dictated what should appear on each double-page spread of the book. Each spread was a text space that might or might not contain other spaces within it. The book also contained illustrations and tables that were part of the overall pattern. Together with the designer, I produced a book that was icon-laden as well as full of text.

What I created, however, was something that on the page became fixed. The reader had to take what we had designed and follow our pattern of icons. Such is the case with the readers of any book. They can turn the pages fast or slowly, skip, browse, or stay with one page for hours, but they cannot manipulate the physical text with the freedom that the author and compositor had. As readers of hypertext, however, our relationship to the written word shifts as we take greater command and can move through the spaces in a different fashion from that of the original authors or even differently from the prior reading. We are not mere slaves to the words on the screen, but we are compositors as well as authors and, as such, assert our authority.

But, what are we manipulating other than our view of the text? What is on the disk may not change, only that which is in the "memory" of the reader, or possibly with the use of a trace program retained in the memory of one's own computer.

Implications of Seeing the Text as Image

To some extent the text itself became an icon and even an idol long before the electronic era. This was often true in those religions—such as Judaism and Islam—that prohibit physical representations of the divine. Then the Koran or the Torah became themselves iconic, and even the lettering and the formation of the scroll became a representation of the divine. You do not have to read the book's contents when you put your hand on it to take an oath. The physical book itself is the icon. It is so much of an icon that we forget that it is one.

The iconic nature of the visible text has long had its secular aspect, as well. At many points in the history of our consciousness the truth has seemed to be equated with being in print. "I only believe what I read in the papers," say many. Scholars and graduate students that I know will accept as truth anything that has been published. In *The World on Paper*, David Olson shows how, with the advent of printing, there emerged the idea that what was on paper, such as a map, necessarily accurately represented reality. The paper version takes on a metonymic character, where the word stands in direct relationship to the object. We can read the map and thus get a "true" picture of the world.[12] At the same time, we know that the map is necessarily both a distortion and a selection. A map takes a sphere and transforms it into a plane. It also fails to include all the detail as it changes scale. So, too, a text distorts thought or the mental meaning into a conventional format of letters, words, paragraphs, and the like, and it includes only segments of the immense capacity of the mind. Good texts, like good maps, are things of beauty. Bad ones falsify and discourage. Both are images, simulations of the world; the value of the image or in the image lies in the user, not the object.

The image, like the text, can be metaphoric or mythic, the two stages that Northrop Frye describes in his book *The Great Code* as antedating the metonymic view of the text, which I described in the previous chapter as the view of text before the time of printing.[13] In the mythic relationship, the words and images are used as a sign for a whole complex of ideas and concepts. A map suggests a concept of the world but not a set of directions as to how to get from Paris to Rome. This is the world as Logos. In the metaphoric relationship, the words consist of analogies to things. We read the text to get an idea of the world to which the words refer, but we know that the words are not the world; the map is "like" the world, as is the image, but the two are readily distinguisable.

When the printed world of text or image is seen as standing for the "objective world," one can manipulate that world and thus believe that one manipulates the objective world. Thus, we can see the road in a particular map as a particular representation of certain reality —not just the idea of roads. We tend to take the map as a literal representation of reality. Such an acceptance of this relationship of written language to external objects is what enables science to be codified and nature to be ordered. Mathematical or chemical symbols are treated the same as the objects or elements they represent. They may be manipulated in formulae, for example, and what is manipulated is a version of reality. Similarly, objects in nature can be placed in taxonomic systems such as those of Buffon or Linneaus. This ordering of objects helps to give us a mental picture of the relevant relationships and the objects' key features that predetermines how we actually see the objects—or don't see them. If one were to shift the place of a particular plant from one genus to another, many botanists would undertake to see the plant very differently. No matter the real plant, the plant's place on paper is what counts most with some. Such is the view of many who argue the literalist position of sola scriptura.

I have worked for several decades with statisticians, who sometimes translate human behavior into numbers that they can then manipulate mathematically. They appear to believe that statistics can accurately portray actual relationships between people or between facets of their behavior. Some statisticians that I have known have sought to establish that family background has a statistically significant relationship to reading outcomes. Therefore, if such a relationship is found, it becomes a matter of determination in the real world.

Such a view of the world on paper as an idol rather than as an image is similar to reading the text literally. A literal reading is, in effect, a form of idolatry since it takes the image conveyed through words and treats it as the same as that which it represents. In *Hard Times*, Charles Dickens inveighed against this literal, taxonomic view of objects; so, too, did William Wordsworth when, in "The Tables Turned," he had his character Matthew say:

> Up! Up! my friend and quit your books;
> Or surely you'll grow double . . .
> Come forth into the light of things,
> Let Nature be your teacher.

But the literalist view has persisted. A form of nominalism, it is the view that the world on paper is literally (that is, in a readerly fashion) the world of things. It is a view that is prevalent in the modern scientific world, a secular form of sola scriptura. Such a view benefits science, but it also leads to a particular kind of reader, one who accepts the literalness of particular texts. Not the writer or the reader, but the text, becomes a particular kind of authority, no different from the authority of a table of logarithms or the periodic table. All of them are expressions of literal reality. All are maps to things, ideas, and God. In fact they are seen as better pathways than might be contained in images. In actuality, however, they are idols. And many who idolize print are iconoclasts when it comes to images. Print is the truth, images lie, is their constant refrain. Such a view, I think, has to change when we come to accept that the text is but one kind of image in a world of hypermedia.

TEXT, SCRIPTURE, IMAGE

Many of the scholars of prehistoric art maintain that the drawings on the walls at Altamira or Lascaux are sacred images. They point to the use of sacral images in other religions. Although St. John argues ontologically, "In the beginning was the Word," from an anthropological perspective one might say, "In the beginning was the image." The image becomes a part of the religious ceremony, and the book is both the container of words and an image in itself.

As I mentioned earlier, it would appear from the early history of writing that the written text was seen as an image. In fact, the first recorded writing, that which was created in ancient Sumer, was the image of an image. Traders made little clay symbols of the goods that they were trading (whether a vat of oil or some grain). By doing so, they could barter the image without having to carry the actual goods around. They then put these images in little pouches to store them. Soon they realized it was useful to mark the outside of the pouch with a visual symbol of the contents. In this way writing was born. The word as pictograph or image of an object, action, or idea later became stylized and then related to speech through a syllabic or alphabetic connection. But the original iconic and graphic impulse was not entirely lost.

For many people, the religious text as a physical object became important as an icon in its own right, not simply for the written words and sentences that it contained. The scrolls of the Torah, the codices of the Gospels, the writing and illumination of the Rig Veda or of the Bible, the script of the Koran—all of these became objects of veneration for themselves. Today, we often recognize Bibles, missals, or prayer books by their binding, so that the object itself may readily become the idol.

The revering of the physical book has its counterpart in the religious icon or any other image of the deity or the sacred. Sacred and sacral objects abound in all religions, and they become important symbols of the concepts and myths that sustain believers. Even in the world of Islam, where pictorial representations are strictly banned, the physical letters and other patterns painted on the walls of mosques serve the function of an icon. The image is castigated as an idol, and the text is established as an icon; but it too may easily turn into an idol.

The text that contains icons is itself an icon.

Icons and Iconoclasts

Throughout the history of religion in the West, particularly the monotheistic religions, there have coexisted two traditions: one of image making and one of iconoclasm, the breaking of the image. The latter has surfaced at various points in the history of religion, from the time when Moses ordered the destruction of the Golden Calf to later instances where prophets destroyed images and idols. In place of these idols, the Ark of the Covenant became the center of the religion of Israel, but it too became an icon, as did the temple that held it.

Icon building and iconoclasm coexisted throughout the history of Christianity. Early Christians appear to have disliked icons, although they began to adopt symbolic ceremonies, particularly the Eucharist. They also used the sign of the cross, the fish, and the χρ, or *chi rho*, as means of identifying members of the new community. As the religion became established, additional icons and symbols began to appear. The symbolic outpouring in church design grew steadily, and the churches became places where people could observe a variety of images in order to recall particular people and events and to enhance their worship. Iconoclasm was equally strong, as some people came to see the images as threatening to the contemplation of God directly and were concerned that the icon had become an end rather than a means to an end. One of the high points of iconoclasm occurred in the late Middle Ages with the founding of the Cistercian orders by Bernard of Clairvaux, who wanted a simple icon-free monastery. It was continued in the Protestant Reformation by Calvin and Zwingli, whose followers destroyed stained-glass windows and statuary as forms of idolatry. It was continued in the Puritan churches of New England. The iconoclasts of the Old Testament and the Reformation set up the text instead of the image as all-important. The text was what all communicants were to read and through which they were to find salvation.

In *The Humiliation of the Word*, Jacques Ellul observes that "the God of the Word cannot tolerate the gods of the image."[14] I think that Ellul's gods of the image are closer to seventeenth-century philosopher-scientist Sir Francis Bacon's "Idols of the Market-place." In the

Novum Organum, Bacon describes sets of idols that inhibit and prevent our thinking. The Idols of the Market-place are "idols which have crept into the understanding through the alliances of words and names. For men believe that their reason governs words; but it is also true that words react on the understanding" (p. lix). Such idols are those words and images that become so closely identified with an object that they are no longer a doorway to contemplating the object but rather an inhibitor of thought and imagination. Words and images of this kind can, in their commercial counterpoints, lapse into slogans and logos that evoke prejudice rather than understanding.

So many of these idols, of course, come from the actual market-place. Certain images, logos, and brand names can emerge to become objects of admiration, as do such celebrated creations of mass culture as Michael Jackson, Elvis, and Madonna. They become idols, that is ends in themselves, rather than merely musicians or artists. They are promoted as being on some sort of transcendent plane, and they even become the objects of pubescent and prepubescent worship. They are clearly secular, and their cults are often evanescent, replaced by marketers with the next new rage.

To Jacques Ellul, the idol conceals the symbolic and limits it, and thus confuses truth and reality. In an instance where an idol replaces that which is symbolized by the icon, it can illustrate the problem of a world where the word is not seen as metaphor or myth but rather becomes a direct representation. To a person like Ellul, the iconic nature of hypertext would tend to treat as "true" what is the apparent reality of the text, although the text is no longer palpable-visual, but electronic. But what Ellul is talking about is not the icon but the idol.[15]

As I have argued throughout this chapter, icons are idols only if people persist in making them so. And it is a sad fact of this literal world that many people do indeed treat the icon as an idol. The iconic text in hypermedia is a metaphor on the screen for the interconnectedness of languages within the larger network that is the web of meaning. Such icons could be misleading if we idolize them and treat the hypermedia as anything but a web of metaphor and myth. We need to probe this web deeper in order to find something of its reality.

Television and the New Iconoclasts

The debate about icons has resurfaced in the past generation thanks to television. Television has placed moving images in virtually every household in the industrialized nations and its penetration is fast growing throughout the rest of the world. The icons of the marketplace can be flashed throughout the globe, and their widespread familiarity transcends language and culture. These images purveyed by television are ubiquitous, and, it has been argued, act powerfully on the human sense and imagination. The art critic and theologian Gregor Goethals argues that television is highly conducive polarization of belief, conversion, charismatic leadership, and sacramentalism.[16]

Goethals suggests, as part of a theological critique, that in the contemporary mass media, based on images, we do not have prophecy but myth in the secular sense of false image. Marketers seek to create in mass media images figures some sort of sustaining myth, even if only a materialistic one. Because television can bring the individual into the living room, such people as Rev. Billy Graham, Bishop Fulton Sheen, or Rev. Jesse Jackson become as important as their message—if not more so.

Television, Goethals continues, lends itself to Manichaeanism and a clear right/wrong view of the world and of human behavior. Because of its basis in time, the nature of fleeting time, and because it constantly juxtaposes images, television necessarily simplifies. There is a new sacramentalism induced by television, moreover, whereby the trappings of a religious show—whether T-shirts, bumper stickers, or pledge cards—become a part of the identification of the viewer with the text.

Conversion, or metanoia, is where Goethals finds the secular and religious to converge in television and elsewhere. The viewer is to be turned around, to make a decision and a confession of faith to a hemorrhoid treatment or a spiritual leader. How does conversion relate to brainwashing, programming, or advertising?

Goethals's conclusions seem apt for to a single show, but what happens when we go beyond the individual to the larger network or the multiplicity of channels? How will these options change matters? Do we see the network as merely a complex arrangement of the simple or something altogether different?

Latter-day iconoclasts include such diverse critics as Jacques Ellul, Neil Postman, and Ivan Ilich. Like Goethals, they see the image and the icon as degenerate manifestations of television and all that is pernicious in our culture. And they see the degeneracy as persisting into the world of hypertext and hypermedia.[17]

But with the sudden onslaught of digital media there is the

addition of question how religious leaders can retain their charisma in a media glut. Radio enhanced the charismatic voice. Television did the same for the face, body, and voice. What will happen with hypermedia?

Image, Reality, Truth

As we have seen, Jacques Ellul argues that the image is false in its relation to reality—it cuts up reality and divorces it from the world of sight. It is as if we were to take one dot in a pointillist painting and make it the whole painting.

Ellul examines the Orthodox theology of icons, where the theological doctrine argues that "the icon is 'an image which leads to something else,' a prop in a mystical and transcendent quest." Ultimately Ellul finds that view unsupportable:

> Fundamentally the theology of icons involves first a switch from signs to symbols, because the icon is essentially symbolic. Then, the icon is inserted into an entire liturgy. It implies a theology of the concrete presence of the spiritual realm, and a divine light, which can be symbolically retranscribed and which is the image of glory itself.
>
> We have said enough to show the degree to which this theology is diametrically opposed to everything that seems to me to be of importance in biblical thinking. . . .
>
> Because of my Orthodox friends I am sorry to say so, but this theology of the icon seems to me to correspond exactly to what we are prohibited biblically from doing: it is idolatrous.[18]

To Ellul and others, the iconographic falsifies the world. It is the world of the sound-bite and the quick take. It simplifies and acts to distance us from the truth, from communication and communion with God. It simplifies to make the world intelligible, but at the risk of both truth and reality. These critics cite the destruction of the Golden Calf in Exodus and the parallel destruction of the tablets inscribed with the Ten Commandments, because they too ran the risk of becoming an idol. So, too, with the prohibition of religious art in Judaism and Islam as well as some forms of Christianity. To these critics the icon automatically becomes an idol, and their view of the literal, and of the image as metonymy, casts them in the role of literalists and iconoclasts.

But to Trubetskoi and others, the icon is only an idol to those who would see it literally. The theologian Aidan Nichols claims that the problem with people like Ellul is that they accept the twentieth-century positivist view of the icon.[19] Positivism led to the idea of objective empiricism, which in turn led to the destruction of the artistic and iconographic spirit (or saw it as delusion). Goaded by the success of the photograph in portraying what was thought to be "the actual," the impressionists tried to make art scientific and deal with the surfaces of light. The postimpressionists—Cézanne, Gauguin, and Van Gogh—each broke through this and created an art that sought out the transcendent order of the seen world. In doing so, they (like Trubetskoi) rediscovered the world of the icon and reinterpreted it for us.

Nichols quotes our old friend Gadamer:

> "The power of the artwork suddenly takes the person experiencing it out of the context of his life, and yet relates him back to the whole of his existence. In the experience of art there is present a fullness of meaning which belongs not only to this particular content or object but stands rather for the meaningful whole of life. An aesthetic experience always contains the experience of an infinite whole."[20]

Nichols goes on to write this ringing defense of the icon and the image from both an artistic and a theological standpoint:

> The revelatory event breaks in on a man, as the aesthetic experience arises in a moment of communion from the art object in gallery or church, and he finds himself reorganizing his own world of meaning, what counts for him as "the real," in its light. In the course of that, just as the artwork can shape an existence, moving us to the suppression of self that fidelity to ultimate values may replace the distortions of the relentless ego, so the revelatory event proves able to place us in touch with an absolutely satisfying and complete hold on the reality that blesses us with its own truth, even if it call on us for a painful reshaping of our lives. The revelatory event satisfies our nisus towards transcendence by disclosing to us the inexhaustibly satisfying reality we call "God" drawing near to meet us.
>
>   . . . this it does, secondly, through the mediation of signs. Just as the artwork communicates its full meaning only in the context of iconology, an interrelating set of images, so the reciprocities between events that we may suspect to be revelatory in force—their typological connections—are what give us the full meaning of the revelatory event which

is never to be looked at in isolation, as lone image uncontextualized in its iconology.[21]

It is upon the ideas of Nichols, Lossky, and Prince Trubetskoi, as well as those of the postmodernist aestheticians, that we must build in the new world of hypermedia—which will be, willy-nilly, a world of images and textual images.[22]

A Positive Theology of Images

Despite the cosmic nay-sayers, I think there is a positive theology of the image or a theology that incorporates the image and so accommodates and even welcomes hypermedia. Hypertext tends to emphasize the character of image (a manipulable visual representation). As image, text seems divorced from both the written word and that which it represents—the oral word, or logos. But the text has always been an image. As a result of the transformation from pictographic to ideographic to syllabic and phonetic writing, people in the West tended to divorce text from image and relate it to speech or to make it unique. Throughout this book, I have been arguing against this transformation, this suppression of the original heritage of text, which is coming full circle now in the form of hypertext. I have also argued against suppressing the imagination, that immense capacity that humans have of visualizing and seeing in the mind's eye based upon what we hear and what we read.

To that end, we need to reconsider the image.

To some thinkers, the image is like a sacrament: an outward and visible sign of an inward and spiritual grace. An image is a ceremony, but a ceremony frozen in time or taken out of the world of time and put into the world of space. The transformation of the senses is not necessarily in itself a degradation. Nor is the movement from time to space. When YHWH said "Let there be light," he created space–time, a continuum that become virtually impossible to disentangle. The priority of time and the oral is historical, not theological.

Icons are indeed only the images of God and originally were never confused with God. In Christianity, Christ is the image of God (imago Dei) in humanity, but Christ is not man, not like us. Jesus was both human and divine, and could be so as Christ, the image. In this way religious symbols or icons may lead us to the reality and the truth. They do so if we let them be icons and not stay only on the surface.

We should not read icons too literally but rather should consider them representational function. Take the example of a map. It uses a large number of icons—red lines, blue lines, black lines, green patches. Once get under way, we immediately notice that the read is not red, blue, or black, but a sort of mottled beige. Yet, we feel secure that we are on the road. There may be numerous forests along the way, but the one marked in green on the map is no different from the others except that it is the property of the state. The map is an iconic world, but too many map readers view it as not a metaphor for the world, but as the world itself.

They do the same with icons such as the cross, the portrait of Mary, the Star of David, or the figure of Ganesh. These are representations, metaphors, icons, "outward and visible signs of an inward and spiritual Grace," as the *Book of Common Prayer* tells us. So to with the sacred text; it is a map, one to be read and reconstructed by the reader who is in search of the Divine. To quote St. Thomas Aquinas again: "Man cannot understand without images [phantasma]; the image is a similitude of a corporeal thing, but understanding is of universals which are abstracted from particulars." The image is a key to memory and the key for access to ideas and thereby to God. If we consider such books as the various books of the hours, these are compendia of images to enable the barely literate worshipper to reach toward the Divine; so, too, with stained glass windows, statues, and even the cruciform church building itself.

It is only when the icon becomes the object of worship rather than the medium for worship that idolatry can occur. The same is true of technology itself; that, too, can become idolatry. In one of his first books, *The Technological Society*, Jacques Ellul made this point only too clearly, observing some forty years ago that people came not to use technology but to be its slaves and to worship it for what it was rather than what it does.[23] This has certainly been true of people in the past, and it continues to be true. People all too easily view television, satellite communications, computers, or even information in general as the solution to a problem, as the end to be pursued and valued for its own sake. We love our toys and our tools, and we forget they are tools. Ellul's later criticism, to which I have alluded frequently in this chapter, is, then, addressed to our idolatry more than to the image. The other critics of the image confuse the object with the viewer and therefore icons with idolaters.

So, too, the icon of hypertext or the Internet is only a way of moving through information, which is a way of moving through ideas and images and of communicating with one another and of understanding ourselves, our world, and our God. It is no different from the written text, which is only a way of storing something of the ideas and information that people have expressed about their world, themselves, and the divine. Both are simply a web of printed symbols that can lead to an understanding of the important webs of God only at our intellectual and spiritual peril do we dare make them idols.

In Moving Forward, We Return

We need, I believe, to return to a balance between the worlds described by Giordano Bruno and Peter Ramus. Both were extremists. Bruno took the image and made it the focal point of an elaborate hermetic system. He indeed tended to make an idol out of what he had created and worshipped it beyond the bounds of reason. Ramus, the iconoclast, who saw in every image an element of the Golden Calf, sought to create a structure of words on the page, of tables and lists; these too emerged as idols, for the text on the page came to be taken for what it represented, and the world on paper was worshipped as much as the world represented by the paper.

Such is always the problem with a technology; it comes to be seen as the end rather than the means. Widespread attention to Marshall McLuhan's observation that "the medium is the message" has led many to confuse the technology with what it carries or serves. Although we need to understand technology, we do not need to be its slaves.

Both image and text are ways by which people reach the Divine. They become paths to the idea or The Word; they are mediators. The iconic view is a way of allowing people across space and time to see the text as an interpenetration of idea and image and a way of enabling our imaginations to transcend the limitations of a particular language and move to the mind of the Maker, the divine author (as Dorothy Sayers described God). But text and image must be seen solely as mediators, or means, and not idolized. The icon on the screen is seen as an entry point. So is the image of text in a hypertext. Although we play with the images and move the icons, we must remember that they are simply portals to the idea. They are the tools of rhetoric and not ends.

In its profusion of images, hypertext may be seen as a festival, a necessary excessive celebration of the life of the mind and the lives of humankind. There is a long theological pedigree to this celebration, as Harvey Cox argues in his monograph *The Feast of Fools*.[24] The world of the feast is also a world of fantasy, and the world of fantasy is a world of images—a riot of images, which are themselves anarchic and not hierarchic.

The image, then, is a means of revelation rather than simply of objective signification. Is this true of the image world of hypertext? Yes, for the text as image becomes a revelation of the totality of the expression and its complexity, more than we get by reading word for word or line for line in the literal manner of the printed text. The text may be a map, but the hypertext is an icon to the world of the writer and a revelation to the reader of the world he or she has coauthored.

CHAPTER FIVE

The Web of Text in the Web
of Culture in the Web of Text

Though world of literacy does not exist in a vacuum; it never did.
When writing was first developed in the Middle East, it accompanied
the development of towns with their specialized trades and forms of
labor, and was part of a communication system that included camels
and donkeys as well as some form of water transport. Systems of writing
and the various means of inscribing and storing information in text
form changed; those changes accompanied, followed, or led changes
in the way society organized itself and thought about the world. From
crude marks, people developed syllabic, ideographic, and alphabetic
systems that enabled them to write increasing amounts and kinds of
information. They saw the potential of storing laws as well as accounts,
and once they start that, their whole way of thinking about relationships among people changed. One might argue that the whole concept
of property depends critically on a written system to record ownership.
Clay tablets were replaced by papyrus and parchment in the Middle
East and bamboo rods by paper in China; as a cause or as a result,
people could store not only laws and property deeds but also stories,
religious documents, and philosophic treatises—not to mention, in
their time, jokes and recipes. Later the idea of movable type was
brought from the Far East to Europe and was combined with the press
so that many copies of a text could be produced. Books and broadsides
became ubiquitous; so did paper currency, wedding certificates, postage
stamps, and other forms of storing and transferring information that
accompanied the development of capitalism, nationalism, and the
modern age.

As these changes occurred, they accompanied such changes in

transportation as the development of the paved road and of courier systems; the opening of sea-lanes; the coach, the steam engine, and the railroad; the automobile; and the airplane. The two technologies went and continue to go hand in hand, but nowadays they may be on the verge of parting as we seriously begin to consider the implications of have discovered the virtual meeting, the conference call, the ability to write a newspaper on one side of the globe and print it on another. The technology of communication may have outstripped the technology of transport. With satellites doing the traveling for us, we may stay in one place but simultaneously send our image and thoughts anywhere or everywhere.

Forms of communication are intimately related to transport, which is simply another way of moving information from one place to another. I can go visit someone, talk to her on the telephone, write her a letter, or send her an e-mail. Each accomplishes the same purpose—albeit with many differences. Writing and e-mail have an advantage over other forms of communication and transport, however, in that they can be stored outside of my memory for later retrieval. I am able to archive my virtual visit in a way comparable to how a camera or camcorder archives an actual visit. With the advent of the television camera and the audiotape, the virtual visit can include pictures and sound. Firsthand experience seems almost superfluous in this context—but our physical selves wisely crave it!

As its members grew in number, a community moved from being a set of isolated villages and towns to being a city–satellite system and later a megalopolis, which tends to have no center. This shift is not unlike the movement from writing to printing to electronic communication. Both shifts have shaped the ways in which we think of ourselves in relation to others, a central authority, and the deity. The shifts in transportation and communication have brought with them shifts in consciousness. Such shifts have also been brought about by changes in our knowledge about the world. Copernicus and Galileo changed our consciousness about the earth, the heavens, and our place in them. Harvey's elaboration of the circulation of blood changed our consciousness of our bodies and their fluids. Darwin and Freud have certainly changed our consciousness of life and of the mind. These are ideas that slowly and profoundly changed the way we see the world and think about the human place in the cosmos. A different sort of profound change was brought about by Buddha, Christ, and Mohammed. Thus, both scientists and religious figures have affected our consciousness in and of the world. But the secular figures operate on our perceptions of the external world, while the religious figures affect our perceptions of the unknown and that part of our internal being that we call the soul.

The foregoing scientists are more noted as shapers of our consciousness than are the comparatively lesser-known technicians such as Johann Gutenberg, James Watt, Thomas Edison, Alexander Graham Bell, the developer of the autobahn or his American counterpart, Robert Moses, the cartographers, the people who developed mechanical clocks, and countless others who have forged our technological progress over the years. The most recent developments in technology, particularly those relating to digitization, are radically changing our consciousness today, and it is some of those changes that I will take up in this chapter.

LINKING PEOPLE THROUGH PATHWAY/ROAD/TRACK/TEXT

One might well postulate that the earliest human pathways on earth linked people to the nearest waterholes, hunting grounds, and other villages. The pathways became byways, usually tracing the most direct route between points. The villages were generally self-contained and self-sustaining, and they formed natural social groups that grew out of kinship systems. Slowly the villages spread and might or might not remain connected to one another. As Colin Renfrew observes in his account of the spread of language, often children who moved away to form a new village would lose contact with their families and even begin to speak a "different" language and create a "different" set of religious stories and ceremonies.[1]

As more and more people used it, the byway became the road. Its markings became clearer, and the widest roads connected those places to which people most frequently traveled. The road appears to have become part of a trading system as people began to develop more elaborate artifacts and craft specialties. The beginnings of specialization of labor and trade brought with them the development of written language and the establishment of towns in place of villages. Roads, therefore, came to be associated with towns and, as towns grew, with cities. These towns and cities were connected over time by a network of roads that brought rural goods into the center and sent processed goods and tax edicts back out, and they had a literate or scribal group that held the people together through law, commerce, and religion.

When people came from outlying villages to the town, they came to realize that many of them could not communicate orally, the different dialects had become different languages, and the phenomenon of Babel came to be recognized. With recognition of the difference in language came the recognition of difference of culture and religion.

As empires grew, roads came to lead to main centers. "All roads lead to Rome." Or Jerusalem . . . or Mecca . . . or Benares. The road was extended to the sea-lane, which was patrolled, and thus led to the development of the major maritime empires of Venice, Amsterdam, London, and New York.[2] With the advent of steam came the railroad track, which connected the larger towns to cities and also led from the outskirts into the central city. The hub-and-spoke system became the model of the city as the heart of the commercial political, religious, and cultural empire.

Thus, the suburb was created—not the central-city district but the districts around the city. From the suburban complex came the great metropolises of the world. These became linked by a combination of sea-lanes and railroads until the development of the internal combustion engine and the road networks enabled people to bypass the centers and move from point to point on the periphery. In the modern metropolis, the center or the hub has seemingly become obsolete or quaint. Some urban centers still command our attention for historic reasons. But many who live in today's American metropolises have never even visited the hub (there is just no need to!).

Print Parallels

These shifts in the way people have moved parallel the shifts in the movement of words and ideas. In the world of the pathway, people talked to one another while passing on the path or meeting in the village. It was in talk that they held their various ceremonies. When writing developed, the text could be carried and disseminated to several people. Anthropologists have held that writing aided or was aided by the development of the town culture, the place where labor was specialized and where it was useful to store information on some semipermanent basis. But the problems of reproducing what was written into a large number of copies made the storage places and centers of writing relatively small and concentrated.

Even at the height of the Roman Empire and later, during the Middle Ages, disseminating a decree or an edict widely, or having an exact reproduction of it in the provinces as well as the imperial city, was not an easy undertaking. In many instances the means of transmission was the courier, the person who went with the text and read it to the group. Text and speech went hand in hand to bind the empire together. The couriers involvement ensured the validity of the text. So it was with the priest or the monk who went with the religious text to make sure that it was read in the approved manner.

Printing changed all that. The same text could be reproduced in hundreds, thousands, and eventually millions of copies. The text could be spread from one center to every corner of the globe. It did not require a courier, since its exact replication in so many places in the known literate world helped to assure the uniformity of its reading. Such advances in printing technology and distribution methods coincided with the development of political, religious, and commercial empires with extensive networks of communication emanating from a single center.

With printing, too, there developed various media that increasingly appealed to a mass audience—that is, everyone would read the same thing. This development was slow, encompassing the first three hundred years after Gutenberg, for truly mass media required the development of the steam press, cheap paper, and an avid reading public, which took time. But by the middle of the nineteenth century major newspapers were spreading the same news across many countries, books and particular authors could be read throughout the world, literate magazines and other journals developed, and publishing fortunes were made. People began to amass serious wealth while determining what the world would read. This increasing centralization and concentration of mass media paralleled similar developments in transportation (railroads and the steamship lines).

As radio, film, and television developed, power in many cases came to be concentrated into comparatively few hands. These new media tycoons saw these new technologies as essentially extensions of the printing press in their capacity to distribute information widely from a single source. Although small-scale uses of these media proliferated, the major uses came to be as devices for mass communication. In more recent years, the large television networks have been challenged by the development of cable and satellite systems, radio stations and networks have specialized and proliferated, and independent film producers have come to be a force that Hollywood studios must reckon with. But, so long as a deregulated environment for these enterprises encourages encomonies of scale and concentration of power through mergers and acquisitions, true competition enters the picture only through smaller operators' quicker grasp of the implications of new technology. Thus, new entrepreneurs are now emerging who hold the key to digitization, fiber optics, and the forms that the next new mass medium will take.

The Telephone, the Airplane, and the Beltway

In the past century, three inventions have countered the hub and spoke metaphor that has dominated print and nonprint media. The Swedish anthropologist Ulf Hannerz distinguishes between the mass media and the "non-mass media," such as "photography, tape recordings, the telephone, the fax, the computer, and the good old-fashioned personal letter, all employed in fairly symmetrical relationships with regard to scale and directionality—and also those which are asymmetrical to a degree without being 'mass': specialized books and journals."[3] He continues:

> Without travel and the non-mass media, we would not have a wide range of ethnic diasporas, transnational corporations, jet set and brain drain, tourism, charter flight hajj and other modern pilgrimages, invisible colleges in science. Exchange students, au pair girls, foreign pals as part of growing up, transcontinental families, international aid bureaucracies, summer beach parties of backpacking Interrail-pass-holders from all over, and among voluntary associations everything from Amnesty International to the European Association of Social Anthropologists.[4]

The telephone has become so commonplace a part of our environment that we sometimes forget that it is our primary medium for reaching across space to communicate. In the century since its invention it has brought voices and minds closer together and has strongly impinged upon our consciousness and our conscious ways of communicating. Through it we reach out and touch someone, sometimes dozens of times a day. Its ring means the chance for communion or for renewing old or broken connections.

The airplane originally was used to go from field to field, but as it became commercialized, it went from city to city and from airport terminus to terminus. Along with the bus and automobile, it enabled travelers to avoid large seaports and train hubs. For a while, in the

1950s and 1960s, hubs and spokes became the norm—Rome was replaced by O'Hare. But the large hub in time became problematic, and most airlines, both domestic and international, have now moved to a system of smaller hubs so that travel can be both more direct and more diffuse.

The automobile at first followed the railroad, operating largely on a hub-and-spoke system, but in time the automobile made the city–suburb distinction irrelevant. People could avoid the hub and, by means of expressways and then beltways, move from place to place without going through the urban congestion.

This shift to suburban-style living produced a network of malls rather than adding to the urban center. It produced the megalopolis rather than the metropolis. Together with the telephone, which enables people to order merchandise and information from home, the highway and air networks have allowed for the movement of people and information to be individual, to avoid the hub, and to appear personal and intimate. The next step in the establishment of the non-mass media and the hub-and-spoke system is the Internet.

THE INTERNET AND THE WEB
AS TRANSFORMATIONS OF LITERATE COMMUNITIES

The Internet, one of the names for the electronic superhighway, is the common term used to describe the vast network of interconnected nodes around the world. It is one of a number of networks set up by the United States government originally to connect research centers involved in the cold war. As Howard Rheingold has delightfully described the history in *The Virtual Community*, the scientists using the early networks found that they had many more interesting things to talk about than military security, and they began using the network for a variety of purposes. Rheingold writes:

> The essential elements of what became the Net were created by people who believed in, wanted, and therefore invented ways of using comput-ers to amplify human thinking and communication. And many of them wanted to provide it to as many people as possible, at the lowest possible cost. Driven by the excitement of creating their own special subculture below the crust of the mass media mainstream, they worked with what was at hand. Again and again the most important parts of the Net

piggybacked on technologies that were created for very different purposes.[5]

I remember first connecting to the network in the mid-1980s. At that time I was working on a project to study how well students in fifteen different countries around the world could write. From my office in Illinois, I found myself able to "talk" with colleagues in England, Europe, Asia, New Zealand, and Latin America. The telephone costs were minimal, and we could send notes, papers, and even whole data sets instantly. We did not use the online chat feature because of the time differences, but with the technology we were able to speed our work by months. We could also chat about our respective friends and families, send congratulations, jokes, and bits of trivia back and forth with ease.

During the 1990s the Internet system has grown immensely. The Internet connects sites such as universities or commercial "servers" by means of satellite, and in turn these nodes serve to connect the various terminals that are hooked up to the server by telephone line. On the Internet, terminals may be used by unaffiliated individuals or by whole libraries with their databases. With the World Wide Web, a computer in a particular site can support a "home page" able to serve a large number of users by presenting them with a hypertext or hypermedia "package" on a given topic. Like other hypertexts, it can be added to by the various readers, and with this interactivity comes the possibility for special forms of one-to-one or one-to-many communication.

Through the Internet, I can turn on my computer at home, turn on my modem which is connected to the telephone line and dial up a file server such as my regional nonprofit one or a commercial one like America Online. Once connected, I am plugged into a vast network of people and institutions. I can call up commercial news services, public and university libraries, the bulletin boards of various of interest groups, commercial and nonprofit publishers, and other individuals. I can check the stock market, follow a news story, get the listings for television, place an airplane reservation, pay my bills, talk to a friend, scan the services of a university library, access an encyclopedia, listen to Congress, chat with a famous author or with a friend, read a journal, play a video, or listen to the latest rap song.

I am connected to the rest of the world—if only I can find it. I can understand the connections if I can find the metaphor or metaphors.

The Internet is becoming the non-mass medium of choice. As such it is in the process of transforming even the other non-mass media. We may communicate with one another, read the news from around the world, browse libraries and databases, download much of what we would have asked for by airmail or fax. It can even become our shopping mall; I find it easier to buy books through the Web than to get into a car and go to a bookstore or even to call my local bookstore and have the book sent. A friend is developing a business that enables people to custom cut musical CDs on the Web and pick them up at a local retail outlet.

The Global Village

Considering television's impact on its viewers worldwide, Marshall McLuhan wrote of the "global village." By this term he implied that the mass media, particularly television, could bring everyone in the world together around a particular event (the example he cited was the assassination of John F. Kennedy) and share it instantly. Because television was both visual and aural, the effect was like that of witnessing a local event in a village. Although the media bring people together instantaneously, the resultant global village appears at this point to be not one, but many. There are a number of reasons for this diversity of villages, the most obvious being the multiplicity of channels that satellite technology and fiber optics make possible.

To McLuhan, television serves to unite people, but they are united as consumers rather than as participants. Television did not create a village in the old sense. It is not the center of learning (as with the ceremony of the oral culture). It is a worldwide movie theater where an audience all over the globe can watch the World Cup soccer match, the Olympics, or the trial of a celebrity. Television is an instrument of the masses, but its future implications have little to do with traditional concept of the village. That role has been taken by the Internet.

Together with the opening up of multiple channels and the world of hypermedia, the Internet brought with it certain fragmenting as well as uniting effects. This new Global Cinema has already become the multiplex theater to beat all multiplexes, in that most complex and interactive shopping mall of all. The Internet has created a vastly more complex web of information, services, entertainment, and connections among people than was envisioned by McLuhan in his metaphor of the global village. It is more like a soup than a village. Because of the diversity of options, there is also the opportunity for people to join any one of a number of chat groups, interest groups, or rooms.

The cultural walls around any larger society are permeated by the media. Perhaps centers no longer exist; perhaps they are replaced by nodes on a network.

Electronic Networks

The electronic world has also moved from a hub-and-spoke system to a more diverse one. We have gotten beyond the era of the central radio or television station and the central server with "dumb" terminals.

The "electronic superhighway" may be an inapt descriptor. The highway image is one of a straight line going from point A to point B. (It is an old image reaching back to the Roman times, when all roads led to Rome, the hub of the world.) On the Internet there are switching points, but there is not a central computer into which everything goes. The electronic system is much more complex than the old hub-and-spoke system. Although there may be a physical center for a particular commercial or public switching agency ("service provider" like these are replaced in our thinking by the smaller servers within them. They do not exist within our spatial consciousness, as might an O'Hare or a Heathrow (those vast terminals and switching stations of the jet world). If I sit in my house in upstate New York and connect to the Gopher server at the University of London, I do not see myself as traveling along a highway. The only place I am conscious of is here in my study on my screen. I am not even conscious of the larger web, but only of my set of nodes and home pages.

There is no travel, no going to a terminus and changing planes. The switching is instantaneous and virtual. We have no better image for the phenomenon than the network or the web. It is hyperspace—that which is beyond space even though we are in space.

Connections

Howard Rheingold wrote of the fact that, although widely separated geographically, people on the network tend to form communities in which the people are equally as interesting as their ideas. Thus, through the sharing of common interests, still there comes to be a recognition of individuality and personhood in these self-selected groupings.

A part of my time working on this book has involved me in communicating with people on one of the commercial networks as well as on the university-linked Internet. I find the commercial network fascinating. I had a question about one topic, "Sola Scriptura," and so asked the question on a bulletin board under the kabek "Religion Christianity Doctrine/Theology." Within a week I had 41 responses; within a month, 250. Most of the responses came from four or five people who took my question and then proceeded to undertake an intensive dialogue on the topic and on the differences between Catholic and Protestant theology on this and other matters.

I have since dipped into the larger set of bulletin boards under "Religion" and have found chats on dozens of topics, from abstruse theological points to groups of people discussing particular charismatic experiences. The people clearly get to know one another, if not intimately, at least more than superficially. They come together in a space where they can have a meeting of the minds.

These connections are bulletin boards, places that allow for continuous discussion over long periods of time. But there are also "rooms," where people can meet briefly on line at the same time. The mother of a colleague is able to go into a private room on one of the commercial networks and chat with her children and grandchildren. It saves a long-distance call, enables several people to participate at once—and then can be erased from the computer's memory.

The Network and the Mall

Whether commercial or not, the networks provide a way of dealing with the phenomenon of the mass. They are not unlike the shopping mall in this respect. The mall itself is an impersonal structure, not unlike a bazaar. It is filled with shops that are isolated from one another although physically connected. The shops' networks are linked to sister shops in other malls, not to other shops in the mall.

When I have gone to a stationery shop in a mall to look for a particular ink cartridge for my pen, for example, and the shop is out of what I want, the clerk will phone branches in other malls. If that approach fails, the clerk will send me to a stationery shop in another mall rather than to, say, the department store in the same mall. The network of the shop is a network of stationery shops, not a network of mall occupants, even though they do share space under the same roof. Shoppers treat the mall in the same way, as the location of specialized merchants, not as a department store where one is encouraged to go from department to department.

The network is like the mall. When I go on the Internet, World Wide Web, or America Online, I am confronted by a multitude of boutiques, individual stalls in the bazaar of information. I can pick up the Religion and Ethics set of stalls on America Online, or go to the related but different set under Christianity Today, or I can venture out on to the larger Internet and pursue the various religion stalls there such as the First Church of Cyberspace or the ARIL network. The same would be true of any other interest I have, such as language or fishing. I am "surfing," but more particularly I am looking at a specific community that is networked both in hyperspace and in my brain, which leads me from one part of the specialty to another.

I may return to the central hall of the Web or the Internet in order to determine whether I want to go into another set of nodes on the network. But the hall or the home space of the network is not a village, though it leads me to many villages.

The Market and the Room

The shift from the McLuhanesque global village appears to be toward global villages or the shopping mall. The problem with these metaphors is that they exist within space and time. Of course, we can only understand the new in terms of what we know. How, then are we to see this world of the virtual, where we seem to transcend space and time (if only briefly)?

There is a broad universal vision or set of images in the new communications media, but there are communities that span both space and time in hyperspace. We can go into those communities in a number of different ways.

The interest group or user group approach allows people to enter a world at any time and see who else has been there before they entered. They may then write an answer to or raise a question with any of the previous occupants. Whether they get an answer or not, they can only determine by revisiting the group at some later point. Thus, to truly be a member of the group entails an active dedication to it over time. We must be willing to listen to others whose interests are perhaps only tangential to our own most compelling interests.

A second approach to the Internet is through the chat spaces or the MUDs (multi-user dungeons, a term that is an outgrowth of the game Dungeons and Dragons). These started out as fantasy spaces on the Internet where a number of people could congregate at the same time and become part of a fictional world. They enter a "room" where other people join them and talk within the bounds of a common topic or framework. Some of the MUDs have a particular focus and are open only by invitation. There can be MUDs in which serious discussion on a given topic can take place. In this sort of space, the environment becomes like that of a salon or a symposium. Other MUDs are open to anyone who desires entry—those who misbehave can be thrown out—but otherwise one is free to pick up in mid-course and leave at any point.

MUDs are elaborate kinds of play opportunities, escapes to other worlds—and possibly the beginning of a new art form. As Howard Rheingold has remarked:

> Many of the highbrows of Elizabethan England would have died laughing if they knew that vulgar, nerdy Shakespeare would be remembered as great literature centuries later; who is to say MUDs and other alien suburbs of fandom are not as legitimate as Elizabethan theater? We remember Shakespeare because of the quality of his insight and his use of English, not because his contemporaries considered him to be "a great artist" or "in good taste."[6]

Rheingold's great insight on this world is that it is theater, a new world of drama that grows out of such experiments as the "Living Theatre," where the audience was part of the play and thus helped write it nightly. Just as hypertext enables new types of fiction and poetry, so the Internet permits a new sort of drama, a virtual performance art.

This is a world in which people are both the audience and the actors in a drama that is unfolding. They make their entrances into the room or the stage, and they make their exits. While in the room they don the role of a character and participate in a drama. To some extent they know their lines or at least the premise of the play, but they are improvising, playing off the other characters and lines. The drama may seem to have no beginning and no end. It is an ever-ending, ever-beginning phenomenon for those who participate. It is, indeed, the dramatic version of hypertext, where author, actor, and audience become one.

"All the World's a Stage;
and All the Men and Women Merely Images"

In one metaphor for the Internet, then, we are all actors in an unfolding set of dramas. Like an actor, each of us enters the stage and dons a role in the drama of our choice. It is the play of life or life as play. It is virtual, not real, but we can still hurt others or be hurt. The Internet becomes the avenue to a new form of drama, just as it is the avenue to a library or magazine (in the original sense of the term, as storehouse). The Internet itself may resist a single metaphor since it is itself potentially all of life on a virtual plane, the world on the screen. All of the world is a stage and all of the stage is the world. The two are indistinguishable.

It is a world in which the center of learning is everywhere and nowhere at once. It retains some of the aspects of the ceremony and the library, but it is something else besides those. The network is visible on the screen as it may have been invisible in reality except to those mystics or visionaries who did indeed see that interconnection.

THE DISSOLUTION OF CENTERS OF LEARNING
AND THE RESHAPING OF CULTURE

As I have described them in earlier chapters, within a culture or society, there has always been some center of learning, a time or place whereby the lore of the culture could be passed from generation to generation and where the learning could be added to and modified. It could be seen as the storehouse of information out of which the knowledge of the individual and the learning of the culture could be formed.

Jacques Ellul argues that the center of learning in the oral world is the ceremony.[7]

In the written or print world, it is the library.

Where is it in the electronic world? This is a political and epistemological question of great moment.

Where do I go to be connected to the past, to gain that sense of wholeness that enables me to see how I am related to such entities as my heritage, my culture, my roots? One source that I have often turned to has been my library, the set of books and documents that form the repository of things that I know: my genealogy, the history of America, the classics, the Bible. But I have also turned at times in my life to a variety of rituals, to the ceremony of the dinner table, to the church service, to the classroom, to the annual professional meeting. These too provide a center of learning and culture.

The Persistence of Ceremony

Ellul suggests that in the world of print we leave ceremony behind. I do not think so. It is in ceremony that books take on their full importance. The center of learning may have been the library, but it was also a set of actions in and around the library. When I was a graduate student, there was a "best" time to enter the library, people whom one saw there daily, to whom one spoke. There were customary gathering places for different groups of students. There were rituals of leaving books in particular spaces, of checking out books, of sharing. Even the coffee breaks had their own ritualistic aspects that served various socializing functions.

Centers of learning may shift in accordance with the technology, but that does not mean that the new center forsakes all of the trappings of the old. In the oral world, the ceremony, be it one of birth, growth, marriage, conquest, or death, provided a means for a culture to express its strongest feelings about those things that mattered most—the things that are related to the cycle of life. The ceremonies, rituals, and lore associated with these issues are the primary constituents of culture, according to Giambattista Vico[8]; they are what distinguish one culture from another. They set the patterns for stories, rituals, taboos. In the ceremony the elders teach the younger about the past of the culture and about what makes the culture distinguished from others.

We can see the vestiges of these ceremonial centers of learning in the variety of rituals that cultures have today. The birth, marriage, and death of a culture may be individual or communal. Thus, we can see that the ceremonies surrounding sports events are a part of the learning of the culture of the team and of the sport. The entrance of the teams, the playing of the national anthem, the warm-up, the intervals between action, the victory and defeat rituals—all of these are ceremonies in which the elders initiate the youth, whether as spectator or player.

Similarly, certain ceremonies may be part of the daily routine of a family, such as what happens upon arising, the service of breakfast or dinner, or family devotions before going to bed.

Ceremonies are clearly the center of learning in many religions. What goes on in the service; what books are used when; who speaks; in what tones; what instruments are allowed to be played; where people sit; how they sit or stand. All of these are part of the learning of the group.

In an oral society these ceremonies—daily, seasonal, or periodic—were the foci of all the knowledge of that culture. They remain so as the foci of such cultures as that of a family or a community.

The Library

When Ellul names the library as the center of learning in the print society, I think he is suggesting that the repository for the book, rather than any single book, serves as the true center. The library is the place to which one goes to find the book or books that are reputed to contain the important knowledge of the society. The knowledge is not contained in a single book but in a collection. It is a collection that is gathered over time, just as the ceremony changes over time. The early libraries had rather limited collections in many cases, so seemingly learning was in the totality of those libraries.

Such appears to have been the case of the libraries at Alexandria and at Pergamum, the birthplace of parchment. Such appears also to have been the case of most libraries in the Hebrew temples and particularly in monasteries. There, in the scriptorium, the place where books where kept and copied, lay the heart of the learning and the culture of each monastery. But the monastery library was also the place from which books were taken to be read aloud at the ceremonies and services of the monks or nuns, including at mealtimes, which were themselves ceremonies. Most of these readings were from the sacred scripture, but some also were from the church fathers.

The library served a function within the world of the monastery, so that the learning came not simply from the reading of the book but also from the book's becoming a part of a ceremonial and scriptural process.

The Secular University

The library, of course, expanded out from the monastery and into the secular world. As the universities were created—at Bologna, Paris, Oxford, and Cambridge—they found at their center the library. This building was the repository of whatever was known of importance. It was the place that served as a hub of the university. It was where one could connect to the past—through its records, in the form of books and papers.

But just because the library functioned as a center of learning did not mean that ceremony disappeared. The texts of the library were read by the students and the scholars and teachers. Yet, it is not simply the solitary reading and accumulation of knowledge that have been important in the university; ceremonies around the reading are equally important, so that both library and ceremony lie at the heart of learning.

One form of ceremony is the lecture, the large forum in which the professor, the person of learning, talks about a book that is in the library and that the students have presumably read. The lecture serves as a commentary on the book, a set of notes to the codex of the book, and an addition to it. The book sits at the center of a secular liturgy of talk about what is the meaning or what are the meanings of the book. Thus, the library becomes a source for talk, not just for reading.

Another form of talk about the book that takes place in the center of learning is the colloquium or the seminar. In this learning format, the master reader of the book inducts a group of neophytes into ways of talking about the book. The rules of this discourse are carefully rehearsed and practiced by the students so that they too can become masters. They are not learning to lecture—not yet—but they are taking part in a communal liturgical reading of the text. In some versions, the seminar is formal; in others, it is informal. The end, however, is induction into the ceremonies of learning by means of the book.

Stephen Leacock, the Canadian humorist, once described the peculiarly British version of this seminar, wherein a small group of students comes to the don's study having read the book and waits while the don smokes at them and occasionally grunts. This form is also known as the tutorial,[9] a ceremony that places greater responsibility upon the catechumens.

In all of this activity of ceremonial talk about the secular scriptures of the university, the objective is to increase the size of the library. It is important to learn not only to talk about the books one reads, but to add written commentary on them in the form of notes, treatises, criticisms, and the like. As the process continues, the library swells.

It grows beyond its bounds as it becomes increasingly important for the ceremony to include commentaries from outside the wall of a particular university. So the commentaries from one center of learning are added to others, and the whole swells.

When I was a graduate student in the 1950s, we were told that in order to claim a dissertation topic, we had to read everything else upon the topic and prove that our topic was new—"a contribution to scholarship" was the term used. For that reason, my colleagues in philosophy claimed, no one ever wrote a dissertation on Kant—it was impossible to get through the reading. In literature, this seemed equally true of Shakespeare. People published handbooks at that time to help students find a topic that had not been pursued.

A stricture, to "read everything," could not be applied today in most areas of the humanities, history, or even the social sciences. The amount of information on a topic simply grows too fast nowadays to abide by the old rules.

The library can no longer be the center of learning. Where in hyperspace is it?

The Heart of the Machine

In an age where libraries are connected electronically, where bibliographies and databases are online and updated daily, it is difficult to locate a center of learning. Many universities are cutting down on their actual book and journal purchases in favor of using other sources of information. It is possible to browse the catalogs of other university libraries and thus create a hyperlibrary.

There is no longer any reason for the university campus to be built around a library. In fact, there is no reason for a campus. During the past twenty years there has been a growth in the "open university" or "the university without walls," the campus that has no central lectures or seminars and no library. It is the correspondence school gone high-tech, using television, telephone, and computers to connect students to one another and to faculty. There may be sites where groups can congregate, but, with the advent of the bulletin board and the wide-area-network, these are not as important to the smooth functioning of the open university as they once were.

Another feature of these campuses without walls is that they do not use a permanent faculty of professors and instructors. There may be course designers and lecturers, but they are separated from the mentors or discussion leaders. The faculty, therefore, can be a group of independent "wandering scholars"—it need not be a cozy group of people who meet for lunch at the faculty club.

The electronic university has no tangible center, and the library is no longer a physical center. There may still be ceremonies, but they may well differ from the ceremonies of the lecture and seminar. As yet, we do not know what they might be, although it would seem that there must be some means for talk, the learning of rituals, and other means of certifying the induction of the individual.

But the electronic university, more properly, is one where the center is the circumference. Or rather, there is no center in that all is outside. Learning exists in a Möbius strip or a Klein bottle. All sources of information are available to anyone who has a computer and a modem and knows how to use them. These people can connect with any database, bring into their rooms text, pictures, sound, information on all subjects in virtually all media, and then re-create or combine it in any of a number of ways.

The center of learning is the electric plug or the telephone line.

Perhaps it is the screen or the mouse.

Perhaps it is the hard drive.

But there must be some ways for the individuals to participate in the ceremony of learning. Can they do it physically? How can they do it virtually?

The Library of Cyber Learning

The center of learning is the focal point for the individual to connect to the larger human and social world. When the center of learning lay in the ceremony, it was because through the various ceremonies and rituals people learned what it was to be sociable, what knowledge was worth passing on, what it was that helped constitute a culture. The learning was transmitted from person to person or group to individual. We learned through sight and hearing and imitation by our bodies. With the advent of writing, there came to be the possibility that information could exist outside of the minds and mouths and movements of the people who created that information. The repositories of learning became impersonal; they survived the individual and the local community. The individual could plug into the communal texts or their repository, the library. The people in charge of the library, of course, determined what knowledge was worth having. In this respect they were no different from those who controlled the ceremonies.

As printing enabled the reproduction of texts and their distribution around the world, the information and learning grew too large to be contained by all but a few large libraries with their branches. The scholarly world flowed to the New York Public Library, the Library of Congress, the British Museum, the Bibliotèque Nationale, the Moscow Library, and even began to overwhelm these centers of learning. As the amount of information became too large and unwieldy for any one center of learning, the electronic revolution intervened, enabling us to manage vast torrents of new materials.

First there came library networks and complexes of interlibrary loan. Now the library has exploded into cyberspace. The library itself is a hypertext.

There need not be a physical repository of objects we call books or journals. There can be tapes or chips or disks with digitized language, sound, or images. The physical center that is the library is dissipated into thousands of nodes. The learning is diffuse and infinitely reorganizable into home collections garnered on the Internet, downloaded onto a hard drive or Bernoulli disk, and then read, watched, or listened to.

I do not believe this means that the concept of library is gone. Just as ceremony failed to disappear with the advent of the library, both ceremony and the library remain, both are important centers of learning. They have changed and they take their place enfolded into the new cybercenter. But at they same time they enfold it. Just as the library replaced the ceremony as the center, the ceremonies of the library themselves became centers of the centers of learning. So, too, the cybercenter replaces the library, but the library is the repository of the cybercenter, and the centers of learning with their ceremonies of access and use remain paramount.

Although they have changed in form, ceremony and the library will enfold and be enfolded by the new technology, and communities of learning and of learners will remain as important as communities of readers and writers.

We cannot avoid enfolding the present in the past and holding on to those centers of learning which have worked for us.

THE LOSS OF CULTURE AND THE RISE OF CULTURES

Broadly speaking, a culture is that to which the individual becomes affiliated when brought out of the family (the filial bonds) into some other, larger context. The idea of culture originated in the mid-eighteenth century, spurred by *The New Science* of Giambattista Vico.[10] Vico's scientific and religious approach to the world led him to seek to explain those people who were "gentiles"; that is, how, after the fall of Babel, people who were not the chosen people of God could be intelligent. Out of the principle of self-interest these human beings created villages, cities, and nations, and they forged a concept of humanity and a concept of the divine.

Vico defined a culture by its ways of dealing with particularly vital aspects of the human place in the cosmos—with birth, coming of age, and death—and in those particular events the ways by which the human confronts the unknown. Culture thereby becomes associated with religion and with ceremony.

Culture may have a racial or ethnic basis, but that tie may become attenuated over time.

Culture is that with which a person identifies and which recognizes the person.

A culture may be a community, or it may take on aspects of a public. It is this difference that helps explain the changes that are emerging.

The Public and the Community

Wendell Berry, in *Sex, Economy, Freedom, and Community*, posits a series of oppositions between concepts of "the public" and "the community." He is chiefly describing an opposition between the product of a universal approach to the idea of the mass and that of an alternative approach, one that appears to arise out of the circumstances in which we live.

The public is an abstraction, perhaps a fiction. The community, on the other hand, is (or can be) a palpable entity. Some other differences may be seen in the set of oppositions in the table on pages 153–154.

How Does a Culture Work?

The literary critic Edward Said has observed that "culture is used to designate not merely something to which one belongs but something that one possesses and, along with that proprietary process, culture also designates a boundary by which the concepts of what is extrinsic or intrinsic to the culture come into forceful play."[11] Said goes on to remark of the relationship between culture and education: "What is

THE PUBLIC

Hierarchical The public is arranged in such a way that it is a group beneath those that seek to define it. It is a way by which the minority thinks of the mass. The German term for this sort of structure is *gesellschaft*.

Denomination In religious terms, the broad sects and denominations tend to think of their members as a public. Muslims, Methodists, Mormons—all are ways of thinking of people's religious life in terms of the structured religion to which they belong. The sectarian label seeks to define and place people.

Denies the Individual The public view of people is that they are not individual but are part of a demographically definable whole. The individual is often asked to use check marks to indicate to which of a variety of groups she may belong. Thus the individual is able to be located by coordinates or parameters in a public and as such the individual is interchangeable with another fitting the same characteristics.

Static and Atemporal A public tends to be a fixed entity. It is often seen as existing outside of time and place. Thus, there is a "reading public"— just as their is an "ideal reader" or a "typical NRA member." Each of these is a type, and the type's characteristics tend to stand outside of time.

THE COMMUNITY

Shared The community is such that its members think of "we" rather than "we" and "they." All of the members share equally in the community. The German term for this sort of structure is *gemeinschaft*.

Congregation A congregation is a group of people assembled for religious purposes. It is usually a group that comes to one place at one time. This group of people associates voluntarily and tends to share beliefs and structures. There may be Presbyterian or Reformed Jewish congregations but the name may be incidental because many of the attendees may be of different denominations.

Respects the Individual From the perspective of the community a person is an individual with a name. Usually there are both first and last names, which help to distinguish the person from his siblings or children. For the community this name and the associated face are important and central to the functioning of the community.

Evanescent and Dynamic A community is always changing. People come into and leave it. There may be a mass influx or exodus from time to time, and the com- munity may shift in form and configuration. One metaphor for the community is the jellyfish that moves through the water without seeming to move, yet whose shape never stays the same.

continued

Fear The public is controlled through fear. Often it is fear of those who manipulate and control the group; at other times it is fear of those who constitute a threat to the group—some outside force or alternative public.

Love Communities tend to develop through love, through a sense of respect for the individual and a sense that the community cares about the individual. The community shares many parts of its group life and through this sharing exhibits a kind of love.

Taxonomy A taxonomy is an ordered and hierarchical way of viewing phenomena. It is established by a scholar, a group of scholars, or some designated authority, and everything is neatly placed in the structure of the taxonomy. It is a set of nested boxes that can be made into an organizational pyramid. One may move only up or down, given a strict taxonomy.

Hypertext A hypertext has no fixed hierarchical order; in fact, any order that appears is the once order of the person originating the hypertext, which may be changed and modified by the next person who comes along. There may be an ad hoc or recommended order, but it is not a mandatory one and is simply a temporary holding place. One can move from any one place to any other place.

Dependence If the world of the public is all that we have so far defined, then the place of the individual in the public is a place of dependence upon the group and the structure of the group.

Independence In the community each individual is connected to the others but is independent of them, free to move about to separate from the community (she will be missed) or to join another (she will be welcomed), but allowed to come or go.

---

more important in culture is that it is a system of values *saturating* downward almost everything within its purview; yet paradoxically culture dominates from above without at the same time being available to everything and everyone that it dominates."[12]

Education is one of the primary vehicles that we have for sustaining a culture, and it does so through one or a combination of the centers of learning. At some time before puberty in a village culture, the young are initiated into the culture through a variety of means. Sometimes it is separately by gender, with the boys and girls being taken through a period of initiation into the roles and responsibilities of the adult community. Many of them had some inkling of these roles and responsibilities by virtue of having tagged along after their elders and watched them as they worked in the fields or in the village. The society tends to set the limits of the consciousness of the individual. This limitation is, quite simply, culture.

In a society where there is text, a major part of the acculturation accompanies learning to read and write. Over the past three decades, I have studied the ways in which this acculturation takes place in a number of countries around the world. It is clear that there is a "trickle down" of culture through the formal educational system. At the top are the intellectual minority, those who write the textbooks and train the teachers. They have their internecine wars, which are fought in the scholarly journals or the halls of academia, but they often share a vision of what is important to know and to do. They may argue at the fringes of our consciousness, but they do not often succeed in changing our consciousness; that is left to other, less cerebral forces such as technology and the acceptance of scientific ideas.

My studies have shown me that schools are often used to indoctrinate students into the culturally approved texts, the local canon, and also into the ways of reading and writing. They teach the ways of using these texts as scripture. Across cultures there may be a consensus that people should be able to decipher the words on a page or write legible and grammatical text. But this similarity masks differences in the ways students are instructed to organize their writing or to ask questions about the books and poems they read. For writing, schools in the United States encourage a logical organization and an impersonal style, while those in Australia emphasize a metaphoric or imagistic organization and a personal style. For reading literature, schools in the United States encourage the hunt for symbols and morals, while schools in England encourage discussions of form and imagery.[13]

One can argue that the American culture of reading and writing has been a combination of the scientific and the puritanical. It is moralistic and literal, following in the tradition of the map. It is thoroughly modern in its view, as well. It represents the forging of a reading and a writing public rather than a set of learning communities.

Schooling, Culture, and Media

When schools took the student outside of the family bonds and focused him or her on a mission of acculturation and affiliation into the community, they had a relatively clear notion of their mission and an acceptance by the community that this was their proper role. In many systems of education, there was a commonality of beliefs and values of school, church, and community. This mission was particularly effective when the primary medium was print; then, the child learned to use the medium of acculturation in a culturally sanctioned location. Children learned to read by reading texts that supported the society's social and cultural values and that sustained the main cultural myths. Early-twentieth-century American readers were told of our own Revolutionary War leaders' righteousness in creating the country and separating it from England, of early colonists' depredations at the hands if "savage natives," and of the glorious God-fearing men and women who were to be most revered in our nation's pantheon of readers.

People who learned to read from these books developed a vision of the culture and found themselves bonded to it. These bonds were further strengthened by the sorts of books that were to be found in many American homes: the Bible, Benjamin Franklin's autobiography, *Pilgrim's Progress*, and, at least among the more well-to-do, perhaps one of the many compendia of the "classics" like President Eliot of Harvard's "Five-Foot Shelf," which reliably contained all that a cultured household needed to know. Immigrants and the upwardly mobile could readily purchase the necessary texts of the culture—perhaps even comic book versions of them, as well.

This bookish, educated culture become separated from the popular imagination of folktales, folk songs, charms, and even the religious culture of the popular churches such as that of the Pentecostals. Whether from the right or the left, the bookish minority has tended to disparage or patronize the popular arts. As a result, this minority consciously shaped the culture in the direction of those who knew and were devoted to the books that were part of the syllabus of secondary and higher education, thereby defining the predominant American canon as largely a Greco-Roman culture, a culture that celebrates a particular kind of print.

This sort of culture was the culture of the minority, not that of the masses. As a result of the intrusion into the home of other media besides print—first radio and then television—whole bodies of new information became available to the child. In the United States, with private broadcast stations, the information was unregulated as to content. These media (for which no schooling was required to be a member of the audience), helped create a large popular culture that operated independently of the formal educational institutions. Only grudgingly and belatedly has the minority culture begun to recognize this vast reservoir of images as having any cultural legitimacy whatsoever.

A 1994 article by J. Peder Zane in *The New York Times* began: "It was bound to happen. Like a ravenous Klingon, television has already devoured much of popular culture."[14] Zane cited the widespread popular preference for MTV (Music Television) over normal music, for television reruns over most new films, and for books arising out of such TV series as *The Partridge Family, Seinfeld, Mission Impossible,* and *Home Improvement.*

Such books had long been popular with the adolescent market, and they appear to be dominating the adult market, as well, these days. They do so in part by treating early television programs as a part of the cultural heritage, with studies of *The Partridge Family* and *The Addams Family,* for example. Zane humorously quotes Robert J. Thompson, a professor of television: " 'If you back me against a wall, I would say ostensibly, as a piece of art, "Hamlet" is in some ways superior to "Lou Grant," ' he says, referring to a drama written by the English playwright William Shakespeare. 'Television is our modern art form. It is where the national dialogue is being carried on. Rather than fight this, we should recognize it and embrace it.' "

How Long or Broad Is a Culture?

There are those who seek to assert an historical unity to a culture, and for many of the larger cultures there are certain defining events that tend to hold people together in the public sense of a culture. Whether they hold them together in a community is problematic—the community bond tends to be more local.

The community bond is perhaps best defined in the intermingling of readings and stories of coauthoring and sharing. The community may partake of a larger culture while yet retaining its own distinctive characteristics.

The breadth of a culture is also a problematic issue. There is a desire to make broad claims for a cultural unity—whether speaking of one's Jewish heritage, or African American heritage, or Hispanic/Latino heritage or tradition.

This search for breadth, however, is a way of making a person a member of a "public." Although a cultural label is a convenient way of dealing with the stranger, it may not have the sustaining power of either a community or a state of anarchy.

Culture/Community

What is the relationship between a culture and a community? There are broad affiliations that define a public culture, but are they so broad that they finally fall apart? If we examine the history of a culture, we find it takes on a self-dividing nature. The affiliations become attenuated over time.

In the world of text, these attenuated affiliations held together in such concepts as nation, denomination, and perhaps ethnicity.

They were often held together by language and by common knowledge that was shared information.

Nowadays people seek to draw attention to common affiliations through such devices as shirts or jackets of sports teams. But that no longer works as a cultural identifier; the jackets are worn not for cultural identification, but for their color or design.

In this age the large cultural groups are not sustainable—people define themselves as members of a community, not as a public and not as the mass.

THE MASSES AND THE MINORITY

At many times in our lives, I suspect, we become suddenly aware of the mass of people. It may be when we go into a shopping mall during the Christmas rush, or when we enter a bustling city after having spent time in the country or a small town, or while visiting a country like India or Japan for the first time. We are surrounded by hordes of people; for many of us, our personal space is seemingly invaded by the teeming mass of humanity. We may be repelled, fascinated, or even excited by this swarm of people; after all, we are social creatures. But the immensity of the hordes in some places seems almost too much to bear—even for the most gregarious.

There is a significant difference between a large accumulation of people and the idea of the masses. There may be a large number of people on the earth or in a city, but we are not necessarily struck by any feeling that they are faceless, undifferentiable—what we might think of as the mass. In the early nineteenth century, William Wordsworth wrote of his first encounter with the crowds of London:

> O Friend! One feeling was there which belong'd
> To this great City, by exclusive right;
> How often in the overflowing Streets,
> Have I gone forward with the Crowd, and said
> Unto myself, the face of everyone
> That passes by me is a mystery.
> Thus have I look'd , nor ceas'd to look, oppress'd

By thoughts of what, and whither, when, and how,
Until the shapes before my eyes became
A second-sight procession. . . .
   . . . lost
Amid the moving pageant, 'twas my chance
Abruptly to be smitten with the view
Of a blind Beggar, who, with upright face,
Stood propp'd against a Wall, upon his Chest
Wearing a written paper, to explain
The story of the man and who he was.
My mind did at this spectacle turn round
As with the might of waters, and it seem'd
To me that in this Label was a type,
Or emblem, of the utmost that we know,
Both of ourselves and of the universe . . . [15]

In this powerful description of the blind man standing out in the crowd but simultaneously serving as an emblem of the blind mass of humanity, Wordsworth is one of the first poets to express the sense of both the enormous concentration of people in the city and their simultaneous collective anonymity. Later in the same book he writes:

Oh! Blank confusion and a type not false
Of what the mighty City is itself
To all except a Straggler here and there,
To the whole Swarm of its inhabitants;
An undistinguishable world to men,
The slaves unrespited of low pursuits,
Living amid the same perpetual flow
Of trivial objects, melted and reduced
To one identity, by differences
That have no law, no meaning and no end . . . [16]

Even in Wordsworth's time, the masses of people in the city had become an overwhelming phenomenon, a massive swarm of indistinguishable and undistinguished humanity. Earlier poetic descriptions of city life had focused on individual people or caricatures of people. Here they become a public, and so they are to remain for nearly the next two centuries.

The Concept of the Public as Mass

In the 1920s the Spanish philosopher and critic, José Ortega y Gasset posited that at the end of the eighteenth century there emerged the masses, hordes of people who combined not so much voluntarily as involuntarily into some sort of nameless, faceless agglomeration. The masses not only constitute a large number of people, but also come to encompass a concept by which we often think of ourselves and of others. He opens his book *The Revolt of the Masses* this way:

> There is one fact which, whether for good or ill, is of utmost importance in the public life of Europe at the present moment. This fact is the accession of the masses to complete social power. As the masses, by definition, neither should nor can direct their own personal existence, and still less rule society in general, this fact means that actually Europe is suffering from the greatest crisis that can afflict peoples, nations, and civilization. Such a crisis has occurred more than once in history. Its characteristics and its consequences are well known. So also is its name. It is called the rebellion of the masses. In order to understand this formidable fact, it is important from the start to avoid giving to the words "rebellion," "masses," and "social power" a meaning exclusively or primarily political. Public life is not solely political, but equally, and even primarily, intellectual, moral, economic, religious; it comprises all our collective habits, including fashions both of dress and amusement.[17]

For Ortega y Gasset, as for others, the mass is something about which we become aware as we look around us. The mass is the "other," distinct from the family or the tribe into which we are filiated (connected by ties of kinship) and from the culture or community into which we are affiliated through education. We talk about the downtrodden masses, and we talk about mass media, mass education, and mass culture. Mass culture appears to differ from popular culture. The idea of mass art differs from that of folk art. "Folk" seems tied to an indigenous group, to a particular geographic area or perhaps to an ethnic bond; "popular" is tied to the common people, as opposed to the aristocracy or the intellectuals of a society. Both "folk" and "popular" carry with them a sense of springing from the group itself. "Mass," on the other hand, has the sense of being external to oneself. The masses exist as objects of our consciousness rather than as a group with which we can identify. The mass is, quite simply, a public.

The Critical Mass

In the eyes of many, the masses in the twentieth century have reached a critical mass, with the resultant potential for an explosion readily likened to that of a bomb. It is this mass that is the focus of

Ortega y Gasset's discussion, for he was among the first commentators to notice that the urban masses' influences albeit comparatively anonymous, was actually greatly compounded through enhanced communication with the mass of people on the whole planet. The mass becomes a critical mass when it is possible for everyone on the earth to be aware of the same phenomenon at roughly the same time.

"Critical mass" may also be associated with other modern-day phenomena. Many communities, for example, are painfully aware of the mass of garbage and trash that engulfs them, perpetually outdistancing their best efforts to create new landfills fast enough to contain the problem. Most Americans are painfully aware of the amount of mail and other paper that daily crosses their threshold—thanks largely to mass marketing and bulk-rate mail. For the past two decades, such futurists as Alvin Toffler have alerted us to the onset of the information explosion, that is, the accumulation of and ready access to massive amounts of information. Our libraries and databases expand at a phenomenal rate. Databases and the electronic world appear to take care of the problem, but their sorting systems are in fact strained. Even the Internet and such service providers as America Online are beset by the mass of products, goods, and services they must contend with. The new form of mass e-mail is called "spam," the much-derided "spiced ham" canned meat product. The Internet community adopted this term because of the way spam was ridiculed on the British TV comedy series *Monty Python's Flying Circus*.

The Ethics of the Mass

In earlier times, it was thought that the masses could be made good by being made literate. It was this idea that lay behind much of the popular proselytization that occurred during the Middle Ages and the Reformation. When the Calvinist reformers promulgated the idea of sola scriptura, they appear to have assumed that, by the widespread distribution of a text through the new invention of the printing press and through increased literacy, they could promulgate much more widely an enlightened mass ethic as well as a ready means of conversion. The Bible and tract societies that suddenly sprang up at the end of the seventeenth century and proliferated thereafter operated on the basis this belief. The text was sufficient in itself for redemption, and the fact that the same text reached more and more people meant that all were under its rule.

At the beginning, this approach to the masses was a democratic one. During the period 1600–1900 literacy spread from the clergy to the laity and from the aristocracy to the merchant class and then to the working class. In some seventeenth-century societies, such as Sweden, virtually every adult could read and write (it was a requirement of marriage or to have one's children baptized). Schools were established and flourished throughout these three centuries, and workingmen's institutes supplemented the schools to provide adult education. Immigrants to the United States became literate first in their own language and then in English, often thanks to popular newspapers and ethnic institutes. Although these educational efforts were attacked by Marxist critics, who saw in them certain exploitative elements, both the intention and the results were benign and built on the idea that an educated public was a discerning and active one.

But there emerged a different sense of the masses at the end of the nineteenth century and growing through the twentieth. This is a sense of the masses as a consuming mass, not a discerning one. Ortega y Gasset sees the masses as spoiled and materialistic, but one must wonder whether they were encouraged in this attribute through the efforts of the earliest advertisers and purveyors of mass entertainment and media.

The mass ethic has become one that would establish a world of conformity to a single norm. It is one that has been satirized and written about from the early nineteenth century on. It is the world of the machine-made object and the machine-made human, a world in which there is little room for either the individual or the community. It is also a world frightened of anarchy—and of community.

Mass Media—Mass Marketing

The increasing availability of inexpensive print, paper, and distribution methods enabled the mass media to burgeon during the nineteenth century. Soon, these media were succeeded by film, radio, and television. These media all emanated from central points of distribution, whether a publisher, film studio, or broadcasting station or network (not in the sense that I use the term elsewhere in this book). The executives controlling each of these media tended to define the masses as an audience, a public, a readership—and, in general, to pitch their appeals to the lowest common denominator among them. As an audience, as a public, and as a readership, the mass is a passive group, one that receives the medium and the messages contained within it and through it. Success in these media is measured by the number of people reached, not the quality of the experience or the intrinsic quality of the newspaper, book, film, or show. Through advances in electronic and other technology, the mass media have tended to upgrade their operations, so that nowadays newspapers publish the same edition simultaneously around the nation or even the globe, television shows are beamed to viewers in all parts of the earth, films routinely get worldwide distribution, and even logos and T-shirts carry the same message across national boundaries.

Rupert Murdoch and the late Robert Maxwell, among others, have seen the vast amount of power that can be had if one controls the media of print and television. They have developed chains of newspapers that re linked to television networks that are linked to book publishers that are linked to record companies and film studios. Maxwell even owned a football team, as if to make the circuit of mass entertainment complete. Murdoch has done the same and is now in the process of seeking control of the digitization of the media. His entrée is through the technology and through sports—which remain a "mass attraction."

More recently, there have been attempts to control the non-mass media, as well, through the rapid concentration of market share by such plutocratic corporate giants as Microsoft, America Online, and Sun Microsystems, to name but a few in the realm of the Internet. But the users of online networks have thus far resisted attempts to be dominated by any one corporate entity or group of companies. These services are "consumer-driven."

The mass media are asymmetrical; they do not allow for an interchange except on the terms of the purveyor. People can "vote with their feet" and not watch or not read, but they have little direct effect on the makers or producers of the media. That is, indeed, why they are mass—they are a public as opposed to a community.

The Mass Dystopia

In much literature and art of the past two hundred years, the mass society has been the dystopia. A utopia is the creation of an imaginary heaven, a dystopia the creation of an imaginary hell. In the mass society, the protagonist strives to retain individuality, just as in the earlier society the protagonist struggled to find an appropriate relationship with the deity. The anonymous mass replaced the angry God. We may observe this shift in comparing the plays of the Greeks or even of Shakespeare with the poems of Byron, the novels of Dickens, Hardy, or Dostoevsky, or the allegories of Aldous Huxley, George Orwell, or Ayn Rand. In the works of Franz Kafka, the mass society and the angry God become fused into a single construct like The Castle. The mass is the antagonist of much modern literature. It is often cited by critics both liberal and conservative as characteristizing the "worst in modern society."

Jacques Ellul suggests that it is the phenomenon of the mass that produces the spread of evil, the absence of love, the growth in violence, and many other conditions that we consider maladies of our society.[18] These phenomena arise and spread in part because of the crowding of the planet and its urban spaces but also because it seems easy to lose one's sense of the importance of others and the sanctity of life.

The mass media have fueled this loss in that they have made the mass appear attractive by praising crowds in amphitheaters doing the wave, or cheering each other on in talk and game shows, or conforming in dress or moral codes through ever popular T-shirt slogans or mindless bumper stickers.

The mass constantly produces a sense of "the public" as opposed to "the community." It has also produced a number of responses on how to deal with the overwhelming number of people involved. This set of responses has urged a move from a centralized to a decentralized approach.

Minority

If there is a mass, is there necessarily a minority? In *The Revolt of the Masses*, Ortega y Gasset suggests that there is; so, too, had people like Matthew Arnold before him. In *Culture and Anarchy*, written in the latter part of the nineteenth century, Matthew Arnold had argued that the minority was a cultured group that knew the best that was thought and known, that could steer a course between overintellectualization and impassioned change. In the 1920s Yeats expressed his lack of faith in this possibility in "The Second Coming." To Ortega y Gasset came the same doubts, hence his book. The minority, like the masses, is a psychological fact as well as a sociological one. If we think of others— even one other person whom we may meet—as part of the masses, we are the minority. The minority is that which is the other, the stranger, that which is suspect to the mass. We think of minorities in two ways, one positive, one negative.

The Positive and Negative Minorities

Observers like Arnold and Ortega y Gasset define the (I would say positive) minority as that voluntary group that shares a sense of purpose and a sense of ideals.

In his discussion of community, the philosopher Glenn Tinder argues that such a division makes community impossible. When the minority is separated from the mass, the division between the two perpetuates a we-they sense that is hierarchical.

The negative minority is that group which is not us, not in the mainstream, whatever that might be. It may be linguistically, racially, or religiously different. Ethnic, cultural, linguistic, or religious minorities are usually not self-defining, but they are defined by the majority, by the mass, as that group which is not us. In the United States there have been minorities that have become virtually invisible. Once a despised minority, the American Irish have for the most part entered the mass; so have the Italians, the Greeks, and other European groups. Asian, African, and Latin American groups have themselves tended to remain a part of the minority. In Canada, the French-speaking are a minority in Ontario, the English-speaking a minority in Quebec.

The rise of a multicultural view puts a number of modern notions to the test among them the idea of universality. Many institutions are affected, not least the educational system.

The treatment of social or ethnic minorities is an ideological issue, varying according to the ideological beliefs of those in power, usually the majority. In many parts of the world the issue is one of language policy, inevitably a political question. Educational options have included: assimilating the new groups into the existing population (e.g., the United States in the early twentieth century and France and its colonies); creating a new unifying "culture" (e.g., Indonesia); ignoring the subgroup as uneducable (e.g., Finland and Hungary's treatment of gypsies); establishing separate educational systems (e.g., Belgium's two school systems, for the Walloons and the Flemish); or accommodating the unassimilable minorities by including their culture in the curriculum and thus redefining culture).

This last possibility confronts at least some school administrators in the United States today, and is paralleled in countries like Canada, New Zealand, and the United Kingdom. The situation in the United States and Canada, I believe, differs from that in Europe in that the dominant cultures in both Canada and the United States are themselves immigrant cultures and they themselves are culturally and linguistically diverse. In the United States as well as other parts of the world, there is the fact that some of the minority cultures are what the anthropologist John Ogbu calls "caste cultures," people who came or were brought as slaves or indentured workers. Although they could be compared to the "guest workers" of modern-day Europe, I believe their status is actually quite different. The Turkish population of Germany is viewed—and views itself—as temporary residents. Such obviously, was never the case with either blacks or Chinese in the United States, both of which have attained legal equality if not socioeconomic equality.

As the historian Rhett Jones has observed, before Americans disavowed slavery entirely, in 1865, the African people were subjected to what seems a deliberate attempt to take their centuries-old regimen systematically deprived slaves not only of their status as human beings but also obliterated any remnants of family and cultural ties to Africa that the slaves had, forcing them to develop a new plantation culture that was cut off from African origins and so had to create a new set of myths.[19]

This group was treated differently from Native Americans or any of the other immigrant populations, except possibly the Chinese railroad workers of the western United States, the "coolie labor" at times drew the wrath of California politicians, for example, but which never forced this minority to break ties with their country of origin or to forge a new identity.

The Scribal Minority

There is yet another minority, the group that appears to be the controlling force of the mass. This group is also a "they," a group that sets itself apart from and seeks to remain in control of the mass. Whether it is a positive or negative force remains a question.

The minority in a literate society is the group of scribes, these who have fully mastered the tools of reading and writing and so serve as intermediaries between the world of text and the world of people. Scribes today have diverse occupational titles: lawyer, accountant, editor, copywriter, journalist, teacher. Whatever the label, they serve the function of manipulating the world of text and therefore of controlling and shaping information.

This minority has much of the same function in a secular world as does the priest in the religious one. In a theocracy, the priest and the scribe formed a common class. As job specialization grew and the world increasingly divided into its spiritual and secular aspects, the two found their own special places: the pulpit and the lecture hall. But the functions of each remained similar, however different or even antagonistic their separate spheres might be.

As images tend to replace realities and images tend to be controlled by those who control the media, latter-day scribes naturally wish to preserve and assert their minority control. They do this through media images, through control of the "highways," through the attempt to assert universals, and through doctrine. This is the new generation of scribes, and they are as suspect as scribes have always been. But they tend to be controlling. And they tend to assert that the only access to the web is through them and that their web is "The Web"—the truly "authoritative" source par excellence.

The Potential of a Scribal Majority

But their assertion of authority has the potential to be thwarted. Anyone with a computer and a modem can (with a little effort) create a home page. The Internet and the World Wide Web are not, as the image makers would like us to believe, a mass medium but rather a non-mass medium. Just as anyone can talk to anyone with a phone, so can people form communities and networks with their computers and web pages. They already do so with chat groups, list-serves, and news groups. There are some problems with this ideal, to be sure. I can create a web page and then forge a link to the First Church of Cyberspace, but there is no guarantee that the First Church of Cyberspace will necessarily return the favor. That is to say, the link is only one-way at this point; whether it can be two-way remains to be seen.

Conceivably, however, the scribal group in the world of hypermedia is vast, nearly as vast as the network of readers and writers. One example is the large group in France that can access Minitel with their touch-tone phone and a television. Such systems allow for a vast network of interconnected scribes sending and receiving images to large and small groups. Once touted as a key to modernity, today's electronic web is actually a key to the postmodern world.

THE DISSIPATION OF THE MODERN

The modern age is said to have begun with the defeat of Napoleon in 1815. According to Paul Johnson, the historian, several technological, political, and intellectual forces converged around that time to frame the world and dominate the imagination of people in all walks of life.[20] It was an era that was to last something over one hundred years. During that time a set of beliefs came to reside at the center of thinking in western Europe and the United States. We may see these beliefs as attempts to deal with the emerging phenomenon of the masses. It is an era that we have left, but we have not fully shaped the intellectual framework of the world to replace it. When we started leaving it is a matter of some conjecture—perhaps with the inventions of Bell and Edison, perhaps with the First World War, or perhaps with the dropping of the first atomic bomb in 1945.

Citing numerous other scholars, Harvey Cox defines modernism as "the attempt to come to terms . . . with the modern world, the world supported by . . . the 'five pillars' of modernity." These are:

1. the nation-state;
2. science-based technology based on a positivistic idea of science;
3. capitalism in the sense of "the quest for profit maximalization" or perhaps materialism;
4. bureaucratic rationalism or structuralism as a mode of organizing thought; and
5. the secularization of religion.[21]

To these I would add what I have described earlier, a literal and text-bound view of the world that posits external reality as conforming to what is on paper.

All of these views form part of what Owen Barfield would call the modern consciousness, the lens through which the world is perceived and to some extent conceived.[22] It was a world consciousness engendered and nurtured through the seventeenth, eighteenth, and nineteenth centuries, and it is a view that is challenged by hypertext, other non-mass media, and decentralized transportation.

The Nation-State

The nation-state is the political entity of choice that first emerged during the Renaissance but gained its greatest strength in the tumultuous wake of the French Revolution. Nationalism, the forging of a distinct geopolitical entity that sought separation from the ancien régime (Old World empires), became a rallying cry throughout Europe in the nineteenth century and the rest of the world in the twentieth century. By the end of the Second World War, nation-states had multiplied severalfold in the two preceding centuries. The nation-state was a political attempt to deal with the mass. Nation builders sought to forge a polity that could claim the allegiance of a large number of people and could in turn provide them with those necessities and luxuries that had been provided by the village, the church, or the feudal lord.

A nation might be subdivided into administrative units, but both the planning and execution of policy were generally centralized. So it was that the bureaucracies of government grew. These bureaucracies demanded loyalty and conformity so that all in the nation could be served. The bureaucracy thrived by advocating in behalf the public, as well as by making the public dependent upon it. Thus, the bureaucracy became the special province of a scribal elite—the clerks in the Circumlocution Office of Charles Dickens's *Our Mutual Friend*, at one fictional extreme.

Science-Based Technology

In *The Revolt of the Masses*, Ortega y Gasset asserted that technology helps to create a dependent (he used the term "spoiled") populace. Technology builds upon scientific advancement and comes to be seen as separate from the tools that people normally use. In the modern view, technology includes any thing dependent upon steam power, electricity, or the internal combustion engine, but not such things as hand weaving or writing with a stylus on cloth (techniques that predated these technologies). Technology is the world of biomedicine but not that of herbal remedies or healing through prayer. Technological advances are produced by an elite that then distributes them to the masses, who become users of the technology rather than masters of it. Thanks to advertising and marketing, the technology itself is venerated and becomes an idol, so that people become dependent on it. This is the vision that Ellul foresaw over thirty years ago, a world in which the means becomes an end and the icon the idol.[23]

Capitalism/Materialism

The modern world is, as the historian Fernand Braudel has amply demonstrated, a world of capitalism that created the civilization of Europe that has tended to dominate our ideas of how the world should and must be.[24] It was a world in which the production of goods became centralized and specialized so that few could be "self-sufficient." The people became users of tools, goods, and materials supplied by others. They thus became consumers domestically as well as at work. As they became consumers, they found it necessary to have more and more material goods and became increasingly dependent upon them. Materialism was spawned by the mass media, whose very ethos ends up substituting the idol for the icon.

Structuralism

Structuralism is an approach to the variety of phenomena around us that is essentially rational and that assumes the world to have universal properties. It is often tied to the approaches of empiricism, the gathering of data based on sense impression and then the use of inductive reasoning to order and explain those data. Structuralism begins with the Cartesian "cogito, ergo sum" ("I think, therefore I am"), and from that basis of the knowing intellect (which is representative of all rational beings, particularly human beings) it can discern relationships and structures in phenomena and can therefore make predictions about the ways in which the world can be changed.

In the world of the intellect, structuralism assumes an inherent order in the universe or the particular phenomena under study. It also assumes a literal approach to text and object—that the text represents the world in a metonymic fashion. This order or set of structures can be known, and through such knowledge, the relationship of any individual piece of data to the whole can be assessed. From structuralism in literature, for example, come the ideas of genres, themes, myths, and archetypes. Structuralism is a world created on paper that then can be applied to the world outside of the book. Structuralism has had great effect on our knowledge and on our sciences. It is what allows for such taxonomies as those from Buffon and Mendeleev to be useful.

The Secularization of Religion

As with any generalization about an era, this one is dangerous, but there has been an increasing divorce of spiritual and secular learning that began with the Renaissance. Traditionally religious institutions such as the university became state or private institutions; religious trappings have remained with government functions, but they have been diluted. What had been important religious ceremonies have developed commercial aspects, and ceremonies that began as secular ones have taken on even more obvious commercial trappings. In the United States, Christmas, Valentine's Day, Mother's Day, and Halloween have become virtually indistinguishable over the loud din of ringing cash registers.

In addition, the churches have lost some of their social functions. They are no longer the sole place where marriages and funerals become sacramental. They are no longer the locus of charity; the National Football League is the largest private donor to the charity, the United Way. Parish life is no longer the center of civil life, and taxation has become the new form of tithe. (I shall return to many of these phenomena in the next chapter.)

Universalism

Universalism, or universality, is the set of beliefs growing out of the encyclopedist and scientific movements of the seventeenth and eighteenth centuries. The root ideas, however, are those of the Greek (and particularly the pre-Socratic) philosophers, those people who sought to posit universal laws of human behavior, government, economics, and even ways of doing science. As an ideology, universalism formed the intellectual side of imperialism and the secular side of the missionary movement. It can said to be the backbone of liberal thinking. This is a sort of thinking that makes publics, that treats people as groups, and that focuses on such concepts as the individual, society, law, or morality. Many have argued that it is peculiarly European, although one can see elements of it in the thinking of other cultures that assume a "self-centered focus," such as those of China and India.

As Mahmoud Hussein has written:

> The European Enlightenment ushered in a new conception of humanity, based on the idea that certain fundamental characteristics—the need for

individual autonomy and freedom, the ability to think for oneself by exercising the power of reason, the aspiration for progress—are common to all human beings. Over and above all differences of race, nationality, region, or class, the individual was acknowledged as belonging first and foremost to universal humanity.

This truly modern view of the individual seen independently of all his or her religious and social affiliations was developed in the West from the time of the Renaissance onwards and assumed its final form in the eighteenth century.[25]

Hussein goes on to argue that Europeans actually betrayed this idea in their dealings with their colonial administrators and subjects. In that context, the autonomous individual was strictly the European male. Still, the idea of the universal has persisted in much European thinking, particularly thinking in the social sciences and philosophy. It is the universal mind-set that helps create the idea of "the public."

Universalism has come to be challenged in the postcolonial world, although it still has a strong hold on thinking in its manifestation as the idea of "development," where all societies and cultures are seeking to be like the Eurocentric capitalist society. It has been challenged culturally, scientifically, and in many other ways. One form of the challenge is that of the "fundamentalists" of other religions and beliefs, those people who resist the European definition of democracy.

Paradoxically, one of the universal ideas that has arisen has been the idea of individualism. This is the idea that there are individual characteristics and natures as well as individual rights, and a necessary corollary is, that which is individual cannot be divided.

We turn to what cannot be divided, to the self (although psychiatrists have tried breaking it down while calling the integrated self the healthy person). A turn to the self has happened in literary criticism, in anthropology and other social sciences, and to a great extent in religion as well. But, the leap of faith is individual—it is the point of my conversion as an individual.

Just as in the material world the ideal in the United States has been the Horatio Alger hero, the individual who by luck or pluck can find success and salvation in the material world, similarly, in the world of the universal, the individual can find intellectual or spiritual success through absorption into the whole. But individualism and the self and consciousness of the self can become self-centeredness. We are centered on ourselves, of course, but being self-centered leads to narcissism.

Christopher Lasch and others have argued that individualism—
that quintessential American idea—masks narcissism and solipsism.[25]
Emerson's individual was an independent and interdependent member
of a community, not a narcissist. The right of the individual becomes
the right of me as opposed to all others. It is not anarchy but quite
the opposite. It asserts that what is universal is the self and the selfish
self at that. And capitalism's apologists from Hobbes on have argued
the virtue of self-interest, many of them citing—and perhaps misin-
terpreting—Jesus's second commandment, namely, "to love your
neighbor as you love yourself" (Matt. 22: 36–40).

The Response of Diversity in the World of Hypermedia

The increasing response to the idea of universality has built on the
idea of the individual and the particular but has radically modified the
universalist definition of the individual. In political, psychological,
social, and humanistic thinking, there has emerged a set of challenges
to the universal. Clearly a major set of challenges has come from the
so-called Third World, which has asserted its independence politically
and intellectually from the Eurocentric universal.

Although trapped by the economic power of the West, these
people have tended to throw off intellectual imperialism.

The Postmodern

We might define postmodernism as an age of counter-universalism,
counter-positivism, counter-secularism, counter-structuralism,
counter-materialism—which is to say, an age that rejects the domi-
nance of any one idea, movement, aesthetic, or text.

It is also a world in which we see certain assumptions challenged
and the realization that humans are creatures of habit. It is an age in
which we see the importance of the relationships we think of as
cultural and therefore different. There is a lack of linearity, but not a
simple relativism that posits some sort of unifying umbrella.

There may be an umbrella, but we are never sure that we can see it.

What are the new habits of the world of hypertext and nonlinear-
ity. How will they change us?

Counter-universalism. The postmodern age is one that looks at
differences, at marginality, and at the plurality of worlds. It tends to
accept such a plurality as preferable to any attempt to lump or people

or things together unwarrantedly. Thou shalt not "-ist" any one, postmodernists should cry, but unfortunately too many of them use universalizing labels.

Counter-nationalism. We have witnessed a breakdown of the nation-state in two distinct ways. The first is through nongovernmental organizations (NGOs) and multinational corporations. The second way nation-states are breaking down is through the rise of regional groupings or ethnic elements with the country that seek separatism of one kind or another. The first tends to lend itself more to the notion of hyperspace and the virtual community than does the second, although the second uses hyperspace as a means of gaining allegiance (witness the use of fax and e-mail for "revolutionary" purposes, be they revolutions of the right or the left).

Counter-structuralism. The poststructuralist position is one that views objects in a logocentric way but does not view them in terms of the Logos. One of the tenets of poststructuralism is the idea of difference, or distinction, and marginality. It leads to an examination of opposition, to a view of the text in terms of what is said and what is not said. It leads away from the page and toward the world lying off the page or in the white spaces as well as in the print. It also leads to an oppositional view of text and a view of text against text. It can be solipsistic in the extreme. But it is a view that enables one to disengage from the rigid literalism of the modern view.

Counter-materialism. A part of the counter-materialist movement is seen in the revolt against the large corporation and the attempts to resist domination by the multinationals. It is also seen in a distrust of the image that is projected in the secular world. The notion of liberation is partly a liberation from the economic power structure that appears so inexorable. It may be a failing attempt, but it is one that is being engaged in by a large number of intellectuals as well as people who would deride the intellectuals. It appears in the various ecological movements, in the resistance of many to television, in the home-schoolers, and in those who seek a variety of alternatives. It is a movement of the minority, but thanks to some of the non-mass media, it may become a movement of the majority.

Counter-secularism. There have been both liberal and conservative critiques of secularism, and the revival of the "religious [right's]", or the fundamentalists', attack on the secularization of the arts (the Salman Rushdie affair is a good case in point) has been a counter-secular force. This has had the effect of producing a new censorship that is related to an attack on the eroding notion of canonicity. Other evidence of the critique of secularism can be seen in the popularity of "new age" or "twelve-step" approaches that speak to a spiritual need. So, too, are Pentecostalism, Liberation Theology, and other forms of spirituality. The various experiences of the countries of the former Soviet Union have shown the latent spirituality and spiritual drive of people whom the modernists thought had been "freed from religion." This aspect of the postmodern is the focus of the next chapter.

Tying It All Together

I believe that many of these new cultural signs—the revolt against the masses, the rise of multiculturalism, the distrust of universalism, and the broad movement that is called postmodernism—are abetted by and accompany the technological changes that are signaled by hypertext and the non-mass media. Which is cause and which effect is difficult to say. Just as the Renaissance and the Reformation straddled the invention and development of printing and new forms of transportation and cartography, so these changes in our thinking and in our consciousness cross back and forth over particular inventions and developments.

I believe that there are forces seeking to retain the universal, mass, and modernist view of the world. These are the groups that seek to control, to retain the hub-and-spoke system, to retain the literal view of the world, and to retain a tight grip on culture and the various forms of expression. They would not like readers and viewers in cyberspace to be coauthors. They want to retain the libraries, because that is where knowledge lies. They want to retain copyright, because that makes the workings of the writer private property appropriate to commercial development. Their grip may remain for a few more years, perhaps, but I think it will be forced to disappear in reality if not in law. The so-called "pirates" will have too easy a time, and their creation of a new order will bring about a multitude of particular uses of goods and objects as well as of ideas and the arts.

CHAPTER SIX

Suspended in the Web of God

As I have worked through my understanding of the changes that have been wrought in our consciousness by the advent of hypertext, I have frequently referred to religious practices. I have done so for reasons both intellectual and personal. The intellectual reason I have set forth earlier in saying that the changes in our consciousness reflect changes in theological consciousness because so much of our world has for so long been affected by if not conditioned by religious practices. I argue this with particular respect to literacy, which, directed by the habit of scripture, is a set of practices using text and thinking about text and being part of a textual and now a hypertextual society. I shall return to this point at the end of the chapter. Now, I want to turn to the reciprocal, the influence of hypertext on our consideration of our religious nature and practices in the postmodern world

The personal reason is that, in writing this book, I wish to bring together the world of my intellectual life and the world of my spiritual life. I wish to seek and share a sense of harmony. So, let me turn directly to religious practice, and begin briefly with mine to set the stage, then move to a brief history of the Church and an exploration of its new directions in the world of hypertext.

A CHURCH: THE IDEA OF ECCLESIOLOGY

I go to church; in fact, for my particular church in upstate New York I am a warden, one of the lay people charged with the care of the church building, finances, and activities. I have gone to church since I was a child. Nearly all the churches I attended were part of the Episcopalian denomination, the American offshoot of the Church of

England, that church that seceded from Roman denomination at the time of Henry VIII—but did not count itself a part of the Protestant Reformation. I should qualify this profession of faith by saying that I attended two non-Episcopalian but church-related schools, a Quaker school from grades 1 through 5 and a nondenominational Protestant school in grades 10 through 12 with required Christian chapel for all students, regardless of their faith. In both institutions, I had to attend the worship service—Wednesday meeting at the Quaker school and daily assembly (with prayer) and Sunday service at the high school. There was a period during college when I did not go to church, and there has been a period in my adult life when, for geographic reasons, I attended a Methodist church where I lived. In the summers I am involved in a nondenominational chapel and even conduct one of its services. I am also involved with certain church-related groups and organizations, and I am a "member" or at least a subscriber to the First Church of Cyberspace. I am enrolled in a four-year course in Education for Ministry and have been trained to be a mentor in the same program. But during all this and for all my life, I have considered myself simultaneously a Christian, a member of the Episcopal denomination, and a member of a particular church congregation.

For me, as for many, the word *church* is multifaceted. A church is an *ecclesia*, a gathering together of people for the purpose of worship, and ecclesiology is the term used for studying and defining the structure of churches, denominations, and sects. A church is a building. A church is also a group that in worshipping employs scripture and ceremony. As I wrote this chapter, there was a wave of bombings of church buildings in the United States. Many have noted that it is not churches that are bombed but church buildings. The church, even the church with a particular name like St. Paul's Church, exists whether its building stands or falls.

Church is, to go back to a theme I have discussed earlier, the word we use for the continuity of a particular form of scripture across time and space. It is that which contains the scripture and defines the ceremony. It may be more or less organized. Some churches, like the independent storefront Pentecostal churches, are small, independent, and intimate, seeing themselves as unique in time and space; others, like the Roman Catholic Church, are broad-based and have elaborate administrative and fiscal structures similar to those of a huge multinational corporation. "The Christian Church" is used as a metaphoric term for the Church universal, the large umbrella covering the diverse churches that bind themselves to one another by avowing a belief in the divinity of Jesus—although they may disagree as to how they define that divinity. A similar loose definition of *church* could apply to the different kinds of Judaism, Islam, or Buddhism, but the term is usually reserved for Christianity for historical reasons. It is the universal identity that is dissolving before our eyes.

A church was seen in earlier times as a physical gathering that engaged in the ceremony of worship; for Christians it was notably the Eucharistic meal. When St. Paul and St. John wrote to the churches, they were writing to discrete groups of people in particular places, who had probably no fixed meeting place (given the temper of the times), gathering in various houses or other places marked with the icon of the fish or the cross to disguise it from hostile neighbors. Thanks to writing and later print, the church grew beyond a set of semi-isolated gathering places into a network connected by a common text, the Gospels. By having a text that was common across places and by having an organizational structure to the ceremonies that was written and so could be followed and replicated in many different places, the church grew from a gathering place to a religion or a denomination.

A denomination is a subgroup of a religion of the book (to use Jack Goody's phrase)[1] that remains tied to other denominations in sharing both a sacred text and a set of preferred ceremonies that have been codified and, in many cases, written down in a manual of practices. Thus, we can see denominational differences in Orthodox and Reform Judaism or in Catholic or Methodist Christianity. They may share the same basic text, whether the Torah or the Old and New Testaments, but have differing manuals that define the scriptural practices of the denomination. A sect is a denomination that tends to set itself further apart from other groups and is seen as being bigoted in its separateness; it is the pejorative alternative to "denomination."

Most of the denominations have a governing body that adjudicates disputes and sets policy concerning belief and practice. These bodies have at times been strong and decisive about a variety of issues of belief or issues in society. Recently, however, they have come under attack and are faltering. Many of today's denominations are ill defined in the sense that their walls are porous and their sense of missions occluded. A part of their transformation may be in the growth of the home church movement and of televangelism, both of which affect the "mainstream" churches. In *A Generation of Seekers*, Wade Roof suggests other manifestations of the transformation of the larger (or mainstream) denomination, such as the "new age" spiritualities, the various pentecostal movements, and the twelve-step programs.[2]

These ideas had been prefigured in the mid-1950s by H. Richard Niebuhr in *Christ and Culture*, particularly where he writes that our religious decisions are made

> on the basis of relative insight and faith, but they are not relativistic. They are individual decisions but not individualistic. They are made in freedom, but not in independence; they are made in the moment, but are not nonhistorical.
>
> They depend on the partial, incomplete, fragmentary knowledge of the individual; they are relative to the measure of his faith and his unbelief; they are related to the historical position he occupies and to the duties of his station in society; they are concerned with the relative values of things.[3]

Both Niebuhr and Roof argue that some of the broad, firm structures of both church and denomination no longer are holding, yet the religious impulse is still strong though diffuse. The picture they paint is similar to the one that I described in Chapter 1 when citing Loren Mead's discussion in *The Once and Future Church*.[4] It is an age of uncertainty about the firmness of structures and principles as well as institutions that is a part of the postmodern malaise. It is a time when the principles that led to the rise and power of the denominations have come under the same sort of challenge that hypertext has brought to literacy and postmodernism to other intellectual and social structures. How they will respond and what new shapes the religious impulse will take is the subject of the rest of this chapter.

DENOMINATIONS UNDER QUESTION

Like many other institutions of our times, the Christian denominations and, to some extent, their Islamic and Judaic counterparts developed over a long period and burgeoned in their present form in the nineteenth century. There were splits and divisions among the Christian groups that led in the late fourth century to the division between the Eastern and Western churches of Byzantium and Rome. Some of these and later splits resulted from language divisions as much as they did from differences in doctrine. But despite these splits or

within them the denominations tended to develop a single hierarchical structure that paralleled the imperial and later the national structures of politics. It is this kind of structure that has come under attack
from a variety of sources.

Denominations as Religious Cultures

Can we talk of a religious culture, such as the culture of Islam, or
Judaism, or Christianity? There are, indeed, ties within these religious groups, just as there are among Buddhists or Hindus. They tend
to be public ties, but they tend not to form a spiritual community.
They are probably fractionated. And they seem to have been separated from the broader culture that is seen as national and from the
elitist culture that for the past century has tended to echo the
Marxist view that religion is the opiate of the masses. In doing so,
they have perpetuated a paradoxical situation. Stephen Carter has
done an excellent job in documenting the ways by which official
policy has tended to promote a curious dissociation of religion from
schooling and therefore from the culture as a whole.[5] The schools
and other official and semi-official bodies have kept some of the
ceremonies of religion—such as a religiously oriented calendar—and
have retained some religious documents in the canon of the library,
but the official posture has tended to deny the religious impetus and
any serious commitment. Christmas music in the malls does not
create a theocratic culture. The culture of "the masses" is tepidly
secular. The religious soul is in the minority.

What the Denominations Built

The Roman Church, to take the major Western Christian example,
developed an elaborate hierarchical structure that connected the
remotest parish or monastery to the local hub, the Diocese of the
Bishop or Abbot General, and thence to the Archdiocese or Province,
and through the College of Cardinals (most of whom were also Bishops
or Archbishops) to the Pope in Vatican City. It was a network with a
single center, and it was a network that could be clearly seen as an
hierarchy. At many points in its history, it blended or fused the
spiritual and the temporal.

Communication was primarily one-way. Written documents were
promulgated in Rome and sent out. Appeals were made through the

hierarchy to Rome. At times, local groups that sought some form of autonomy were declared as heretical and were routed out through a variety of means, including wars of extermination. The system worked despite a fair amount of corruption, which was purged occasionally. It worked because it depended on a scribal hierarchy that controlled the production and dissemination of information to a less literate populace. This group had the additional advantage of being literate in the common tongue of the hierarchy, Latin, which remained the language of power as well as the language of the Bible.

With the advent of printing and the spread of literacy, that sort of hierarchical control could be and was circumvented. Although some translators of vernacular Bibles like William Tyndale were killed as heretics for their pains, Martin Luther escaped such a fate and found himself the leader of a new denomination. Thanks to Luther, the printed vernacular Bible could circulate among the people without the intervention of a priest or scribe. All it took was a literate audience, not a learned one. So it was with the aid of print that a variety of new denominations arose from the end of the fifteenth through the nineteenth centuries. Each one had a version of scriptural activity; each one claimed a number of adherents. Some remained local and others developed into hierarchies not unlike that of Rome.

Several of these denominations spread across languages, national borders, and even continents. They did so through the process of promulgation and translation of the central texts of the denomination, namely, its particular version of the Bible and the manual for worship, or turning the text into scripture. This process of evangelism tended to follow national trade and exploration to the New World, so that different denominations came to dominate the lands where the colonials spread. We thus have a complex network of denominations in the postcolonial world that are vestiges of larger national networks of trade or conquest.

Although the system of control differs from denomination to denomination, there remains a pattern of unity and uniformity of scriptural practice from individual church to individual church. A person can go into the church of a particular denomination in any part of the world on a given Sunday and find close to the same service with the same Biblical readings. The language might change, but scripture as an activity does not. This uniformity extends through a large number of the denominations, and although a few such as the Society of Friends, or Quakers, deliberately include individual worship in their meeting, structure there remains a vestigial hierarchical form of governing among the various meetings.

The Modernist Gain

The system of the denominations has generally worked well. Splinter groups that might form would develop their own hierarchical structure as the church membership spread. Others would often die out. It was a Darwinian situation that appeared to work, and it worked well in the modernist world with its system of hubs and spokes and its approach of universalism. All Roman Catholics were considered the same and treated the same way ostensibly. It was, of course, a system that rode roughshod over the particular nature of the group practicing the religion. No matter where the church might be, for example, the Anglican Christmas pageant would feature a winter setting with snow around and the animals resembling those on a typical Sussex farm.

This aspect of denominational activity adapted itself easily to the modernist idea of universalism. The evangelicals, in particular, saw themselves as promoting a Church Universal that was the same in whatever climate and with whatever people. Only the language of the text would change, but not the concepts. Although the denominational system appeared to work well structurally, it has proved unable to survive a number of attacks from other facets of the modernist world. Certainly one of the negative forces has been the modernist practice of secularizing institutional religion. During the nineteenth century and into this one, the churches steadily lost control of a variety of social institutions that they had under their wing. Schools and universities, hospitals, homes for the poor and for the aging devolved to the state, which appeared to be more democratic and available to all than the various denominations.

If the denominations began to become irrelevant to certain previous social involvements, the theology also tended to become more suspect. Like other intellectuals, theologians have long both led and followed the history of ideas and changes in consciousness. In the course of twentieth-century thinking, theologians followed in the structuralist tradition and tended to develop a universal theology that was as "scientific" as were the other branches of learning. Paul Tillich was the great architect of systematic theology—the title of his treatise on the subject.

God was to be put on paper and objectified and treated as though

He were a map, just as were animals, language, the stars, governments, and all other phenomena. But to put God on paper is to kill God. As Wordsworth wrote in the early nineteenth century, "We murder to dissect." In the process of systematizing theology and putting God in a text, people began also to analyze the Testaments as texts as well and subjecting them to the varieties of objectifying textual criticism that they applied to poems, novels, and constitutions. The Testaments as well as other religious texts have long been known to be a combination of myth and history. Disentangling the two versions of truth is a dangerous business if you see the various ways of reading a text as antithetical rather than complementary. So, the search for the historical record became separated from the spiritual journey of a believing people. And the search for that record and the historical Jesus can also lead people to say that they are killing God.

God is indeed dead if He can be dissected and analyzed. And the idea of the Death of God permeated the late 1950s and early 1960s, the heyday of modernism.

THE POSTMODERN NEW ECCLESIA

Although Harvey Cox attempted to resurrect God and to reconcile belief and modernism in *The Secular City*, it was not just an intellectual revolution but a concatenation of forces in the past decades that have changed the nature and structure of the denominations and of the religious impulse that helps to define the human race.[6] Without going into great detail on any of them, I would cite: the changes in civil consciousness; decolonization and the development of indigenous states; the rise of multiculturalism; the horrors of war; the rise of women and deep ecology and a host of other controversial accompaniments to the postmodern world and the world of hypertext. All of these serious matters have been roiling during the course of this century, and the idea of cause and effect or a distinct chronological chain is hard to establish. Let us begin by considering the background of textual change.

The Loss of Text and the Lapse of Liturgy

The denominations had going for them a scriptural tradition, a way of combining text and ceremony that enabled continuity and the sense of stability if not a sense of touch with the eternal. But for many it was seen as old. Such was particularly true of those religions and denominations that used a nonvernacular language as the language of scripture. It tended to set people off from the text. There is clearly a tension between the continued liturgy—which has become to some an image and to others a vestige—and those liturgical forms that are "from the spirit." The denominations had the strength of tradition and a liturgy and set of ceremonies that went back beyond print to the time of early writing and scripture. But these liturgical traditions did not appeal to a large segment of the population, which wanted to find a new form of worship. This shift is liturgical but also both textual and scriptural. Such was particularly the case with members of any denomination who lived far from the seat of power.

In the 1960s the Roman Catholic Church made the biggest break with scriptural tradition of all in giving up Latin. That alone set forth changes that have become irrevocable. On the one hand, it allowed scripture to become acclimated to the new populations; on the other hand, it tended to allow them to redefine scripture and thus to redefine worship in ways that tended to be highly disruptive of the denominational fabric.

One of the most interesting examples of this sort of tension has been occurring over the past thirty years within the Episcopalian Church. It is an example that is paralleled in other denominations. Up until the mid-1960s, the central document of the church was the 1928 *Book of Common Prayer*. This book was a descendant of the first such book, produced in the sixteenth century by Thomas Cranmer. In this book were the text of the major and minor services, the psalms (one of which was to be read at each service), and the passages of the Bible to be read on each Sunday. There was also a perpetual calendar and a copy of the historical documents of the Episcopal Church. The *Book of Common Prayer* was indeed a book, a self-contained text that included all that was necessary for the people to participate in the liturgy. The book was such that people read it as a book (if not going through it from beginning to end, at least using it as a common reference). Each Sunday, everyone across the nation was at the same point in the book. This pattern of uniformity was followed in many denominations, both Christian and Jewish.

In the 1960s, it was decided to produce a new edition of the book. This was at a time when there was also a desire to reconnect with the Roman Catholic and Eastern traditions and to seek to incorporate some of the flavor of early Christian services that had been unearthed or rediscovered. After several years of trials and tentative editions, a new *Book of Common Prayer* was released. The volume retains the historical documents, the psalms, and the calendars. But for many of the services the new "Book of Common Prayer" contains both a traditional version (which is close to the original) and "new" versions of them. The new versions contain alternative sections or a variety of other options.

The "new" *Book of Common Prayer* is not a book—nor is it common. It is close to a catalog, an anthology, perhaps a hypertext. It exists as a hypertext on some Web sites, in fact. It is a volume that is not to be read but to be selected from. Today, there is no surety that everyone across the nation will indeed be reading the same things—except the psalm and Bible passages appointed for the day, and even these are set in a three-year rather than an annual cycle. The result is an uncommon hypertext of which each parish priest each Sunday—and every other day of the week—coauthors the scripture.

Without a central authoritative text, the priests and lay people have become free to create their own services. This lack of textual authority, has been accompanied by a change in the nature of ecclesiastical authority as well.

This shift is paralleled in other denominations and sects, as well, where a common text, be it a prayer book or translation of a sacred text, is lacking. The only common text is that to be found in every hotel and motel room in the nation.

Multiculturalism and Liberation

With the breakup of the old political empires, the denominations have had to struggle to adapt to the new way of doing things. There was no longer a political counterpart to the religious structure. Some denominations had already established a loose federation rather than an empire, and the result seemed relatively effective. Other denominations had created a hierarchy that itself became reified and was seen as more important than the reality that it represented. It assumed that there was a necessary connection and line of authority emanating from the seat of power down to the individual church and the individual worshipper. The denomination, the Church with a capital C, was the true church.

In many parts of the world racial and social tensions strained the denominations. Too often they were politically vested with the power groups rather than with the people. Such was true in the American

South during the struggle for civil rights; such was also the case in Latin America, Africa (particularly South Africa), and Asia.

One response was that of a group of Jesuits in the 1960s and 1970s. This group began to develop the idea of the base community. The village was a unit that cohered. It could organize itself, provide its own social services, and direct its liturgy at the issues that most pertained to the people. The Jesuits saw the virtues in a network of small units rather than a hierarchy. Like much of the civil rights movement and other causes of the day, it was a grassroots approach to social and religious problems. Theologically it appeared to recapture the flavor of early Christianity and the beginnings of other religions— small, local, intimate, addressed to the needs of the particular. Through the particular it could rise to a sense of the divine. Liberation theology paralleled liberation pedagogy.[7] Just as the individual reader coauthors and thus authorizes the text, so the individual worshipper or participant in the base community reconstrues the church, redefines the ecclesia as a coauthor in the larger network of worship rather than as a recipient of the hierarchical truth and structure. Both connect the immediate and present experience to the larger tradition.

At first the Vatican encouraged the growth of the movements and the principles of Liberation Theology, but it has since come to see how disruptive of the hierarchical structure change can be and has sought to minimize it. But, if that movement has lost momentum, a larger movement to give more power to indigenous dioceses is growing. These recognize that, for example, the United States Church is not the same as the Nigerian Church or the Nigerian Church the same as the Zambian Church. Problems, issues, practices, and even scriptures may vary. How far this divestiture of authority will go and how soon it will move farther will be interesting to watch.

The Fracturing of the Denominations into Sects

Even within a nation or a culture, there has emerged a variety of single-issue groups. Both inside and outside the denominations and the churches, certain issues are political and social foci. Sexuality and abortion are clearly important issues in the United States. The environment is also an issue for some, as may be the care of the poor or the homeless. Around these issues have emerged certain interest groups, and the denominations have been far from immune to the rise of such groups. These groups seek to control the agenda of a denomination, and on these issues the very foundation of the denomination may be seen to rest. Those taking one side or another may also see that orthodoxy is under attack.

The classic distinction between denomination and sect asserts that the denomination is the unifying phenomenon and the sect a fractionating one. There appears to be a proliferation of sects based upon the increasing diversity of feelings, opinions, doctrines, social issues, and the like. These sects appear to be like spaces on a hypertext: one can trace their connections through elaborate networks, but they remain distinct boxes, spaces, rooms in hyperspace. It is hard to find the web easily, for at one level there are no links between the web sites of the sectarian groups on one side of an issue and those of the groups on the other side.

The sects often run the risk of believing they are the whole of hyperspace, that their icon is the reality and the truth. Their particular view tends to force others out, and the struggle for control of denominations is bitter. It may finally dissolve the denominations into sects that can only bite their own tails.

Pentecostalism

As Harvey Cox has observed in his latest work, *Fire from Heaven*, the pentecostal movement began in California at the beginning of the twentieth century and is one of the most powerful of movements in this century. Primarily Christian, it has its counterparts in other religions, notably Judaism and Islam.[8]

Pentecostalism is broadly defined as the belief in the possession of the human by the Spirit of God. It is a nonrational, nonmodern fire in the soul that produces a number of effects, ranging from a sense of devotion to the deity to speaking in tongues or other manifestations. It tends to be individual, although it can work on a group, and for many it can be contagious. It works less through the media than through personal contact. It does, however, use the non-mass media. There was a song of the 1920s, "Hello Central, Give Me Heaven." Was this a way of reaching the divine, a direct communication that might have helped expand the pentecostal movement?

Pentecostalism is directed at individual salvation rather than salvation of the group, and it leaves the individual in an ambiguous relationship to the traditional church. It is often related to the term *evangelical.* The theological historian R. G. Hutcheson distinguishes three types of evangelicals: the fundamentalists, the charismatics or Pentecostals, and the neoevangelicals.[9]

The fundamentalists are a group of evangelicals who tend to differ from the neoevangelicals and the charismatics in their emphasis on literalism in interpretation and on an antiscience perspective. They also tend to take sanctification further than do neo-evangelicals and extend it to various forms of behavior. They tend to be people who rely on the concept of sola scriptura. This is the group that finds its strength in modernism and its approach to text, to society, and to the world.

The neoevangelicals represent the broad movement toward evangelism within a denomination, and they are less identifiable as a group than the other two.

The charismatics or Pentecostals are the spearhead of the new churches. They have spread throughout the world, and there are large numbers of pentecostal churches in Latin America and Asia, particularly Korea. In Latin America, as Harvey Cox tells us, they have assumed the mantle of liberation theology and have established of base communities; not so in Korea, where they are highly conservative politically.

Pentecostals are also the group that appears to be most in tune with hypertext and the new view of literacy. Following from the idea that the individual receives the Holy Spirit or the divine inspiration directly and is thus empowered, the charismatic view coincides with the view of the reader as author or coauthor. The text is not outside but rather what I read and therefore in me. When the charismatic reads the gospel, she is highly aware that she is the reader, she is an empowered spiritual person engaging with the Word of God, not following what she reads as if it were a map but responding to it as it strikes sympathetic chords in her mind and soul. The Word, although divine, is only what I know and see; it is filtered through my consciousness. The charismatic is also not averse to images, because the idea of the vision, the image of God in and through the Word, come together. Word and icon, image and text, are all stimuli to the religious and divine spark of knowing that is my consciousness.

The Denominations Respond: A New Orthodoxy

With the alienation of the denomination from the culture has come a new orthodoxy within many individual churches and within divinity schools. In several denominations this orthodoxy has led to some of the schools becoming associated with particular sets of beliefs and making their students and graduates toe the line of those beliefs or else go to another school.

It has been asserted that theological and social speculation appear to be declining in the face of a new move toward a centrist orthodoxy in the denominations, but this claim may be an illusion, or it may be that there are calculated attempts on the part of some denominations to grab the center and not take a stand on some of the concerns of the fragmenting culture surrounding the denomination.

The broad church liberal-rational consensus seems to have been eroding, certainly in the issues concerning social justice. It is becoming increasing difficult for the denominations to hold firm to their liberal beliefs in the face of declining parishes and church attendance in the inner city and rural areas. By holding on to these beliefs they may lose parishioners and a broad base of support, and they may find themselves beset with division. Gender and race are part of this division, but also clearly sexuality and social justice generally (e.g., the issue of building new prisons). The issues of social justice as they are expressed within the denominations may be seen to mask the issue of social control and power. A new sort of ecclesia appears to be in order. Perhaps the denominations are up to a redefinition of their role. Certainly some appear less resistant than others. It would seem incumbent upon them to redefine themselves as ecclesia in order to fit into the new world of hypertext.

Postevangelism

There has been appearing over the past decade or so a new type of religious person, what is called the postevangelical.[10] These are people who are dissatisfied with the rigid modernism of the evangelicals and wish to find a spiritual life that acknowledges the facts of the post-modern world. In England, which is the focus of Tomlinson's book—although parallels abound in other parts of the world—they participate in churches in pubs, open their arms to people who are different or outcast in one of a number of ways, are willing to countenance people from different religions as sharing in their faith as well as their scripture. They view the Bible as a hypertext, not a map, and coauthor it in a number of ways. This group seems to me to be the group that most clearly has taken the world of the new media and of hypertext into the realm of worship (see Figure 6.1).

Doonesbury   BY GARRY TRUDEAU

FIGURE 6.1. The church and the new media. "Doonesbury" © 1996 by G. B. Trudeau. Reprinted with permission of Universal Press Syndicate. All rights reserved.

New Ecclesia: From Hierarchies to Networks

Many recent studies of church membership have spoken of a decline of the traditional denominations and the rise of new pentecostal or evangelical churches, churches only loosely tied to denominations. They are local, independent, and at the same time spreading. One thinks of such movements as the Vineyard, the Promise Keepers, or the new pentecostal churches. One also thinks of the megachurches and the postevangelical churches such as Tomlinson's "Holy Joe's," which meets in a London pub.

These movements are similar to those that burgeoned in the world of television, and we see them in various media efforts. But they appear to be more closely related to the new information networks and to hypertextual presentation of scripture rather than the traditional mass media. The world of the televangelist broadcast to the masses may have fallen less as a result of scandal and more because of the failure of the medium in the face of the new non-mass medium of hyperspace.

The reconfiguration of the churches appears to have taken on two forms that are often confused. Both of them come from the idea of the shopping mall, that image of transportation and communication in our society. One sort of church is the church that is itself a shopping mall. There have emerged a number of "megachurches," church institutions that will have a complete array of worshipping styles under one roof and simultaneously. These churches may have a large traditionally shaped church space, but there may also be an auditorium, playrooms, places for encounter groups of one kind or another, church classrooms, and other activities. The whole is planned to provide a spiritual reality for a consumer culture so that one may enter the theme-world and at the same time find one's particular niche in it. The discussion of those who run these churches is of the audience, the customers, the mass who attend. They are differentiated according to taste and interest, but they are treated as consumers of religion. These mall churches appear to be as carefully programmed as the churches of television, whose popularity is still strong but perhaps waning as people resist being a part of the mass audience. Within this new ministry is the television minister. Some television evangelists use images of the traditional church; others use images of the home, office, or talk show.

A second image of the mall church is one of the franchise, in which the people come together in a small and specialized Pentecostal or charismatic church, which may have a relatively small number of members. There this people enacts a scripture. They are an important focal point for their own community and the immediate neighborhood. They are local. But they are loosely connected to other similar locals. This is like the individual store in a mall, which is independent of the larger mall; its connection is to the similar stores in other malls rather than to the other stores in the mall.

In the megachurch, if the customer does not like the formal setting, he simply goes out of that church space into the room next door, where there is intimate meditation. In the franchise church, the people come because they are attracted to that franchise, not to the whole mall, and they know that if they go to another community, they will find a similar but not identical franchise outlet. The franchises are locally owned and controlled and will have their individual stamp on them, but there will also be the link of the same type of scriptural activity.

The Impetus behind the New Ecclesia

There seems to be a tendency toward spiritual renewal and those aspects of "60s" spirituality that have begun to permeate the center churches. Cursillo, meditation, Faith Alive, the Alpha Course, marriage encounters, and the like tend to bring a new idea of the spiritual to bear. These movements bear a resemblance to pentecostalism that is both inside and outside the "established" church hierarchies. They also bear a resemblance to the search for new communities within the established ecclesia.

These newer groups seek to create not an extension of the church but a new ecclesia. Some of the characteristics of this new ecclesia include:

- With regard to text, the principle of the reliability and final authority of the textual tradition in matters of faith and practice is emphasized rather than the literalist authority of sola scriptura.
- With regard to doctrine, key features include: the centrality of personal faith in Christ as the savior and of commitment to Him; the belief in sanctification without a belief in taboo; an interest in social concerns; a friendliness to science and to other forms of religious expression such as Buddhism, Hinduism, or shamanism.
- With regard to organization, there is a separation of clergy and laity but a joint responsibility to witness and a shared priesthood; the churches tend not to be hierarchical (i.e., with bishoprics and a variety of orders), but rather are joined in a network rather than a hierarchy.
- An adaptation of the idea of the base community and liberation theology generally puts the churches in opposition to forces of development, which are seen as undermining community integrity or self-sufficiency or as downright exploitative, an idea engendered by a greater public consciousness.

All of these signs suggest that there is occurring in contemporary religious structures a diminution of power by the central office of the church and perhaps even by the papacy and bishoprics. The congregational community—replacing the traditional geographically bound parish—may reassert itself as the primary ecclesiastical unit, in which case the network among congregations may further evolve and strengthen. Finally, the distinction between clergy and laity may fade as all participate in a coauthoring ministry.

Both God and religion are far from dead. There are a number of signs of growth in a whole variety of spiritual and religious institutions, but they appear to differ greatly from those that are familiar in the history of the church. They appear to be part of a new Reformation, different in nature but similar in force to that which followed the invention of the printing press and the vernacular Bible.

This reformation is less concerned with changing the old institutions of the denominations than with forging a new church, so that we may think of it as a new ecclesiology rather than a change in the traditional ones.

Like the earlier reformation, this one is seeking to return to the roots of faith and to recapture the spiritual quest that was part of the origins of the religions of the Book. It is concerned with the enthusiasm of the earlier churches and is less concerned with some of their issues or with forging a new administrative superstructure along the imperial model.

The new ecclesia are only in part religions of the Book; they are primarily religions of the new media. Brought into being in the age of the telephone and the early film, the new ecclesia have spread thanks to radio and television, and they are religions of the hypertext rather than the text. Many of these new ecclesia have developed intricate web sites, such as those of The First Church of Cyberspace or the groups in and around local churches or synagogues or temples.

The Twelve Traditions as a Model for the New Ecclesia

We may see in such organizations as Alcoholics Anonymous one possible typology of the new ecclesia. The organization is loose. It is, perhaps, ill structured, and it is not hierarchical. Each meeting is independent, and although the liturgical structure is the same, it is varied in that it is participatory, not dictated by a priest or by a text. It is scriptural, but the scripture is hypertext, and the ceremony allows for individual authoring and coauthoring.

An individual may enter a meeting anywhere and be welcomed, but the individual is not attached to the physical location of the meeting or even to the same people. It is a drop-in ecclesia. In this respect, it lends itself perfectly to the idea of the virtual community. The bulletin board or the group is the virtual ecclesium to which people may attach themselves for a period and share space–time either synchronously or at different times.

In considering the "franchise church" and the ecclesiastical model it embodies, no better example of the structure comes to mind than Alcoholics Anonymous, which is the first among hundreds of models of the new and dynamic ecclesiology. It is, of course, known for the establishment of the "Twelve-Step Program," a superb way of enabling people who are in bondage to a particular addiction to move away from that bondage without denying its existence. Perhaps less well known than the twelve steps are the parallel Twelve Traditions, which define the organization's structure and thus have enabled it to become the powerful worldwide church that it is. Here is a somewhat paraphrased version of the Twelve Traditions:

1. Our common welfare should come first, the personal depends upon unity.
2. For our group purpose there is but one ultimate authority—a loving God. Our leaders are trusted servants; they do not govern.
3. The only requirement for membership is a desire to stop drinking.
4. Each group should be autonomous.
5. Each group has but one purpose [evangelism] to the alcoholic.
6. A group should never lend its name to an outside enterprise.
7. Every group should be self-supporting.
8. It should remain nonprofessional.
9. It should never be organized, but may have service boards.
10. There is no connection to other issues (the group does not participate in public controversy).
11. Public relations are based on attraction rather than promotion.
12. Anonymity is the spiritual foundation of traditions, principles come before personalities.

These might as well be the principles of base communities in liberation theology, of the house church, of Cursillo, of prayer and Bible groups. They are the basis for so much of the reorganization of religious institutions. Counter to the traditional view of the church as a centralized religious structure, they offer an alternative in which the scripture is the basis of a local activity. They dispute received interpretations, such as those conveyed through councils and fiats, or strict interpretations such as that upon which the idea of sola scriptura is based where the text is an object, not the center of an activity.

The new ecclesiology asserts clearly that scripture is an activity, a humanly constructed set of ceremonies around a text that is conceived as a hypertext, where the words and the icons are fused. The scripture is text, icon, activity, and the participants reconstruct it in their communal images. Rather than being one text handed down from a central agency, it is multiple, multifaceted, and re-created continually at the local and communal level. The scripture of any one congregation, any one church, is connected to that of any other— connected by the distant authority of words—but at the same time always re-created at the local level.

This reconfiguration of scriptural activity is enabled by the new media, which help diverse people around the world create indigenous churches that are connected to one another in a series of networks rather than through one of a number of hierarchical hubs. Such a reconfiguration must be accompanied by a rethinking of what it is to have or to share in a doctrine, for the very idea of doctrine seems threatened by hypertext and the new world of information.

THE IDEA OF DOCTRINE IN A WORLD OF HYPERTEXT

In theology as well as in many other forms of intellectual life, the question of doctrine looms large. A doctrine is what is taught; therefore, it has come to be thought of as that set of principles or beliefs that are important or even essential to be taught as the basis for other beliefs and for action.

We often tend to think of doctrine as belonging to the realm of religion. The reason for this is that the religious institution and the school were closely allied for centuries, so that what was taught had a religious bent. The school was the place for ideas about the nature of God, sin, belief, and the good life to be presented to the young so that they could be in*doctrin*ated. In early Christian circles the newly converted became catechumens, those who were to receive instruction. The term means "the instructed," just as *doctor* and *doctrine* come from the Latin, meaning "to teach." In the Christian world, both teaching and learning and the matter to be taught or learned were seen in religious terms. But the terms are broader today. We refer to a variety of people, not just the religious, as being doctrinaire or as establishing or following a doctrine. Secular doctrines abound as the principles behind various disciplines.

Secular and Spiritual Doctrines

What is a doctrine? As I said above, it is what is taught, but doctrine is not simply the facts. It is the set of principles or, to use the currently fashionable term, theories by which a particular group is supposed to look at the world. There is something called Marxist doctrine, as well as neo-Marxist doctrine, feminist Marxist or materialist feminist doctrine, womanist doctrine, conservative doctrine, Freudian doctrine— the list could go on and on.

I subscribe to a doctrine that the various media, the extensions of man (to use Marshall McLuhan's term), do indeed affect how we live and work and even think. I also subscribe to the psychological doctrine that the human mind is active, not merely the passive recipient of stimuli. I subscribe to Darwinian doctrines, the doctrines of plate tectonics and the "Big Bang theory," the doctrine of relativity, and the doctrine that our lives and perceptions both shape and are shaped by patterns.

In a sense, I survive in part because I subscribe to doctrines. Doctrines, like conventions, help me get through the day and the year. They help me plan. But there are many doctrines (like those related to various "isms") that are not necessary to my survival. They are more like a set of beliefs or values. Political and social doctrines would figure into this group, as would artistic or personal ones.

Then there are religious doctrines. These are the principled beliefs of a religion or a denomination. They may be called the "Articles of Faith," as in the Anglican Church, or the Creed, the Deuteronomic Code, or The Way. They may be relatively simple or complex.

The Validity of Doctrines

One major issue concerning doctrine in the current age is that of validity. Hypertext seems to challenge the traditional notions of validity, for validity is found not in the author or the text, but in the reader, the creative soul who is authoring, spinning a web of understanding of the religious text, who is making a complex scripture. How is doctrine asserted in the face of what appears to be a set of conflicting ideas and beliefs?

In *The Nature of Doctrine*, the noted theologian G. A. Lindbeck argues that, from its own premises, theological doctrine can be thought of as based on the propositions of rational argument and the truth claims that the doctrine makes, on the felt experiences of believers (which have an expressive or existential truth regardless of their rationality), or on a combination of the two.[11]

Like Lindbeck, I question both the propositional approach and the expressive approach and opt for a new approach, which I would call psychosocial. That approach is one rooted in the idea of culture. Although either of the first two can be asserted within a given culture or philosophical milieu, there can be difficulties in reconciling doctrines that come from quite different ways of seeing and thinking about the world. The propositional and the expressive approaches have the failing of claiming a universality that may not be appropriate to them in an age where the monolithic nature of universals is challenged. The two approaches run the risk of letting doctrine become an idol, a map for the world that may tend to shape our thinking about the world in such a way that we idolize the doctrine rather than what it is supposed to illuminate. That is what being doctrinaire is all about. The idol of the propositional approach is the structure on paper; the idol of the expressive approach is the solipsistic self.

Lindbeck argues that a cultural–linguistic approach to doctrine makes sense both intellectually and theologically.[12] Becoming religious is analogous to learning a language, or becoming literate. We do not learn language, we learn New England American English or Puerto Rican Spanish. Similarly we learn to read certain kinds of texts in certain places as part of a particular literate community. Only incidentally do we become "literate." So, too, with doctrine and religion: there are specific local circumstances that always mediate the religious instinct. We become a particular sort of Evangelical Christian or Reform Jew rather than simply religious, just as we learn a particular dialect of a particular language. It is a communal phenomenon that shapes the subjectivity of the individual. That is why it is important for me to have begun this chapter as well as this book with important autobiographical details. That is the way I understand everything around me; it is where I must start because it is where I started.

We don't learn about religion, but how to be religious in a particular way. Lindbeck argues that it is the ultimate dimension of culture[13] In this perception he picks up an idea of Giambattista Vico's that one aspect of culture is an instinct for the divine and thus that to hold a particular set of doctrines is to be part of a culture. This concept of culture suggests the idea of a religious instinct that is much like a language instinct. As we learn a particular dialect and thus become part of the language community, we gain the possibility of networking to other dialects within a language system; we also gain the possibility of becoming multilingual.

While we have comparatively little chance of becoming bicultural or "bireligious" even if we gain an understanding and appreciation of other religions, that is, because we still have the "home" faith. But we do not assert that that faith is right to the exclusion of all others, or that there is some sort of superordinate ecumenical faith, but rather that there are a plurality of expressions that must be seen as valid for the people who have developed them. This is the ecumenical vision that the theologian Diana Eck says is the only possible one to be held by those who truly hold to their religious principles.[14]

So, too, we may connect our doctrine to those of others and become part of the network. This position raises interesting questions about ecumenism and its possibility or even desirability. It also raises the question about the role of the denomination and the structure of the church that can survive in the world of cyberspace.

Pluralism and Ecumenism in Doctrine and Text

Ecumenism is a liberal universal idea in that it implies a unifying or universal principle that holds all churches, sects, and religions together. It is the idea behind both the World Council of Churches and the United Nations. It implies unity, a set of common beliefs or ideals, or values. But does ecumenism make sense?

Many countries in the world are members of the United Nations, but does this mean that the countries hold common values or common beliefs about humanity or government or the rights of minorities? Not all of them necessarily subscribe equally to the concepts embodied in the United Nations Charter.

Many Christian congregations or communities (like their Jewish, Hindu, Buddhist, and Islamic counterparts) are clearly parts of a worldwide network of churches, but this does not necessarily mean that they are moving toward unaterably ecumenism. There will also be a tendency away from the centrality of single center and a rise of Third World sees. There may well be, in time, an internationalization of theology and a rethinking of the global mission of the Church—but that cannot be gainsaid.

If we think of church doctrines in the cultural-linguistic framework, what these churches have in common are certain core structures (as Giambattista Vico argued in the eighteenth century) embodied in the major ceremonies of death, birth, and the cosmology, which are parallel to certain language constructs such as nominality and predication. But such common forms are in the structures of our common humanity rather than in the substance. The remaining differences are real, not simply apparent.

Thus we may be attempting to go too far back or to be too abstract when we try to be too ecumenical or, alternatively, when we try too passionately to hold onto a strong denominational tie. In thinking about society, the nature of text, and our own role as literate beings in a world of hypertext, we should be on guard against universalism and modernity, against the ideas of the public. Instead, we should think in terms of community, pluralism, and networks. To that task I shall turn in the final chapter.

CHAPTER SEVEN

Inconclusion

Finding Ourselves in the Web of Text
and the Web of God

The modern consensus has eroded: that is how I would summarize what we have said so far in this volume. That consensus has been unable to deal with the mass—whether it be the mass of people or the mass of information. It has been unable to comprehend the world of the new technologies of hypertext and hypermedia and of the potential for anarchy that appears within the mass. As individuals, we cannot control even the idea of the mass, just as the minority cannot, in general, control the majority. In spite of this, however, the mass psychosis described by Ortega y Gasset is indeed breaking down. The numbers of people and the amount of information are overwhelming, to be sure, but we are doomed to failure in control and coping if we think of the mass as a mass, as an *it* different from ourselves. We must find a means of identifying with the mass, of which we are a part.

We are at the point of seeking a new consensus. How can we find it in a world where there is no text but hypertext? How can we find it when there is no principle for making knowledge canonical? How can we find it when the library is no longer the center of learning? When there is no culture but multiculturalism? No doctrine but a multiplicity of doctrines?

How can we find consensus in the gutters of the comic book of the world?

My answer to this lies in the five links that I mentioned at the beginning of this book (in the Preface) and which I see as a counterpoint to the themes of its chapters. The themes themselves both delineate the nature of the issue and point together toward a way of coping with the future—namely, *by means of* hypertext, the electronic super-highway, the shopping mall world, and the numerous independent and seemingly fragmented spiritual groups. They serve not only as points of departure, helping to define contemporary problems, but also as indices of hope, possible ways of resolving those same problems.

ANARCHY

When we initially encounter the term *anarchy*, we probably think of people in trench coats carrying bombs as big as bowling balls. Anarchy is frightening. It takes away the nice stable hierarchical order. In the Renaissance it was feared as a threat to the Great Chain of Being, which descended from God through the angels to humans, animals, fishes, insects, plants, rocks, and finally slime. The new sciences were viewed as likely to contribute to anarchy, as far as the clergy were concerned.

In "The First Anniversarie," penned in 1611, John Donne described the unsettling effects of the new science (heralded by the Gutenberg revolution and spurred by the Copernican revolution) on people's perspectives:

> For the world's beauty is decai'd, or gone,
> Beauty, that's colour, and proportion.
> We thinke the heavens enjoy their Sphericall,
> Their round proportion embracing all.   (lines 249–252)

Earlier he had exclaimed:

> 'Tis all in peeces, all cohaerence gone;
> All just supply and all Relation

Clearly, Donne's expressing the view that the whole sense of order in the world had succumbed to anarchy, a circumstance that brings with it great ugliness and disproportion.

In the early twentieth century, W. B. Yeats was even more explicit about the lack of order seemingly evident in the political, social, and intellectual worlds—this time, brought about by the variety of mass movements as well as the rapid proliferation of the new media. In "The Second Coming," he wrote:

Turning and turning in the widening gyre
The falcon cannot hear the falconer;
Things fall apart; the centre cannot hold;
Mere anarchy is loosed upon the world,
The blood-dimmed tide is loosed, and everywhere
The ceremony of innocence is drowned;
The best lack all conviction, while the worst
Are full of passionate intensity.

Although these two poets express horror at political, social, and intellectual anarchy, there is a positive side to anarchy, as well. Jacques Ellul defines "that anarchism which acts by means of persuasion, by the creation of small groups and networks, denouncing falsehood and oppression, aiming at a true overturning of authorities of all kinds as people at the bottom speak and organize themselves."[1] Ellul argues throughout his slim volume that there exists a connection between anarchy and Christianity, what we might call an affinity between the two in that both are communal, antiauthoritarian, and respectful of the individuality of the members.

In this sense anarchy is best seen as a counter to rigid hierarchies. Anarchy less implies the overthrow of a large government or of an established set of mathematical, scientific, or aesthetic propositions than it does the sheer ignoring of them. Anarchy values a different ordering, not one that is completely nihilistic nor individualistic, but one that tolerates and even celebrates diversity and co-equality. Anarchy's order can be seen in chaos theory and "fuzzy logic," as well as in hypertext, the new media, and some of our most powerful cultural and religious institutions.

In the world of information storage and retrieval, anarchy exists when there exists no clear principle of hierarchical structure. In a library, the Library of Congress or Dewey classification system is hierarchical, while the card catalog is not. The card catalog is ordered, but also anarchic in that the alphabet has no structure and dumps authors, titles, and topics into the same heap; for that reason libraries using car catalogs most often use three sets of catalogs—for authors, titles, and topics. The electronic catalog is even closer to being anarchic in that it can be entered in a number of different ways.

So too is the hard drive of my Macintosh computer. I may view my files by icon, type of file, date, size, or name. Any one of those orders is an order but the fact that the drive allows for any or all of them (and perhaps others such as color) means that the computer presents one with an anarchic environment.

Similar observations apply to hypertext. As I have explained, this volume is not hierarchical or sequential, it is anarchic. The principle of order and coherence must be fabricated by you, the reader, working together with me, the author.

According to Howard Rheingold, the author of *The Virtual Community*, the electronic network is often referred to as an anarchy—not in the sense of being disorganized, but in the sense of having no central governing hierarchy at either the policy or the technical level.[2] It appears disorganized in that it has multiple sets of organizing principles, all of which are complex and any one of which can be brought into play. There may be rigid rules for signing on or getting a document onto the World Wide Web or America Online, but once on, there is freedom to browse, surf, stay in one area, or leave. The architecture of these vast networks and their principles is not immediately apparent, so that the whole appears anarchic.

Anarchy is not random. It is, however, playful. It disrupts systems because it is asystematic. Since it is also atheoretical, theories quail before it. Anarchy challenges any attempt to impose a superordinate structure; it thumbs its nose and says, "Ah, but look at me—I don't fit your neat scheme."

AUTHORITY

The word *authority* has as its root *author*, from the Latin *auctor*, and its suffix is from the verb *ago*, "to do," which suggests that the one who has authority is the one who writes—or creates the person who writes. In Genesis, YHWH is the author of the universe, but he gives Adam authority (doingness), authorizing (enabling) him to name the animals. Writers are namers and are authors. They are thus granted authority. This includes the writers of laws, the writers of religious texts, and various other kinds of writers. Authority is often seen as granted, and it differs from power, which is too often taken or seized. People are authorized to do things or to sign documents, to be authors.

Authority often implies control over something or someone; it also implies respect by those who acknowledge the authority.

L. William Countryman defines authority as having three constituent elements:

1. a sense of identity and hope;
2. a set of norms for belief and behavior;
3. some external checks to tell us how we stand in relation to hopes and to norms.[3]

In Sacramentum Mundi, Countryman tells us, authority is defined as first referring to people in terms of Roman law; then it moves to the idea of personal authority, official authority, and finally the derivation into the authority of things like texts. Within societies or cultures, there is also authority inherent in such entities as grammar or spelling. Conventions have an authority. Since the text comes from a person, it is given the weight of being that person's words. People develop sets of decision rules by which they give authority to things such as texts. They canonize them, which vests authority in the texts. We can then have an "authorized version" of the Bible. This version becomes a person, an official.

This concept of authority seems tied to the idea of culture, wherein groups define themselves in relation to authority. When we give a person or an institution authority, we bestow our hopes on that entity and tend to identify with it. We may give authority to a group or to a culture as well as to an idea or a person. Authority is a matter of belief, mostly an intellectual belief. When we believe in a person or an idea, we give him/her or it authority.

A traditional aspect of rhetoric is the argument by authority. By citing a previous writer on a subject who happens to agree with us, we assert a line of continuity between our ideas and the ideas of past thinkers. It used to be that the further back one could go in tracing a line of authority, the stronger the argument. The authorities were the authors of books. Today, with the information explosion and the distrust of the past, the best authority is often the most recent. Today's authority may be the subject of the writing rather than the author of it—or even a performer. The argument by authority nowadays, to judge from TV commercials, consists in endorsements by popular sports figures and film and music stars. The authority is a figure recognized, revered, and trusted.

Authority is intellectual in that we give or recognize authority in our minds, and it regulates and organizes our thinking about our social and cultural world. Since authority is granted by people to people or objects, in an ideal sense, those in authority respect and promote the freedom of those who have submitted to the authority within the limits set by it. As an example, when we submit to the authority of English spelling, we have the freedom to deviate from it in order to achieve a special effect. For example, *kwik* is misspelling (however "cute") because of the authority of *quick*. E. E. Cummings's poetry is effective because of its anarchic playfulness with the authority of grammar and spelling (see p. 56).

When those in authority fail to exercise it, they abuse it and stand in jeopardy of losing it. It is at this point that those in authority forget that it is authority and they seize power.

Abuse of authority can also apply to things, particularly when people claim that the authority exists independently of those who originally granted it and who renew the grant generation after generation. In such a straightforward case as punctuation in writing, a compact of printers and writers gave authority to a set of marks to determine separation and connection of words. Thus was born the comma and the rules of its use. As time has passed, the comma's rules are too often seen as having divine origin and their authority has been abused by grammarians and teachers.

This is a simple abuse of the authority of things; but many would argue that there are more complex abuses, like that of fundamentalist readings of scripture.

Or the tyranny of universals.

COMMUNITY

How do we define a community? It is a popular term. It implies coming together, commonness, sharing.

In *Community: Reflections on a Tragic Ideal*, Glenn Tinder says that community has the ideal of perfect unity.[4] It involves respect for the members by those willing to join it, and a perception of value.

It involves a common inquiry.

It involves shared space and proximity.

It involves connection in time—perhaps a synchronicity, although diachronous communities have been attempted (the convent).

It is threatened by death and by lack of respect for others and for the individual.[5]

To this, Jean Vanier, the founder of L'Arche Community for the mentally handicapped, adds: "A community must have a project of some kind. If people decide to live together with neither specific goals nor clarity about the 'why' of their common life, there will soon be conflicts and the whole thing will collapse."[6]

He adds that communities need love and forgiveness.

Living in a world where communities are a tragic ideal is a strain, according to Tinder, for it means "living within circumstances far different from the simple and hopeful situations proposed [by many religions and ideologies]."[7]

Tinder argues that in Christian terms community is "affirmed [in the standard of love] but indefinitely postponed."[8] He goes on to write:

> If our inmost being calls for community, while inalterable conditions deny us community, our need is for strength and sobriety. This is indicated by the three types of civility [aesthetic, political, religious]. Each one prescribes a solitary and difficult life—a life of political activity without ultimate hope, a life of dispassionate rectitude, and a life of adherence to an ideal deferred to the end of historical time. [Are we] capable of disciplines so onerous? only if we answer that [we are] not will the cost—for all the evils of the past—have befallen us, for then we shall have accepted despair.[9]

Communities such as those Tinder describes are, perhaps, a tragic ideal, but we live in and form small, less permanent ones. To many, a classroom can become a community; to others, a church; to still others, an electronic billboard. In fact, it is possible for us to be members of several communities at the same time. These have the attributes of the ideal community, and they may gather a deepening strength over time. In the world of reading and writing there have been a number of different kinds of communities over the years. Among them have been the community of the monastery, the coffee house, the literary society, the writing circle, and the fan club. All of them share a common text or set of texts the reading or writing of which binds them together.

We even talk of broader communities such as that of a discipline (like law) or a professional association, but these may be less like the other reading and writing communities because of their larger size.

The reader should now again reference the distinctions between "the public" "the community" that I set forth in Chapter 5, based on Wendell Berry's work (see pp. 153–154).

At the music event Woodstock 1994, the commercial interests and the promoters sought to create a sense of community out of a media event. They did it by selling T-shirts and other paraphernalia, by creating a variety of artificial icons that were the bonds of the group. The reports of the people who went to the event were that there was little if any feeling of community among the participants.

In fact when I attended the only people to whom I spoke who reported a sense of community were the people who worked as concessionaires, and their community was with the other concessionaires, primarily prior to the public's arrival.

A public cannot become a community simply through the purchase of T-shirts.

In fact, by licensing and distributing to a mass market a community's logo, the T-shirt industry has taken the idea of community and turned it into a public. This has happened to universities, teams, and clubs. This sort of community is perhaps best seen as a pseudo-community, the commodity of advertisers, not the coming together of people.

True communities tend to be leaderless or to have a shifting personal authority. This raises the question of the authority of, or in, the community. If we assume that authority is granted, so too is the way of authoring the text. The community chooses to read the text as catechumens, and so to bind themselves to a set of authoritative readings.

Does the impossibility of "true" community persist as long as minorities such as scribes set themselves apart from the mass? It seems to have been true in the past, when the book challenged the priest. How does hypertext challenge the new priestly or scribal class (the theologians who believe that only they can bring the text to the community of catechumens and their secular counterparts in academia and in the print and other media)?

What, then, is the role of the scribe (priest, teacher, lawyer) in the community if the scribe is not the dictatorial authority? Is the scribe the radical innocent? the questioner? In what sense is the scribe the representative of authority?

The connection among individuals that respects their individuality and that is not linear or hierarchical is what is often referred to as a community. A community respects the individual and yet finds common ground. A community may be a human counterpart to hypertext. Certainly there are parallels. We may argue that a community is in some sense related to anarchy.

IDOLATRY

Of my five links, idolatry was the most clearly negative, but it has its positive aspects. I have defined it as the worship of the icon in place of the object represented by the icon. In Moses's time it was the Golden Calf. But the idol has taken many forms—sometimes the figure of an animal or a totem, sometimes the figure of a human-like deity, sometimes even humans, such as Alexander the Great, Julius Caesar, Napoleon Bonaparte, Karl Marx, Joseph Stalin, Queen Elizabeth II, Jackie Kennedy, Martin Luther King, and Elvis Presley. In each case and many others, the image or even the evocation of the image is supposed to cause the viewer to accord a form of obeisance to the idol—even if one knows nothing of the deity's or person's qualities that caused the creation of the original icon.

But there have many other sorts of idols, and these are the ones that are more subtle in their effect than the elevated statue or the elaborately framed portrait. These are the idols such as the Bible or the holy text, when it itself becomes an object to be revered even by those who may have no idea of what is inside it. Kissing the Bible to protest one's truthfulness is such a form of idolatry.

Idolatry is taking the thing seen for that of which it is an icon or image. I have already cited the farfetched example of the map readers who believe that the road was not the color depicted on the map. Owen Barfield offers his own definition:

> [I have] sought to show, firstly, the evolution of nature is correlative to the evolution of consciousness; and secondly, that the evolution of consciousness hitherto can best be understood as a more or less continuous progress from a vague but immediate awareness of the "meaning"of phenomena towards and ever-increasing preoccupation with the phenomena themselves. The earlier awareness involved experiencing the phenomena as representations; the latter preoccupation involves experiencing them non-representationally, as objects in their own right, existing independently of human consciousness. The latter experience, in its extreme form, I have called *idolatry*.[10]

For Barfield, the evolution toward idolatry is what has produced most of modern science. It has enabled us to see objects as detached from ourselves and treat them as such. It has allowed for all sorts of brilliant structural descriptions of phenomena, including language, writing, and machines. It has enabled the technology that produces hypertext. BUT . . .

But it can be taken too far, I believe, for it is a kind of thinking that prevents us often from seeing both–and instead of either–or. Not only does this "objective" consciousness see nature as distinct from the perceiving mind, but also it sees technology as separate from the humans who created it and use it and sees it as having a life and will of its own. This is indeed idolatry in its ugly form. Idolatry sees the means as an end. It sees the map as the world, the taxonomy as nature, the physical law as the movement of nature, the text of the Bible as God. The modern consciousness, which has developed a modern view of text, told us that text was its surface, or literal, meaning. We see a text as an object that has meaning without seeing that we are the persons who make the meaning. We see the words on the page as having an existence of their own without realizing the extent to which we are coauthors-readers and namers of what we read and what we see. We see the world as if it were what we had made it on paper, in our models, statistics, and programs. We do not see these as images or icons, to pierce through to a deeper understanding of that world. Or, if we do recognize them as icons, we taken them as objects to be venerated in their own right.

Such an idolatry has derived from the literal reading of the text and the world, as Barfield described; it also can emerge from the newer forms of text and image that are hypertext and hypermedia and reify them. Just as a young child cannot fully be consoled by a parent's telling her, "It's only a movie," so we often seem to forget that it is only an image, only a text, only a tool made for storing and retrieving information, for piercing through to the mind of the Maker and meeting ourselves in the journey.

NETWORKS

Decentralization appears in the world of text, in the world of the media, in the academy, in government. The empire or the single force or unifying agent appears to be replaced by the network, the web created by the electronic superhighway, the hypertext.

Networks have long existed. They are informal; they are hard to pin down; and they are fragile. We use networks almost without being aware of them. As Jane Jacobs has observed, networks are what enable us to take a letter of credit to a foreign country and have it recognized. Networks enable the mail to be delivered—most of the time. Networks are bridges of trust across chasms.[11]

Networks tend to connect individuals and small groups. They are those neural links that enable us to communicate with one another across space and time. Language may be said to be a network. It is a system of symbols by which two people may connect. Different language groups, therefore, have different networks. Writing conventions are also networks, ones that work over space and time. A hypertext itself is a network of texts. It is a way of seeing the various text spaces connected to one another. One may argue that a library is also a network of texts. It just works differently.

Networks may be physical as well as social. A telephone line is part of a network, so are the binding and pagination of a book, or a highway, or an airline system, or a gutter in a comic book. Each of these is a pathway between places, spaces, or people.

The advantage of a network is that it keeps people connected even though they are distant from one another. A network enables the members of real communities to identify one another. It also enables virtual communities to form in hyperspace.

The main disadvantage of a network is "out of sight, out of mind"; the individual can abruptly quit a network, perhaps join another.

The links in a network may be broken or reforged with new groups. But this appears to be the case of so much of human life, that is, we move in and out of community relationships to a great extent because we are not linked to a specific geographical spot. Wendell Berry finds this to be the greatest loss, the loss of a rootedness.[12] Without rootedness we need to find other sorts of community. But is a desire for rootedness really a part of human nature? Only in certain agricultural worlds. We are also pastoralists, and hunter-gatherers, and nomads. We look for different kinds of rootedness. One kind might be an attachment to the nodes on the network or the spaces on the webs in hyperspace.

In hyperspace, there is not one network, but a network of networks, as the Swedish anthropologist Ulf Hannerz has noted in an article aptly titled "The Global Ecumene as a Network of Networks."[13] The word *ecumene* is the noun of the more common adjective *ecumenical*, which comes from the ancient Greek word referring to the inhabited world (the root of which means "house"). The ecumene is the inhabited world, the world of people, not necessarily the physical world. As a habitation, it is, in Hannerz's sense, not a house with rooms and common meeting places, but a network. He quotes the anthropologist Alfred Kroeber's remarks:

> While any national or tribal culture may and must for certain purposes be viewed and analyzed by itself . . . any such culture is necessarily in some degree an artificial unit segregated off for expediency and . . . the ultimate natural unit for ethnologists is "the culture of all humanity at all periods and in all places."[14]

Networks have long existed; they connect people across the boundaries of space, time, and politics. We are now, I think, beginning to recognize their importance as against these constraining forces. We have been able to break through the barriers of space, time, and politics thanks to the non-mass media. These enable us to create networks across barriers that had seemed so formidable in the past. It may be through networks that we are finally able to cope with the vastness and complexity of our society.

SO? . . .

Anarchy, authority, community, idolatry, and *network*—rather than five separate linking themes, are they possibly woven inextricably into a single theme that offers a new vision? I believe they are. Let us explore this possibility in three ways.

A Rhetorical Conclusion

The world of hypertext and hypermedia that is coming into the forefront of our lives is a world in which there is, indeed, anarchy because hypertexts are necessarily iconic as well as textual, multi-authored, and multidirectional. By extension, the nature of hypertext sheds a new light on the nature of all sorts of texts in our lives and perhaps in the lives of prior generations. The text does not come from out there to us, the consumers of it. We are not the audience of mass media (not a public), but the cocreators of the non-mass media (a community), if only we see ourselves as such.

The boundary between reader and writer is broken down. This is a creative and rich anarchy where we are free to create our own relationships and reauthor the texts or hypertexts into meaningful statements or dialogues. Just as you have dipped and scratched your way through this book, deciding on its merits as you go, so you do with what you find in a hypertext on the screen, with the pages both comic and supposedly serious in a newspaper, with a portfolio of the works of a person, with a file or folder on the Internet, even with a new—or old—novel. There is no order, but there is the possibility for you to order what you have to select and make it yours. You are no longer passive but must see yourself as active.

It is also a world in which we are not limited by pages, lists, tables, or all those linear and hierarchical text structures, but where the image or the icon is the focus of our attention. It is a seemingly disordered world, but it is a world where we must indeed make order, and find patterns within and among the various texts and hypertexts that we read and write. We move icons on the screen rather than words on the page. We are not bound by two dimensions. We can manipulate the icons on the screen—opening and closing computer files at will—and through those icons find meaning and the words of others or meet our own words coming back to us through our own earlier contributions to the text and images.

Cyberspace's rhetorical anarchy consists of a creative nonhierarchical set of relationships. In the world of communications, we have entered a place where there is no central post office, no single switchboard, no single network, no file server, but rather a fast-growing menu of bulletin boards, billboards, chat rooms, and other virtual spaces inviting like-minded people to gather and interact on subjects of mutual interest. People may enter or exit them or with the mere click of a button–and change their identity as they go! The virtual world is a web of communities which are webs of people.

What this anarchic state means for us is the chance to assert a new authority by being authors ourselves; authority is divided and shared as the reader and the writer work together with editors, designers, system architects, programmers, and perhaps a host of other people to share in the authority of what we read and what we make into our personal folder and our text in the hypertext of the things we read and images we see on the screen, in print, or over the various networks.

Such an anarchic approach is opposed to our abject surrender of authority to those who control the mass media and would have us become mere consumers or idolaters of the text and the image. That is, indeed, what the scribes who create the mass media would have us do. They would like us to take the text for the thing, the map for the mental view. They would have us surrender to the idols they would like to create. It is easy, but it becomes harder as the number of choices opens up for us. There is the chance for each of us to create our own patterns of what we read and what we watch, to share in the authoring and to see ourselves as having authority over the non-mass media rather than be consumers of the mass media. We must assert our authority as scribes even as we surf the webs of words and icons.

In having authority, we become a part of a community, a sharing relationship with others on the network, in the designing and reading of a text and in the interpretation of the texts that we encounter. We take the variety of texts that we coauthor and set them into the scriptural ceremonies of our secular and our spiritual lives. So, we partake of a direct human relationship with the writer, with other readers, with those who share the reading with us on the Internet. We become equals with those others and develop authority not as individuals but as members of the community. Each of us sees ourself as a member of a reading community or a number of reading communities. As such, we develop a sense of control over the text, over the mass of information, and over the sources of information.

That community of which we are a part is linked to other communities through the network. The Internet as a whole is not a community, and it is a mistake to think of it as one; it is a network of communities. By being members of two or more communities on the network, we form the links among them. We can bring our membership in one community of readers to bear on our membership in another. We do not surrender our uniqueness, but we use that to meet others through a particular community and to form that community. In one chat group dealing with Biblical interpretation in hyperspace, I am simultaneously connected with a Filipino doctor concerned with issues of abortion, with a born-again Christian, with a mainstream pastor, and with several others from different walks of life. Each of us brings our membership in virtual or real communities to *this* community, and we share across the group. So, the community is a node in the network, and we are the links to other nodes. We may also move across nodes to form a complex network of communities to which we are affiliated—that would only be natural, and most likely prove rewarding.

If our role has so changed with respect to the information and text world around us, how does this play itself out in other spheres, the world of culture and the world of the spiritual?

A Cultural Conclusion

As I said at the outset of this volume, I see a number of cultural parallels to this approach to text and hypertext. As our ways of storing, manipulating, and retrieving information change, so too do our perceptions of the world. Our consciousness has shifted and continues to shift and be reformed. The twentieth century has seen the modern approach pushed to the limit and it has collapsed. It has happened in our material existence, in the ways by which we have reconceived transportation, the nature of the city and the village, the media, culture, and the nation-state.

Compared to the world that was so ordered by the encyclopedists, planners, and systems analysts of the modern world (among those who sought universal solutions to the issues of mass), the new world seems fragmented and anarchic. It is indeed scary, but we can make something positive of it.

According to some traditions, the world is made up of one people; according to others, one culture. These, too, are subdivided into many cultures, many peoples. Whereas in the eighteenth and nineteenth centuries, the concept of the nation-state helped people in a world of print counter the previous hierarchies of church and feudal lord, nowadays nations are challenged as artifices that have themselves become overly hierarchical. Todays world is polycultural or pluralistic, with any one culture resisting the domination of others. This leads to a world that is anarchic in that there is no apparent centrality. There is none in transportation, in civilization, in culture, in gender. Unity is replaced by difference. The culture of the shopping mall is one in which there is no center, for each mall is, by design, a centerless miniature world. Each is interchangeable with another, yes, but each forms its own network, joined into ever larger networks by filaments of macadam.

We have seen the relentless dissolution of cities. We have seen fragmentation of all sorts of empires and universals, as well as the establishment of new immense networks of "conglomerates" that both are and are not imperial. We have become increasingly aware that the idea of the European male as the norm has disappeared. We see heterosexuality challenged as the "normal" way of living and being.

We see that the canons and conventions of the universal culture have broken up into a multiplicity of new canons and conventions. We have seen that the icons created by science are useful tools for understanding the phenomenal world; they are our labels and names for things, which we have ordered and authored. They are not the things they stand for, nor are they phenomena in their own right but rather technologies of the mind and the body that deal with the phenomenal world. There is no "best" map of the world. There is no single rule. What is sauce for the goose is not sauce for the gander. One size does *not* fit all.

With that anarchic response to culture there has come a challenge to the authority of a single norm and the diffusion of authority among groups and levels of the citizenry. For the members of those groups, the authority of cultural groups tends to oppose a single larger authority, be it political, social, or intellectual. In a multicultural society, the granting of authority goes to the subcultures first and then to whatever overarching culture there might be. Despite the best efforts of the media moguls, who would set up idols for us in the world of celebrity, people genuinely seek and find authority for dress, behavior, relationships, and tastes within their own communities rather than in a single standard of behavior or taste.

Authority having been lost by a central culture, it has been assumed by the communities that one inhabits. We tend to find strength and authority when we see that we are affiliated to the community or the subculture much more than we are to any larger group. It is more difficult for artists, critics, intellectuals, or even "normal Joes" to see themselves as Americans, much less citizens of the world, than it is for them to see themselves as contributing members to one or more self-selected communities.

A Theological Conclusion

I would accept the traditional idea that God first became manifest in the Logos, the Word of speech and action in speech, and that people found they could approach God through ceremonies that were based on the Word. God's power lies in naming—or in predicating, and people reached to Him by calling to Him in a ceremonial fashion. God's authority was manifest in the ceremonies and rituals enacted by the people. These themselves became icons of the spirit.

Later, God became manifest in the text, the written language that

is God's Book, that which is authored to be read by countless generations of readers in a variety of scriptural languages. The text became
incorporated into the ceremony to form a complex idea of scripture.
In the age of printing, when the text was thought to be able to stand
apart from the oral recitation of it, people thought that the authority
lay in the lines of the text, in the icons of letters, words, paragraphs,
and glosses—that text stood apart from the people who read it. It
became an idol. Though authority had been taken from scribes and
priests and given to the people, the hierarchies of the sects and
denominations remained. In the world of mass media, the television
evangelist creates his (or her) own hierarchy. The idol that was the
text and the literalness of the text become a new idol—the image of
the speaker or the priest or the prophet. The guru replaces the message,
the image on the screen becomes an idol rather than an icon.

We are entering an age where the Word, the image, and the Book
become the hypertext, the collocation, ever shifting, of words, texts,
and images. The reader–viewer can reach through the hypertext or
across the Internet to find a multitude of texts, interpretations, chat
groups, and the like. The religious category on the Web contains
hundreds of groups and communities spun out into an ever widening
set of links. Each of us can find a spiritual home (or even several) in
cyberspace—if we are but willing to surf awhile.

We are at a point where many of the traditional churches face
the phenomenon of anarchy and diffused authority. To some of the
churches, this is highly problematic. They may have had too many
centuries of centralized imperial rule, of centralized evangelism, to be
willing to invite the outside world in. Now they have to cope with a
loss of universality. The postevangelicals want to remain small—ques-
tioning the universal precepts and forging links with like-souled people
across sectarian or denominational lines and even across the lines
demarcating one "religion" from another. They have to see the anarchic spirit within them, a spirit that takes authority from the church
hierarchy and places it in a new setting, within the spiritual community.

This shift in the virtual church matches that of the shift in the
actual churches. The pentecostal movement of the past century has
spawned a multitude of independent and loosely affiliated churches,
linked in much the same way as Alcoholics Anonymous—that is, the
allegiance of members is often to the local community or religious
assembly without any necessary link to other communities. The

authority of these communities lies in the community itself rather than in a hierarchical relationship.

Yet, these communities are often linked into a network. In this way a member of one community may visit another one, say, while traveling. Although the "mainstream" denominations are also linked so that a person can find a service in his denomination while traveling, the relationship is much more heavily structured. In the network of Pentecostals there may be little in common among the different communities. They do not form part of a system, but part of a network.

We need to see how God is revealed in this set of infinite and multivalent spaces connected by links into a web. The links are the creations of human authors, and so are the spaces.

As we maneuver through the spaces, creating our own links to suit our preferences, we are coauthors of our own journey through knowledge.

It is hard to discern the text space of God—the authentic scripture when all is changing and we might bypass some important detail in pursuit of our reading of the text.

Accepting the classic distinction between the Church as a unifying agency and the sect as a dividing one, we seem to be in a time where sectarianism is triumphing. But are these indeed sects? Has the Church disappeared, or is it in the process of reconstituting itself and finding itself in the network called cyberspace?

One might argue that such phrases or statements as "the Church's one foundation is Jesus Christ," or "the Jewish community," or "there is no God but Allah, and Mohammed is his prophet" imply some sort of unity or ecumene. But they are tenuous connections that mask real differences and divisions.

Just as on the Internet there are rooms in the "dungeons" or the "hotels," in the hypertext there are spaces, in society there are communities within the mass and the public, so there are new ecclesia. In each realm, the nodes may be connected in a number of ways and an individual may enter a room or a space or a community or an ecclesium and stay in it for a long time or may move from space to space whether following a thread or moving out of the network and beginning again.

How does this mobility translate into the spiritual or the ecclesiastical worlds? Do people move through sects (and certainly some do) as through rooms in the multi-user dungeon or the spaces on the hypertext? In which room do people find salvation, God, the truth?

If the Word devolves into hypertext and rooms in hyperspace, can it be reclaimed or should it be reconstrued? In the world of hypertext, what appears fragmented may not be.

Is simply entering into the religion hypertext sufficient? Once having entered and found a set of spaces or a place on the network, one finds companionship, spiritual satisfaction, a sense of commitment, faith, whatever else might form a part of the religious impulse.

Is God the network? the hypertext itself? the set of connections among spaces as well as immanent in those spaces? I think God is to be found in the gutters of the comic strip and in the void between the text spaces. God is immanent in the links as well as in the webs of the transcendent spinner.

I shall expand upon this view, as a Christian and as a Trinitarian. God is seen as Father, Son, and Holy Spirit, or as Centrality, Logos, and Emanation, or, as scientists would have it, as Field, Point, and Wave. These views are not separate but simultaneous and overlapping; they shimmer through and around each other like windows in hypermedia. Each window opens to the others, and none can be closed. The idea of the Trinity is one of relationship, of a connection between aspects. God is the creator and the created and the connection between the two. If we look at a tree blowing in the wind, we cannot say God is the tree or the wind, but the connection or linking of tree and wind, wind and tree. God is not in objects or above objects but in the space between and the dynamics of time affecting objects. To take the network and the Web, as a metaphor, God is in the network and above it. God is the windows and the links and the network and the programmer all at the same time. The dancer and the dance cannot be separated; no more so can the program and the programmer, the image and the reality behind it.

The connections are simultaneously immanent and transcendent because we may make new links, new connections, but if it is not the link that is immanent, it is the web—that complex of links and paths among spaces that enable anyone to go from space to space in an infinity of permutations.

God is Whitman's "noiseless patient spider" forever spinning the web, the immense hypertext of which we become readers and participants. God invites us to coauthor the scripture within our community and grants us that authority. In assuming it, we run the risk of becoming authoritarian, which is to assume that we are *the* author when we are not. We interact with our spaces and links, and we modify the web, but we are not the web nor the originator of the web.

The web is a web of words, of texts, of peoples, of cultures, of sects, of communities, of entities in space-time.

Our problem is that we cannot see the web. We are in it and of it, and we may be able to see a set of links, but we have trouble discerning the totality except perhaps through a vague sense of the totality that is fleeting because we are caught in space-time.

Discipleship comes in following the call of the web and of fashioning our own little links and forming communities of connected individuals.

A key to the correct perspective is the realization in us that we are not the center of the web. We are not the spider, we may make links and little pathways and new spaces, but these do not constitute the web.

We seek to understand, to apprehend reality, and to attempt to comprehend the totality because it is a part of our nature. Although as the creatures of our culture we can never attain that comprehension that we seek more than momentarily, we must keep trying.

Notes

*T*his book represents a number of years of reading, reflection, and study. During the course of working on it, I have read and been influenced by a number of writers, many of whom the astute reader will recognize. Rather than clutter the flow of the text with a series of notes or parenthetical references, I have placed them in this section arranged by chapter. I should, of course, first acknowledge certain writers whose work is so pervasive in my thinking, that I cannot but admit that their ideas are in the very fabric of this web of words.

I would begin with two whom I first came to know and work with in the mid-1960s, Marshall McLuhan and Walter J. Ong. McLuhan's *Understanding Media* and Ong's *Orality and Literacy* have shaped my thinking in ways that have become so deep that I barely know when the ideas are mine or theirs.

Among the sources on hypertext, I must acknowledge Jay Bolter's *Writing Space*, Richard Lanham's *The Electronic Word*, and George Landow's *Hypertext*. These books served to confirm some of my ideas, particularly those gained through working on the history of writing and the history of criticism in the twentieth century, two fields that have been my study for the past thirty years. Beyond them, however, there is Michael Joyce, whose hypertext fictions, together with our conversations both real and virtual, his essays collected in the volume *Of Two Minds*, and particularly his collaborative work with Jay Bolter and Mark Bernstein in the development of Storyspace™ have been an integral part of my thinking about hypertext and writing with computers.

In my thinking about authors and writing, I think I have been most influenced by my collaboration with many others around the world in the International Association for the Evaluation of Educational Achievement's Study of Written Composition, and particularly long discussions with my Finnish colleague, Sauli Takala of the University of Jyväskylä and with Gail Hawisher. They pointed me to the work of Roman Jakobson and A. K. Markova.

My thinking about readers bears a heavy indebtedness, of course, to Louise Rosenblatt and David Olson as well as to my many colleagues involved in the 1970s study of literature in ten countries, especially Gunnar Hansson, then of the University of Göteborg and later of Jonköping University in Sweden. Many long evenings of discussion helped me to understand something of the nature of reading. The other profound influence on my thinking must always be Northrop Frye, whom I have been reading for forty years and whose ideas about literature, culture, and scripture have imbued my own.

In turning to issues of culture and religion, my influences lie deep, I think, back to my early graduate school days and work with Marjorie Hope Nicholson. The more recent influences include the work of Edward Said, Mark Taylor (whom I found late), and most especially the work of Paul Braudel and Jacques Ellul, two thinkers whom I have come to admire beyond words. Ellul certainly helped me to understand the patterns of religion and culture in ways that go beyond people like Max Weber and R. H. Tawney and more deeply into the spiritual life of the mind and the society.

During the course of writing this book, I have also been enrolled in the Education for Ministry Program of the School of Theology, University of the South, Sewanee, Tennessee, and have learned a great deal from my reading and participation; that learning also is pervasive in my thinking, for I have come to see the theological ramifications of so much of our present culture. That course, along with participation in the Coolidge Colloquium at Episcopal Divinity School in Cambridge in 1994, where a score of colleagues and I lived, breathed, and thought a variety of interrelated ideas, led me to a number of writers, notably Harvey Cox, whose *Secular City* and *Fire from Heaven*, in particular, affected much of my thinking, and Wilfred Cantwell Smith and his magnum opus, *What Is Scripture?*, and beyond them back to a number of theologians, most notably Bultmann, Lossky, and Lindbeck.

NOTE TO CHAPTER 1

1. As a point of reference for what I intend, I might cite the French philosopher Régis Debray, who coined the term *mediology*, which he

defined in an interview with *The UNESCO Courier* (February 1995, p. 5) as follows:

> Mediology is a discipline that is still on the drawing board. It seeks to examine the relationship between the higher social functions (religion, politics, ideology and mental attitudes) and the technical structures used for the transmission of information. It therefore looks further than the media that actually carry the information. It is concerned first and foremost with symbolic effectiveness: how do symbols—words, writing, and figures—manage to produce specific effects and become material forces in a given society? Communication in the modern sense of the term is a specific, if belated, response to a much more difficult and permanent issue, that of mediation. This is a fundamental notion which has been at the heart of Christian theology. After all, Christ is the archetypal mediator: "And the word was made flesh." The mediological assumption is that it is possible for each period in history—from the Neolithic or the invention of writing to the electronic era—to establish verifiable activities of a human group, its form of political organization and its method of storing and disseminating "traces" (ideograms, letters, characters, sounds and images).

NOTES TO CHAPTER 2

1. Nelson (1982); and Bolter (1991), p. 24.
2. A tape recording, videotape, or film has some of the qualities of a text in that each freezes action or sound and can be duplicated, that is, made into a large number of identical copies. That is one of the reasons that many critics treat films and recordings as texts—as opposed to performances, which are live, fluid, changing, interactions between the performers and the audience. Although hypertexts may use sound and Oquick-timeO video or film images as well as other visual images, I shall deliberately avoid broadening the discussion of text and hypertext to include these and other recordings, as a concession to time and space constraints.
3. Coleridge (1965).
4. Stillinger (1991).
5. Lord (1964).
6. The same effect that Revelation intends can happen when we look at many films and television programs, particularly documentaries or shows that have used montage effectively. Here the set of connections is one made with images and scenes and is more clearly visual. But the principle is the same.
7. McCloud (1993); Eisner (1993); Harvey (1996).

8. Campbell (1982); see also Alexander, Ishikawa, et al. (1977).

9. Heath (1983); Scribner and Cole (1981).

10. Cummings, "Poem 33" (1978).

NOTES TO CHAPTER 3

1. Smith (1993).

2. Smith (1993), pp. 34–35.

3. Freire (1970); Foucault (1970).

4. Bourdieu (1991); Ibsch, Schram, and Steen (1991); Connerton (1989).

5. Freire, Pedagogy of the Oppressed.

6. Gadamer (1976).

7. Culler (1982); Derrida, J. (1974).

8. Stanley (1876), pp. 142–143.

9. Yates (1994).

10. Tyndale (1848).

11. Blake (1957), p. 818.

12. Blake (1957), p. 748.

13. Hauerwas (1993), p. 17.

14. Hauerwas (1993), p. 37.

15. This view was set forth most clearly by Stanley Fish (Fish, 1980), but it had been established by earlier critics notably I. A. Richards, and supported by some empirical research I did in the 1970s. See Richards (1929); Purves (1980).

16. Purves (1973).

17. Ellul (1985).

18. The Letter of Aristeas, quoted in Parsons (1952), pp. 94–95.

19. Radway (1984).

20. Howard Rheingold has an excellent discussion of this aspect of life on the Internet (Rheingold, 1993).

NOTES TO CHAPTER 4

1. McCloud (1993).

2. *The UNESCO Courier* (1995), p. 7.

3. Boureau (1989).

4. Ellul (1985).

5. Trubetskoi (1973), pp. 15–16.

6. Trubetskoi (1973), p. 21.

7. Yates (1994), p. 81.

8. Manguel (1996), pp. 100–103.

9. These ideas are most fully developed in three works (Yates, 1994; Ong, 1958, 1982).

10. See the work of Christopher Alexander, especially Alexander (1993); Alexander, Ishikawa, et al. (1977). Also see Tufte (1983, 1990) for a more direct discussion of the iconography in and of text.

11. Nelson (1982); Bolter (1991).

12. Olson (1994).

13. Frye (1982).

14. Ellul (1985), p. 90.

15. Ellul (1985).

16. Goethals (1990).

17. Ellul (1985); Ilich and Sanders (1989); Postman (1985).

18. Ellul (1985), pp. 102–104.

19. Nichols (1988). See also Lossky (1974).

20. Gadamer (1975), p. 63, quoted in Nichols (1988).

21. Nichols (1988), p. 113.

22. One such writer whom I find supportive is Mark C. Taylor, especially Taylor (1992).

23. Ellul (1964).

24. Cox (1969).

NOTES TO CHAPTER 5

1. Renfrew (1987).

2. Braudel (1984).

3. Hannerz (1992), p. 46.

4. Hannerz (1992), p. 46.

5. Rheingold (1993), pp. 66–67.

6. Rheingold (1993), pp. 168–169.

7. Ellul (1985).

8. Bergin and Fisch (1984).

9. Leacock.

10. Bergin and Fisch (1984), esp. p. 96ff.

11. Said (1983), pp. 8–9.

12. Said (1983), p. 9.

13. Purves, Quirk, and Bauer (1980).

14. Zane (1994), p. 2.

15. Wordsworth, *The Prelude* (1805 Version), Book vii, lines 592–601, 608–619.

16. Wordsworth, *The Prelude* (1805 Version), Book vii, lines 695-704.

17. Ortega y Gasset (1964), p. 11.

18. Ellul (1989).

19. Personal communication, June, 1994.

20. Johnson (1991).

21. Cox (1965).

22. Barfield (1979, 1988).

23. Ellul (1964).

24. Braudel (1982).

25. *The Unesco Courier* (1992), p. 20.

26. Lasch (1979).

NOTES TO CHAPTER 6

1. Goody (1986).

2. Roof (1993).

3. Niebuhr (1956), p. 88.

4. Mead (1989).

5. Carter (1993).

6. Cox (1965).

7. Boff and Boff (1987); Freire (1970).

8. Cox (1995).

9. Hutcheson (1981).

10. The term is used by Dave Tomlinson in his recent book (Tomlinson, 1996).

11. Lindbeck (1984).
12. Lindbeck (1984), p. 33.
13. Lindbeck (1984), p. 34ff.
14. Eck (1993).

NOTES TO CHAPTER 7

1. Ellul (1991), p. 13.
2. Rheingold (1993).
3. Countryman (1990).
4. Tinder (1980).
5. Tinder (1980).
6. Vanier (1979), p. 4.
7. Tinder (1980), p. 12.
8. Tinder (1980), p. 14.
9. Tinder (1980), p. 15.
10. Barfield (1988), p. 142.
11. Jacobs (1992).
12. Berry (1993).
13. Hannerz (1992).
14. Kroeber (1945), p. 9, quoted in Hannerz (1992).

References

Ackroyd, P. R., and C. F. Evans, eds. *The Cambridge History of the Bible: From the Beginnings to Jerome.* 3 vols. Cambridge, England: Cambridge University Press, 1970.

Alexander, Christopher. *A Foreshadowing of 21st Century Art: The Color and Geometry of Very Early Turkish Carpets.* London: Oxford University Press, 1993.

____, Sara Ishikawa, and Murray Silverstein. *A Pattern Language: Towns, Buildings, Construction.* New York: Oxford University Press, 1977.

Amato, Joe. *Bookend: Anatomies of a Virtual Self.* Albany: State University of New York Press, 1997.

Armstrong, Karen. *A History of God: The 4000-Year Quest of Judaism, Christianity, and Islam.* New York: Knopf, 1993.

Arnold, Matthew. *Culture and Anarchy.* Ed. Samuel Lipman. New Haven, CT: Yale University Press, 1994.

Baird, Patricia. "Hypertext Introduction." *Hypermedia* 1.1 (1989).

Barfield, Owen. *History, Guilt, and Habit.* Middletown, CT: Wesleyan University Press, 1979.

____. *Saving the Appearances: A Study in Idolatry.* 2nd ed. Middletown, CT: Wesleyan University Press, 1988.

Barolini, Helen. *Aldus and His Dream Book: An Illustrated Essay.* New York: Italica Press, 1992.

Barth, Karl. *The Doctrine of the Word of God (Prolegomena to Church Dogmatics).* Vol. 1. Part 1. Trans. G. T. Thomson. Edinburgh, Scotland: Clark, 1936.

____. *The Doctrine of the Word of God (Prolegomena to Church Dogmatics).* Vol. 1. Part 2. Trans. G. T. Thomson and Harold Knight. Edinburgh, Scotland: Clark, 1956.

Baudrillard, Jean. *Selected Writings.* Ed. Mark Poster. Stanford: Stanford University Press, 1988.

Bennett, H. S. *English Books and Readers 1475 to 1557.* 3 vols. Cambridge, England: Cambridge University Press, 1965–1970.

Bennett, William J. *American Education: Making It Work* [Report to the President of the American People]. Washington, DC: U.S. Government Printing Office, 1988.

Berger, John. *The Sense of Sight.* New York: Vintage,, 1993.

____. *Ways of Seeing.* London: Penguin. 1972.

Bergin, Thomas G., and Max H. Frisch. *The New Science of Giambattista Vico.* Ithaca, NY: Cornell University Press, 1984.

Berry, Wendell. *Sex, Economy, Freedom, and Community.* New York: Pantheon, 1993.

Birkerts, Sven. The *Gutenberg Elegies: The Fate of Reading in an Electronic Age.* New York: Fawcett Columbine, 1994.

Blake, William. *The Complete Writings of William Blake with All the Variant Readings.* Ed. Geoffrey Keynes. London: The Nonesuch Press, 1957.

Bloom, Allan. *The Closing of the American Mind.* New York: Simon & Schuster, 1987.

Boff, Leonardo, and Clodovis Boff. *Introducing Liberation Theology.* Maryknoll, NY: Orbis Books, 1987.

Bolter, Jay David. *Writing Space: The Computer, Hypertext, and the History of Writing.* Hillsdale, NJ: Erlbaum, 1991.

Boon, James A. *Other Tribes, Other Scribes: Symbolic Anthropology in the Comparative Study of Culture, Histories, Religions, and Texts.* Cambridge, England: Cambridge University Press, 1982.

Bourdieu, Pierre. "Questions of Method." *Empirical Studies of Literature: Proceedings of the Second IGEL Conference, Amsterdam, 1989.* Ed. E. Ibsch, G. Schram, and G. Steen. Amsterdam and Atlanta: Rodopi, 1991.

Boureau, A. "Franciscan Piety and Voracity: Uses and Stratagems of the Hagiographic Pamphlet." *The Culture of Print: Power and Uses of Print in Early Modern Europe.* Ed. C. Roger. Princeton, NJ: Princeton University Press, 1959.

Braudel, Fernand. *The Perspective of the World.* New York: Harper & Row, 1984.

____. *The Structures of Everday Life: The Limits of the Possible.* Berkeley and Los Angeles: University of California Press, 1992.

____. *The Wheels of Commerce.* New York: Harper & Row, 1982.

Bruner, Jerome. *Actual Minds, Possible Worlds.* Cambridge, MA: Harvard University Press, 1987.

Bultmann, Rudolf. *New Testament and Mythology and Other Basic Writings.* Ed. and trans. Schubert M. Ogden. London: SCM Press, 1957.

Calvin, John. *Institute of the Christian Religion.* 2 vols. Ed. John Baillie, John T. McNeill, and Henry P. VanDusen. Trans. John T. McNeill. Philadelphia: Westminster Press, 1960.

Campbell, Jeremy. *Grammatical Man: Information, Entropy, Language, and Life.* New York: Simon & Schuster, 1982.

Carson, D. A., and John D. Woodbridge, eds. *Hermeneutics, Authority, and Canon*. Leicester, England: Inter-Varsity Press, 1986.

Carter, Stephen L. *The Culture of Disbelief: How American Law and Politics Trivialize Religious Devotion*. New York: Basic Books, 1993.

Chappell, Warren. *A Short History of the Printed Word*. New York: Dorset, 1970.

Chartier, Roger. *The Culture of Print*. Princeton, NJ: Princeton University Press, 1989.

Chomsky, Noam M. *Language and Mind*. New York: Harcourt, Brace & World, 1986.

Coleridge, Samuel Taylor. *Biographia Literaria*. Ed. George Watson; Everyman's Classic Library. Boston: Tuttle, 1965.

Connerton, P. *How Societies Remember*. Cambridge, England: Cambridge University Press, 1989.

Countryman, L. William. *Biblical Authority or Biblical Tyranny? Scripture and the Christian Pilgrimage*. Revised ed. Cambridge, MA: Cowley Publications, 1990.

Coward, Harold. *Sacred Word and Sacred Text: Scripture in World Religions*. Maryknoll, NY: Orbis Books, 1988.

Cox, Harvey. *The Feast of Fools: A Theological Essay on Festivity*. New York: Harper Colophon, 1969.

_____. *Fire from Heaven: The Rise of Pentecostal Spirituality and the Reshaping of Religion in the Twenty-first Century*. Reading, MA: Addison-Wesley, 1995.

_____. *Religion in the Secular City: Toward a Postmodern Theology*. New York: Simon & Schuster, 1984.

_____. *The Secular City: Secularization and Urbanization in Theological Perspective*. New York: Macmillan, 1965.

_____. *The Seduction of the Spirit: The Use and Misuse of People's Religion*. New York: Simon & Schuster, 1973.

Culler, Jonathan. *On Deconstruction*. Ithaca, NY: Cornell University Press, 1982.

Cummings, E. E. *Complete Poems: 1904–1962*. Ed. George J. Firmage. New York: Liveright, 1978.

Denny, Frederick M., and Rodney L. Taylor, eds. *The Holy Book in Comparative Perspective*. Columbia: University of South Carolina Press, 1985.

Derrida, Jacques. *Of Grammatology*. Baltimore, MD: Johns Hopkins University Press, 1974.

Diamond, Sara. *Spiritual Warfare: The Politics of the Christian Right*. Boston: South End Press, 1989.

Dillenberger, John. *A Theology of Artistic Sensibilities: The Visual Arts and the Church*. London: SCM Press, 1986.

Drengson, Alan. *The Practice of Technology: Exploring Technology, Ecophilosophy, and Spiritual Disciplines for Vital Links*. Albany: State University of New York Press, 1995.

Eck, Diana L. *Encountering God: A Spiritual-Journey from Bozeman to Benares.* Boston: Beacon Press, 1993.

Eco, Umberto. *A Theory of Semiotics.* Bloomington: Indiana University Press, 1976.

Edgar, Christopher, and Susan Nelson Wood, eds. *The Nearness of You: Students and Teachers Writing Online.* New York: Teachers and Writers Collaborative, 1996.

Eisenstein, Elizabeth L. *The Printing Press as an Agent of Change: Communications and cultural transformations in Early Modern Europe.* Cambridge, England: Cambridge University Press, 1979.

Eisner, Will. *Comics and Sequential Art.* Tamarac, FL: Poorhouse Press, 1993.

Ellul, Jacques. *Anarchy and Christianity.* Trans. Geoffrey W. Bromiley. Grand Rapids, MI: Eerdmans, 1991.

_____. *The Humiliation of the Word.* Grand Rapids, MI: Eerdmans, 1985.

_____. *The Technological Society.* New York: Vintage, 1964.

_____. *What I Believe.* Grand Rapids, MI: Eerdmans, 1989.

Etzioni, Amitai. *The Spirit of Community: The Reinvention of American Society.* New York: Simon & Schuster, 1993.

Finney, Paul C. The *Invisible God: The Earliest Christians on Art.* Oxford: Oxford University Press, 1994.

Fish, Stanley. *Is There a Text in This Class? The Authoriiy of Interpretive Communities.* Cambridge, MA: Harvard University Press, 1980.

Foucault, Michel. *The Order of Things: An Archaeology of the Human Sciences.* New York: Vintage, 1970.

Fowler, Robert M. *Let the Reader Understand: Reader-Response Criticism and the Gospel of Mark.* Minneapolis: Fortress Press, 1991.

Freire, Paulo. *Pedagogy of the Oppressed.* New York: Seabury, 1970.

Frye, Northrop. *Anatomy of Criticism: Four Essays.* Princeton, NJ: Princeton University Press, 1957.

_____. *The Double Vision: Language and Meaning in Religion.* Toronto: University of Toronto Press, 1991.

_____. *The Great Code: The Bible and Literature.* New York: Harcourt Brace Jovanovich, 1982.

_____. *Words with Power: Being a Second Study of "The Bible and Literature".* New York: Harcourt Brace Jovanovich, 1990.

Gadamer, Hans-Georg. *Philosophic Hermeneutics.* Berkeley and Los Angeles: University of California Press, 1976.

_____. *Truth and Method.* London: Methuen, 1975.

Gaur, Albertine. *A History of Writing.* New York: Scribners, 1984.

Goethals, Gregor T. *The Electronic Golden Calf. Images, Religion, and the Making of Meaning.* Cambridge, MA: Cowley Publications, 1990.

Goody, Jack W. *The Domestication of the Savage Mind.* Cambridge, England: Cambridge University Press, 1977.

_____. *The Interface between the Written and the Oral*. Cambridge, England: Cambridge University Press.

_____. *The Logic of Writing and the Organization of Society*. Cambridge, England: Cambridge University Press, 1986.

Goody, Jack W., and Ian Watt. "The Consequences of Literacy." *Literacy in Traditional Societies*. Ed. Jack W. Goody. Cambridge, England: Cambridge University Press, 1968.

Greenslade, S. L., ed. *The Cambridge History of the Bible: The West from the Reformation to the Present Day*. Cambridge, England: Cambridge University Press, 1963.

Hannerz, Ulf. "The Global Ecumene as a Network of Networks." *Conceptualizing Society*. Ed. Adam Kuper. London: Routledge, 1992. Pp. 34–58.

Harris, Wendell. *Dictionary of Concepts in Literary Criticism*. New York: Greenwood Press, 1992.

Harvey, Robert C. *The Art of the Comic Book: An Aesthetic History*. Jackson: University Press of Mississippi, 1996.

_____. *The Art of the Funnies: An Aesthetic History*. Jackson: University Press of Mississippi, 1994.

Hauerwas, Stanley. *Unleashing the Scripture: Freeing the Bible from Captivity to America*. Nashville: Abingdon Press, 1993.

Heath, Shirley Brice. *Ways with Words: Language, Life, and Work in Communities and Classrooms*. New York: Cambridge University Press, 1983.

Hollenweger, W. J. *The Pentecostals: The Charismatic Movement in Churches*. Minneapolis: Augsburg Publishing House, 1972.

Horsfield, Peter C. *Religious Television: The American Experience*. New York: Longman, 1984.

Hutcheson, R. G. *Mainline Churches and the Evangelicals: A Challenging Crisis*. Atlanta: John Knox Press, 1981.

Illich, Ivan. *In the Vineyard of the Text: A Commentary to Hugh's Didascalicon*. Chicago: University of Chicago Press, 1993.

_____, and Barry Sanders. *ABC: The Alphabetization of the Popular Mind*. New York: Random House, 1989.

Inbody, Tyron, ed. *Changing Channels: The Church and the Television Revolution*. Dayton, OH: Whaleprints, 1990.

Jacobs, Jane. *Systems of Survival: A Dialogue on the Moral Foundations of Commerce and Politics*. New York: Vintage, 1992.

Johnson, Paul. *The Birth of the Modem: World Society 1815–1830*. New York: HarperCollins, 1991.

Joyce, Michael. *Of Two Minds: Hypertext Pedagogy and Poetics*. Ann Arbor: University of Michigan Press, 1995.

Kaufer, David S., and Kathleen M. Carley. *Communication at a Distance: The Influence of Print on Sociocultural Organization and Change*. Hillsdale, NJ: Erlbaum, 1993.

Kew, Richard, and Roger White. *New Millennium, New Church: Towards Shaping the Episcopal Church for the Twenty-first Century*. Cambridge, MA: Cowley Publications, 1992.

Kosko, Bart. *Fuzzy Thinking: The New Science of Fuzzy Logic*. New York: Hyperion, 1993.

Kroeber, Alfred. "The Ancient Oikoumene as an Historic Culture Aggregate." *Journal of the Real Anthropological Institute* 75 (1945): 9–20.

Lampe, G. W. H., ed. *The Cambridge History of the Bible: The West from the Fathers to the Reformation*. 3 vols. Cambridge, England: Cambridge University Press, 1969.

Landow, George P. *Hypertext: The Convergence of Contemporary Critical Theory and Technology*. Baltimore, MD: Johns Hopkins University Press, 1992, 1993.

_____. *Hypertext in Hypertext: An Expanded Electronic Edition of Hypertext: The Convergence of Contemporary Critical Theory and Technology*. Baltimore, MD: Johns Hopkins University Press, 1992, 1993.

Lanham, Richard A. *The Electronic Word: Democracy, Technology, and the Arts*. Chicago: University of Chicago Press, 1993.

Lasch, Christopher. *The Culture of Narcissism: American Life in an Age of Diminishing Expectations*. New York: Norton, 1979.

Leacock, S. "Oxford as I Knew It." In *Collected Works of Stephen Leacock*.

Levering, Miriam, ed. *Rethinking Scripture: Essays from a Comparative Perspective*. Albany: State University of New York Press, 1989.

Lindbeck, George A. *The Nature of Doctrine: Religion and Theology in a Postliberal Age*. Philadelphia: Westminster Press, 1984.

Lord, A. B. *The Singer of Tales*. Cambridge, MA: Harvard University Press, 1964. Lossky, Vladimir. In *The Image and Likeness of God*. London: Mowbrays, 1974.

MacKenzie, Steven L., and Stephen R. Haynes, eds. *To Each Its Own Meaning: An Introduction to Biblical Criticisms and Their Application*. Louisville, KY: Westminster/John Knox Press, 1989.

MacLeish, Archibald. *Collected Poems, 1917–1982*. Boston: Houghton Mifflin, 1985.

Manguel, Alberto. *A History of Reading*. New York: Viking, 1996.

Martin, Edward J. *A History of the Iconoclastic Controversy*. London: SPCK (Society for Promoting Christian Knowledge), n.d.

Martin, Henri-Jean. *The History and Power of Writing*. Trans. Lydia G. Cochrane. Chicago: University of Chicago Press, 1994.

McCloud, Scott. *Understanding Comics: The Invisible Art*. Northampton, MA: Kitchen Sink Press, 1993.

McKenzie, Steven L., and Stephen R. Haynes, eds. *To Each Its Own Meaning: An Introduction to Biblical Criticisms and Their Application*. Louisville, KY: Westminster/John Knox Press, 1989.

McLuhan, Marshall. *Understanding Media: The Extensions of Man*. New York: McGraw-Hill, 1964.

____, and Wilfred Watson. *From Cliché to Archetype*. New York: Viking, 1970.

Mead, Loren. *The Once and Future Church*. Washington, DC: The Alban Institute, 1989.

Nelson, Theodor H. *Literary Machines*. Self-published, 1982.

Neusner, Jacob. *Scriptures of the Oral Torah: Sanctification and Salvation in the Sacred Books of Judaism*. San Francisco: Harper & Row, 1987.

Nichols, Aidan. *The Art of God Incarnate: Theology and Image in Christian Tradition*. London: Darton, Longman, and Todd, 1988.

Niebuhr, H. R. *Christ and Culture*. New York: Harper Torchbooks, 1956.

Olson, David R. *The World on Paper: The Conceptual and Cognitive Implications of Reading and Writing*. Cambridge, England: Cambridge University Press, 1994.

Ong, Walter J. *Orality and Literacy: The Technologizing of the Word*, London: Methuen, 1982.

____. *Ramus, Method, and the Decay of Dialogue*. Cambridge, MA: Harvard University Press, 1958.

Ortega y Gasset, José. *The Revolt of the Masses*. New York: Norton, 1964.

Ouspensky, Leonid. *Theology of the Icon*. Vol. 1. Trans. Anthony Gythiel. Crestwood, NY: Saint Vladimir's Seminary Press, 1992.

Parsons, E. A. *The Alexandrian Library, Glory of the Hellenic World: Its Rise, Antiquities, and Destruction*. Amsterdam: Elsevier Press, 1952.

Paulson, William R. *The Noise of Culture: Literary Texts in a World of Information* Ithaca, NY: Cornell University Press, 1988.

Postman, Neil. *Amusing Ourselves to Death: Public Discourse in the Age of Show Business*. New York: Penguin, 1985.

Purdy, William. *Seeing and Believing: Theology and Art*. Butler, WI: Clergy Book Service, 1976.

Purves, Alan C. *How Porcupines Make Love*. Lexington, MA: Xerox, 1972.

____. *Literature Education in Ten Countries*. Stockholm, Sweden: Akmqvist and Wiksell, 1973.

____. "Putting Readers in Their Places: Some Alternatives to Cloning Stanley Fish." *College English* 42: 228–236 (1980).

____. *The Scribal Society: An Essay on Literacy in the Technological Age*. White Plains, NY: Longman, 1990.

____, D. Quirk, & B. Bauer. *Achievement in Reading and Literature: The United States in International Perspective*. Urbana, IL: National Council of Teachers of English, 1980.

Radway, Janice. *Reading the Romance: Women, Patriarchy, and Popular Literature*. Chapel Hill: University of North Carolina Press, 1984.

Reid, J. K. S. *The Authority of Scripture: A Study of Reformation and Post-Reformation Understanding of the Bible*. London: Methuen, 1957.

Renfrew, Colin. *Archaeology and Language: The Puzzle of Indo-European Origins*. Cambridge, England: Cambridge University Press, 1987.

Rheingold, Howard. *The Virtual Community: Homesteading on the Electronic Frontier*. Reading, PA: Addison-Wesley, 1993.

Richards, I. A. *Practical Criticism*. New York: Harcourt Brace, 1929.

Ricouer, Paul. "Preface to Bultmann." *Essays on Biblical Interpretation*. Ed. Lewis Mudge. London: SPCY, 1981. Pp. 49–72.

Roger, Chartier, ed. *The Culture of Print: Power and the Uses of Print in Early Modern Europe*. Princeton, NJ: Princeton University Press, 1989.

Ronell, Avital. *The Telephone Book: Technology, Schizophrenia, Electric Speech*. Lincoln: University of Nebraska Press, 1989.

Roof, Wade C. *A Generation of Seekers: The Spiritual Journeys of the Baby Boom Generation*. San Francisco: HarperSanFrancisco, 1993.

Rosenblatt, Louise M. *The Reader, the Text, the Poem: The Transactional Theory of the Literary Work*. Carbondale: Southern Illinois University Press, 1978.

Ruether, Rosemary Radford. *Gaia and God: An Ecofeminist Theology of Earth Healing*. New York: HarperSanFrancisco, 1992.

Said, Edward. *Culture and Imperialism*. New York: Knopf, 1993.

_____. *The World, the Text, and the Critic*. Cambridge, MA: Harvard University Press, 1983.

Sanders, Barry. *A Is for Ox: Violence, Electronic Media, and the Silencing of the Written Word*. New York: Pantheon, 1994.

Sayers, Dorothy. *The Mind of the Maker*. London: Methuen, 1941.

Scribner, Sylvia, and Michael Cole. *The Psychology of Literacy*. Cambridge, MA: Harvard University Press, 1981.

Sigal, Phillip. *Judaism: The Evolution of a Faith*. Grand Rapids, MI: Eerdmans, 1988.

Smart, Ninian, and Richard D. Hecht, eds. *Sacred Texts of the World: A Universal Anthology*. New York: Crossroad, 1982.

Smith, Anthony. *Software for the Self-Culture and Technology*. London: Faber & Faber, 1996.

Smith, Wilfred Cantwell. *What Is Scripture? A Comparative Approach*. Minneapolis: Fortress Press, 1993.

Stanley, Arthur Penrhyn. *Lectures on the History of the Jewish Church. Third Series: From the Captivity to the Christian Era*. London: John Murray, 1876.

Stillinger, J. *Multiple Authorship and the of Solitary Genius*. New York: Oxford University Press, 1991.

Stiver, Dan R. *The Philosophy of Religious Language: Sign, Symbol, Story*. Cambridge, MA: Blackwell, 1996.

Taylor, Mark C. *Altarity*. Chicago: University of Chicago Press, 1987.

_____. *Disfiguring: Art, Architecture, Religion*. Chicago: University of Chicago Press, 1992.

_____. *Erring: A Postmodern A/theology*. Chicago: University of Chicago Press, 1984.

Terry, Milton S. *Biblical Hermeneutics: A Treatise on the Interpretation of the Old and New Testaments.* Grand Rapids, MI: Academic Books, n.d.

Tinder, Glenn. *Community: Reflections on a Tragic Ideal.* Baton Rouge: Louisiana State University Press, 1980.

Tomlinson, Dave. *The Post-Evangelical.* London: SPCK (Society for Promoting Christian Knowledge), 1996.

Trubetskoi, Eugene N. *Icons: Theology in Color.* Trans. Gertrude Vakar. Crestwood, NY: St. Vladimir's Seminary Press, 1973.

Tufte, Edward R. *Envisioning Information.* Cheshire, CT: Graphics Press, 1990.

_____. *The Visual Display of Graphic Information.* Cheshire, CT: Graphics Press, 1983.

Tyndale, William. "The obedience of Christian men and how Christian rulers ought to govern: wherein also (if thou mark diligently) thou shalt find eyes to perceive the rafty conveyance of all jugglers." *Doctrinal Treatises and Introduction to Different Portions of the Holy Scriptures by William Tyndale.* Ed. H. Walter. Cambridge, England: Cambridge University Press, 1848.

Vanier, Jean. *Community and Growth: Our Pilgrimage Together.* New York: Paulist Press, 1979.

von Balthazar, Hans Urs. *Seeing the Form.* Edinburgh, Scotland: Clark, 1982.

Wilkinson, John. *Interpretation and Community.* London: Macmillan, 1963.

Wordsworth, William. *The Prelude* (1805 Version). *The Prelude: 1799, 1805, 1850.* Ed. J. Wordsworth et al. New York: Norton, 1979.

Yates, Frances. *The Art of Memory.* London: Trafalgar, 1994.

Zane, J. Peder. "News of the Week in Review." *The New York Times,* Nov. 13, 1994, p. 2.

Index